MORE LEGENDARY VOICES

Also by Nigel Douglas

Legendary Voices

MORE LEGENDARY VOICES

Nigel Douglas

LIMELIGHT EDITIONS

New York

First Limelight Edition, September 1995

First published in 1994 by André Deutsch Limited
106 Great Russell Street, London WC1B 3LJ

Library of Congress Cataloging-in-Publication Data

Douglas, Nigel
  More Legendary Voices / Nigel Douglas – 1st Limelight ed.
  000p. 00cm.
  Includes bibliographical references, discography, and index.
  Originally published: London: A. Deutsch, 1994.
  ISBN 0-87910-193-8
  1. Singers – Biography.   I. Title.
ML400.D63   1995
782'.0092'2 – dc20
[B]   95-10323
                                     C.I.P.
                                     MN

Design by Jeffrey Sains
Phototypeset by Falcon Graphic Art Ltd
Printed in Great Britain by St. Edmundsbury Press, Bury St Edmunds, Suffolk

Copyright acknowledgement: the review by Philip Hope-Wallace on page 11
copyright © the *Guardian* 1957; the quotation on page 105 from *My Life*
by Tito Gobbi with Ida Cook reproduced by permission of Rupert Crew Limited

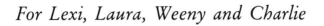

For Lexi, Laura, Weeny and Charlie

CONTENTS

LIST OF ILLUSTRATIONS

Gigli, Chaliapin and Tauber
press photograph, Savoy Hotel, London 1931
(Courtesy of the Mark Ricaldone Collection)

MARIA CALLAS
as Norma, Covent Garden 1952
(Courtesy of Roger Wood)

FEODOR CHALIAPIN
informal portrait

KATHLEEN FERRIER
rehearsing with Gerald Moore
(© EMI Records UK)

BENIAMINO GIGLI
fishing in Central Park, NY, March 1929
(Courtesy of Mark Ricaldone Collection)

MARIA JERITZA
as Marietta in *Die tote Stadt*
(Courtesy of Prof Jürgen Schmidt)

JOHN McCORMACK
singing at New York Police Day,
Sheepshead Bay Race Course, Brooklyn, August 1918
(Courtesy of Mr Theo Mortimer)

LAURITZ MELCHIOR
publicity photograph
(Courtesy of Royal Opera Archives, Covent Garden)

CLAUDIA MUZIO
as Mimi in *La Bohème*
(Courtesy of Virginia Barder)

TITTA RUFFO
press photograph: arriving in America, 1912

ELISABETH SCHUMANN
as Susanna in *Le Nozze di Figaro*
(Courtesy of Gerd Puritz)

CONCHITA SUPERVIA
studio portrait
(Courtesy of the Norman White Collection)

RICHARD TAUBER
informal portrait
(Courtesy of the Bildarchiv der Oesterreichischen Nationalbibliothek)

ACKNOWLEDGEMENTS

Once again I have many kind friends to thank for their help in the preparation of this book, most notably Ilsa Yardley, an unfailing source of encouragement and enthusiasm, Bobby Woodward for his tireless and expert research work, Michael Dealtry, whose practical assistance in several different forms has been deeply appreciated, Norman White, who has allowed me unlimited access to his vast collection of books and memorabilia, Clare Chambers, who makes editing sessions a positive pleasure, and Esther Whitby, who first took the risk of allowing me to try my hand as an author. Then Robert Tuggle and John Pennino of the Metropolitan Opera, Diana Fasoli of the Teatro Colón, Buenos Aires, Francesca Franchi of the Royal Opera, Covent Garden, Professor Jürgen Schmidt in Vienna, Dottore Francesco Ricci in Milan and Mark Elyn in Illinois, all of whom have gone to considerable trouble on my behalf. I would also like to thank Virginia Barder, Mark Ricaldone and Theo Mortimer for invaluable assistance with photographs, as well as Adèle Leigh, Henry Pleasants, Vivian Liff, Sir John Tooley, John Amis, Lord Harewood and many others who have assisted me with their personal memories of various of the singers in the book; and lastly the Bank of England for the provision of various financial statistics.

FOREWORD

When I started to write *Legendary Voices*, back in 1992, my original list of singers consisted of twenty-six names. It soon became evident that this would lead to far too long a book and so I pruned the list to fourteen; the remaining twelve now feature in the present volume. In making my final selection for the first volume I aimed at a balance between ladies and gentlemen, tenors and baritones, Verdi singers and Wagner singers, and so on; in the process many a glittering name was obliged to wait in the wings. The twelve who were left over for the present volume were, in other words, in no sense a second team – lucky the opera house which could have our present dozen as its reserves! Inevitably the first time around there were readers who asked 'Why didn't you include So-and-so?' and I am happy to say that almost (though not quite) all of the most frequently mentioned names are now on parade.

During the last two years the spate of CD reissues of the great singers of the past has continued unabated, indeed new companies have emerged which specialise in this market. The public, evidently, is keen to know how the stars of yesteryear really sounded, and as it is a favourite contention of mine that it is not only singers' voices but also their personalities which form the basis of their art I hope that these brief introductions to some of them as people will help to illuminate readers' perceptions of them as performers. Once again I have preferred not to concern myself too much with the technical side of the various different record companies' re-creations. Some take greater trouble than others to find really immaculate 78s for transfer, and to ensure that everything is dubbed at precisely the correct speed. The methods used to achieve what each company regards as the finest quality of reproduction vary enormously; indeed in specialist circles the subject has become quite a contentious one. I have not written this book from the standpoint of a record critic – suffice it to say that I do not mention any specific CD unless I myself have enjoyed listening to it.

In the foreword to the earlier volume I wrote: 'My selection of singers is a purely personal one. None of them was perfect – singing is too human an activity to countenance perfection – but all of them, for a variety of reasons, are favourites of mine. If reading about them, and I hope listening to them, may infect a few people with the bug of enthusiasm that bit me many years ago, I shall be happy.' That remains my position the second time around.

MARIA CALLAS

GREEK AMERICAN SOPRANO

b. New York, 2 December 1923
d. Paris, 16 September 1977

The world of Grand Opera is one of extremes. Vast vocal and orchestral forces are deployed in enormous theatres to perform works of unrestrained passion, and those who wish to immerse themselves in this sea of sound and spectacle are invited to pay daunting sums for the privilege. Their emotions, unless they are there for purely social or business reasons, tend to be stirred on the same inflated scale. Devotees of straight theatre may say 'I was disappointed by So-and-so's Othello', but opera fanatics let fly *con tutta forza* – 'that tenor trying to sing Otello should be taken out and shot' is a much more likely comment – and where the theatre-goer's favourite leading lady will be regarded simply as a superb actress the opera-goer's favourite soprano is raised to the status of a Diva, or Goddess. This level of hyperbole is reflected in the matter of applause. Whenever I go to a play, even if it is a performance of the highest quality – Shakespeare, let us say, with world-famous names in the cast – the short, sharp curtain-calls strike me as strangely perfunctory in comparison with what we are used to in the world of opera. Operatic audiences, caught up in the heady intoxication of the music, love to shout and stamp and throw flowers, or conversely to boo, hiss and whistle. Occasionally different sections of the public will be indulging in all of these activities at the same time – controversy is a plant which thrives in the rich soil of the operatic garden. It all helps to raise the general level of excitement, and since the Second World War no other singer has engendered more excitement or stirred up more controversy, either as an artist or as a human being, than the incomparable Maria Callas.

More books have already been written about Callas than about any other single singer in the history of opera. There have been serious studies of her artistic status, bar-by-bar analyses of her recorded repertoire and publications principally devoted to the craft of the gossip columnist. There have been some with personal axes to grind and others which have sought with ill-disguised blatancy to cash in on the subject's fame – at one time, after the appearance of *My Wife Maria Callas*, *My Daughter Maria Callas* and *My Sister Maria Callas*, it seemed reasonable to fear that *My Brother-in-Law's Cousin Maria Callas* might well be on its way at any moment. Following on the heels of so much published material all that I would like to do is to set out my personal memories of her as a performer, refreshed by reference to a selected few of her numerous recordings, and in the process perhaps myself achieve a more balanced view of what she really meant to me as an opera-goer. I was lucky enough to hear her quite regularly in several different countries between the time of her sensational Covent Garden début and her final London appearance, and I was baffled by the experience. To me she was a mass of contradictions – it was part of her fascination.

My reactions to other great sopranos of the Fifties and Sixties were less complex – their performances were more straightforward events. When I think of Renata Tebaldi, for instance, I see her making her début in the Vienna State Opera as Tosca, a tall and dignified figure, in the first act so uninvolved in the drama that when she reproved Cavaradossi for embracing her with excessive passion in front of a statue of the Madonna the two lovers were in fact separated by half the width of that enormous stage; but in the second act singing a 'Vissi d'arte' of such flawless beauty that had she done nothing all evening but the one glorious, creamy diminuendo after the climactic high B flat she would have fully earned the ovation which came crashing about her ears, and which lasted for at least twice the length of the aria. When I think of Victoria de los Angeles I see her infinitely appealing Manon in Massenet's masterpiece, the charm of her personality perfectly matched to the silky richness of that lovely voice; or I see her Mimi, the very embodiment of youthful vulnerability, and I feel the sensation of being almost drawn out of my seat by the magnetism of pure beauty as she launched into that bewitching phrase 'Ma quando vien lo sgelo'. These two singers, and many others too – thinking for a moment only of sopranos the names of Lisa della Casa, Elisabeth Schwarzkopf, Irmgard Seefried, Sena Jurinac, Ljuba Welitsch and Hilde Gueden come instantly to mind – were the people who stretched out their hands and led me into the enchanted world of opera, but Callas never reached out a finger to me. I recognised her as the most potent of them all; she thrilled me, dazzled me, puzzled me, infuriated me, but I was never enchanted by her. I felt as if in every performance she was throwing down a dual challenge – a challenge to the role and a challenge to the audience. I was an onlooker in some private battle of her own, a battle which I was sometimes longing for her to win, one which carried me along with its every charge and its every fusillade; but at other times one in which I merely sensed her antagonism, and which left me feeling that as far as I was concerned she could fight it out on her own.

Nobody, as far as I know, has ever pretended that Callas was a restful person, and she did not lead a restful life. Although both her parents were Greek she was born in New York; her father (the family name was really Kalogeropoulos) was a chemist who had emigrated from Athens to the United States, where he only succeeded in making a meagre living as a travelling salesman in pharmaceutical products. At an early age Maria evinced signs of unusual talent both as a singer and as a pianist, and her mother, recognising that she was some kind of prodigy, pushed her as hard as she could go – something for which Callas, robbed of a normal childhood, never forgave her. Unlike her elder sister she was an unattractive child, fat and extremely short-sighted, and in a revealing essay written about her after her death, Walter Legge, who produced nearly all her studio recordings and had a profound influence on her career, quoted this as the reason for what he described as her 'superhuman inferiority complex'. 'This was the driving force', he wrote, 'behind her relentless, ruthless ambition, her fierce will, her monomaniacal egocentricity and insatiable appetite for celebrity. Self-improvement, in every facet of her life and work, was her obsession.'

When Callas had just turned fourteen her mother took her back to Athens and the responsibility for her improvement as a singer was handed over to the Spanish soprano Elvira de Hidalgo, then a professor at the Athens Conservatory. After various student performances Callas made her professional début shortly before her seventeenth birthday in the small but amusing part of Beatrice in Suppé's operetta BOCCACCIO, and within two years she had progressed to the role of Tosca. During the war, under the German and Italian occupations, she was obliged to sing any role which came her way, as well as concerts for which her fee would be paid in spaghetti and vegetables; and although her teacher was determined that her future lay in what one might generally classify as the heavier coloratura roles of the *bel canto* repertoire – Bellini's Norma, for instance – by the time she was twenty she was appearing in such unlikely parts as Leonore in FIDELIO. When she was twenty-three she came to the attention of the man who, after de Hidalgo, probably had the most formative influence on her vocal development. This was the veteran opera conductor Tullio Serafin, a man who had worked with virtually all the great singers of the Italian repertoire since the end of the previous century, and who had had an important hand in the artistic development of Rosa Ponselle amongst many others. He conducted Callas in her first important international engagement, Ponchielli's LA GIOCONDA in the Verona Arena in 1947, and he recognised that she possessed qualities which, with guidance, could make her into something quite outside the usual run of the mill.

Callas's success in Verona was by no means unqualified because the basic sound of her voice fell strangely on Italian ears; it did not fit into any accepted category, and there were ugly patches in it. Engagements did not fall into her lap; indeed without Serafin's faith in her she would have had a hard time of it. He conducted her as Isolde in Venice, Aida in Turin and Norma in Florence; Turandot, too, under the conductor Nino Sonzogno, added to her slowly burgeoning reputation. Then, in January 1949, came the turning-point in her artistic development. Serafin had cast her as Brünnhilde in Wagner's DIE WALKÜRE in Venice, which was to be followed immediately by Bellini's I PURITANI with the famous light soprano Margherita Carosio in the role of Elvira. Carosio fell ill and Serafin himself was later to credit his daughter with the revolutionary idea that Callas should step into the breach – they were all staying in the same hotel, Signorina Serafin had heard Callas warming up with snatches of Elvira's aria 'Qui la voce', and felt convinced that the music would suit her. Callas undertook the assignment, learned the role of Elvira in one week, a week which included three performances of DIE WALKÜRE, and scored a triumph.

Within this story lie, I believe, many of the clues to what was right and wrong about Callas and her singing. Her extraordinary musicianship, her fierce determination and the unprecedented versatility of her voice* had enabled her to achieve a feat of which nobody else would have been capable. Brünnhilde, even when sung in Italian, is one of the peaks of all-out dramatic singing, while the essence of Elvira is the finely spun line of classical *bel canto*. The two roles not only need to be sung in totally contrasting styles, they actually require two different voices, and it must have been as confusing for Callas as it was thrilling for the public to find that she apparently possessed them both.

The 1949 season in Venice gave rise to widespread reports of the birth of a new phenomenon, and these were confirmed when Callas appeared in a concert in Turin, broadcast on Italian radio,

---

* To find anything approaching a precedent one has to go back to the legendary Lilli Lehmann whose repertoire in the last three decades of the nineteenth century extended from light coloratura roles via Violetta in LA TRAVIATA to the Wagnerian heroines, but even she did not undertake two such extremes contemporaneously.

with a programme consisting of Isolde's 'Liebestod', Aida's aria
from the Nile Scene, Norma's 'Casta diva' and Elvira's 'Qui la
voce'. It was almost a declaration that long accepted borderlines
no longer existed. In a sense she was turning the clock back a
century, to the days when Bellini's heroines were entrusted to
singers like Grisi, Pasta and Malibran who had strong lyric voices,
rather than to the light coloratura sopranos who had appropriated
them in more recent times – the only difference being that none
of Callas's distant predecessors had had to stretch their dramatic
range to incorporate the music of Wagner. Eight months later the
Isolde, Norma and Elvira numbers were recorded by the Italian
company Cetra, and if one listens to Elvira's aria 'Qui la voce',
which now features on Nimbus CD *NI 7864*, with the voices
of, say, Lily Pons or Amelita Galli-Curci in one's ear, one can
scarcely fail to appreciate the impact which this recording made
at the time. From the first note of the off-stage 'O rendetemi la
speme', we are listening to a fully grown heroine and the amplitude
of voice results in Bellini's long-breathed, passionate melody (to
my taste his finest) being invested with a depth of feeling which
simply cannot be realised if the singer's basic tone is shallow
or superficial. It is difficult to sympathise with these deranged
bel canto heroines when they sound like witless little girls or
twittering swallows, but Callas's timbre, darkened as if by grief
and suffering, is the stuff of genuine tragedy. The reason why the
light sopranos had commandeered these roles is obvious enough;
singers with full-blooded voices seldom have the necessary agility
at their disposal, but Callas did. When she reaches the coloratura
fireworks at the end of the cabaletta she dispatches them with the
minimum of fuss, crowning a scintillating cascade of chromatic
scales with a meaty and imperious high E flat.

It is not, however, merely the vocal quality or the dexter-
ity which make this performance something utterly out of the
ordinary. There is also a rare musical intelligence at work and an
arresting talent for marrying the words to the music. In the days
before Italian composers had explored the potential of harmony

as a means of dramatic expression the singer carried almost all the responsibility for interpreting the composer's intentions – the orchestra merely sighs along with the vocal line – and the listener can soon lose interest if the singer gives a monochrome performance. By maintaining a legato of tremendous tension throughout the vocal line – I do not wish to sound too technical, but Callas's use of portamento and of rubato is something to be savoured – while at the same time investing every syllable of the text with a colour and emphasis of its own she turns what can become a monotonous piece of melody-spinning into a riveting theatrical event. To give but one example of what I mean, the main aria opens with the words 'Qui la voce sua soave mi chiamava . . . e poi spari' ('Here his sweet voice called me . . . and then vanished'). The opening phrase is sung with an overwhelming sense of nostalgia as she recalls the sound of that well-loved voice, and then with the subtlest shift of expression the word 'spari' is lightened with a minute hint of surprise. It is minuscule, and for all I know it may not even have been conscious, but it is typical of the endless little touches which went to make Callas, at her best, one of the most vivid of vocal actresses.

Listening now to singing as magnificent as this it seems strange to me that I so seldom capitulated to Callas in live performance. There were, I think, two main reasons. The first of these was that by the time I first heard her, as Norma at Covent Garden on 8 November 1952, there was such an air of hysteria and what one would nowadays call 'media hype' surrounding her every step that I felt antagonised by it. This was, of course, unfair to her – she by no means always courted the publicity which accompanied her – but there seemed to me to be a touch of the Emperor's New Clothes about the adulation with which the audience greeted her.* There was an enormous amount about that Norma to admire, especially in the second half, and the occasion

---

* This lack of balance, as I see it, in people's assessment of Callas persists to this day. I recently read in a serious publication the ludicrous statement: 'She alone has ever conquered the operatic stage.'

was one of the most exciting in London's post-war operatic history; but to my admittedly inexperienced ears the 'Casta diva' sounded out of tune, which did not prevent the audience from going wild about it.* From then onwards I always went to a Callas performance with a certain feeling of 'All right, lady, prove it to me', a feeling which no other singer has ever aroused in me, and only twice did I come away completely won over by her – once was as Leonora in IL TROVATORE at Covent Garden in 1953, and once as Lucia in Vienna in 1956.

The other reason why I found myself resistant to Callas was, to put it baldly, her propensity for producing ugly noises. Even when she was singing at her best, as in the 'Qui la voce' recording, the voice was not one which I personally found beautiful – exciting, expressive, astonishing, yes, but beautiful, no. I do not offer this as a piece of objective artistic criticism; if beauty is in the eye of the beholder it is also most assuredly in the ear of the listener, and nothing could be more subjective than the question of whose voice is or is not beautiful. I know, too, that much has been written about her occasional tonal peculiarities contributing to the thrill of her performances, and I think that this is a perfectly fair observation, but what used to prevent me from sitting back and surrendering to La Divina was the knowledge that at any moment she might send a shock through my system by releasing one of her rogue tones. It was a typical Callas contradiction that she was a perfectionist whose singing, particularly in the second half of her short career, was riddled with imperfections. Lord Harewood, who understood Callas as well as anyone, recently said to me, 'She was indeed a perfectionist, but she did not see perfection in singing as involving an avoidance of danger.' Hats

---

* This impression has been confirmed by a live recording which has come to light, and also by a conversation which I had recently with the eminent record collector Vivian Liff. He had been present at the dress rehearsal, at which, in his own words, 'Callas was totally relaxed and sang a "Casta diva" such as one would only hope to hear in paradise. It was not until the third performance that she came anywhere near that standard again.'

off to her for that – it requires an immense amount of courage to go for a rocketing high E flat in front of a packed house if you are not sure that you are going to hit it. Every operatic performance, whether you are in the auditorium or on the stage, has something of the tightrope act about it, and Callas was a tightrope artist who spurned the safety net.

In the later stages of her career Callas was beset by many problems of technique, but I cannot help feeling that the seeds of all these troubles were sown at the very start. Although it was Serafin who later guided her footsteps into the *bel canto* repertoire he must surely have been doing her a disservice by encouraging her at such an early age to tackle Turandot and Brünnhilde. If she had stayed on the path which de Hidalgo had indicated might not that amazing voice have lasted twice as long as it did? One specific characteristic used to puzzle me even in her early days – a strange and disturbing guttural sound which used to distort the vocal line from time to time. There is a hint of it even in the early 'Qui la voce' recording discussed above, when the first syllable of the word 'speme' seems briefly to open up some unrelated cavern of sonority, momentarily threatening to whisk us out of the Elvira voice and into the Brünnhilde. I was interested to note, while researching for this chapter, that almost all the leading British critics were as baffled by these inconsistencies in Callas's singing as I used to be, and one particular review, written by Philip Hope-Wallace in the *Guardian* when she returned to Covent Garden as Norma in 1957, exactly reflects my own reactions at the time of her début:

Mme Callas never fails to hypnotise her audience. She takes the stage as Rachel must have taken it. Visually she is magnificent. Musically she exerts so much will-power and bends art to her fashioning in such an imperious manner that one guesses that even if she were to whistle the music or play it on a violin instead of vocalising it, she would still make us hang upon her every phrase. She is, in short, the very antithesis of your canary soprano, your empty unmusical prima donna. And yet those with critical ears can scarcely fool themselves that she was not often singing sharp on Saturday; that her tutta forza was invariably sour and that her climactic high notes often developed a zagging beat like the sound of a plank being sawn. Moreover the actual timbre of her voice often sounded nasal and 'blocked'. Free emission, the sound of a voice of natural beauty vibrating in perfect harmony, was simply not in evidence. But such is Mme Callas's witchcraft that one was utterly resigned to including her second scene of Act 2 among the supreme experiences of opera. Here – but not in the hooty 'Casta diva' – Mme Callas abandoned herself with perfect simplicity to the lament, which echoes the big cello tune of the orchestra, sitting and singing with her forehead propped on her hand. In the duet 'Mira, o Norma' she gave proof that whatever one may think of her as a singer or as a 'voice' she is a mighty performer.

As I mentioned earlier, the role which struck me as being her finest at Covent Garden was her Leonora in IL TROVATORE in 1953, and here, too, I have found that the critics and I were in agreement – something which cannot always be taken for granted. Desmond Shawe-Taylor, a genuine connoisseur of great singing, wrote in the *New Statesman*, 'The public was right to give her an ovation after her fourth-act aria, for Italian soprano singing of this calibre has not been heard at Covent Garden since the best days of Eva Turner';* while Hope-Wallace, far from being distracted by images of saws and planks, found that 'Her singing of "D'amor sull' ali rosee", trills and all, taken with the most perfect phrasing and a grandiose sweep, was a magnificent thing; the real grand manner again'.

It is interesting to check those memories against the TROVA-TORE recording which Callas made three years later with the forces of La Scala, Milan, under Karajan (EMI *CDS 7 49347 2*); it is obviously impossible for a studio performance to capture the electricity of those evenings in the opera house when Callas was in full cry and everything was going right for her, but the record-

---

* See *Legendary Voices*, pp.251–61.

ing certainly confirms the majestic style in which she undertook this role. She approached it as its earliest interpreters must have, trained as they were in the style of Bellini and Donizetti, not of later Verdi and Puccini. She saw the trills and decorations as an essential part of the vocal line, not as something which can be dispensed with if one finds them awkward, and she moulded the phrases with the same infinite care for detail that is such a characteristic of the early 'Qui la voce'.

The *Times* critic wrote in his notice of the Covent Garden TROVATORE, 'She is not an artist given to gesturing but when she moves an arm the audience sits forward, gripped by the stimulus of a dynamic personality in action,' and it might be supposed that on a recording Callas's celebrated talent as an actress would go for nothing. This is not the case, though, because with her the physical and the vocal acting were inextricably entwined. Again and again, not only in the big set pieces but also through the vocal inflections which she employs in passages which other singers might regard as unimportant, she piles up the little touches so essential for the building of a characterisation. For this reason she was at her happiest when she could work out a performance over a long period of detailed rehearsal with directors, conductors and designers who shared her views and her dedication, conditions which tend to be rare in the hectic world of international opera, but which to a large degree obtained during Callas's heyday at La Scala during the 1950s. The most famous product of these ideal conditions was probably the TRAVIATA of 1955, directed by Visconti, conducted by Giulini and with sets and costumes by Lila de Nobili. To my sorrow I never saw this production, but it has entered operatic myth, and a recording taken at the first night, now available on a two-CD set (EMI *CMS 7 63628 2*), gives us a fair idea of what an occasion it must have been. There was the usual healthy admixture of controversy because Visconti had decided to update the action to the *fin de siècle*, his sole reason being that Callas would look stunning in dresses of that period. 'I staged TRAVIATA solely for her,' he said, 'not for myself. I did it to serve Callas, for one *must* serve a Callas.' Giulini has described the detailed work which she undertook with Visconti and himself in order to achieve 'a complete blending of words, music and action . . . Each of Maria's gestures he [Visconti] determined solely on musical values,' as a result of which 'you felt her inspiration not only in the great moments, the famous arias and duets, but also when you heard her call the name of her maid in a recitative. It could break your heart.'

The recording certainly confirms that this production found Callas at the zenith of her artistic career, the voice still used fearlessly but with much greater control than at her Covent Garden début two and a half years earlier. The make-or-break solo scene at the end of Act I is stunning, not only for the panache of the florid passages (which culminate in a regular bull's-eye of a high E flat) but also for the manner in which she never reverts to being a prima donna with a set piece to sing, but always remains Violetta, riveting the attention even with lines of semi-recitative such as 'abbandonata in questo popoloso deserto che appellano Parigi' ('abandoned in this populous desert which people call Paris'). As the emotional changes are rung throughout this most emotionally demanding of all the great Verdi soprano roles Callas is the mistress of them all. She is vulnerable but heroic in the extended duet with Germont,* overwhelming in the passion of her 'Amami, Alfredo', and the very embodiment of dignified grief in the 'Alfredo, Alfredo, di questo core'; none the less it is perhaps in the last act that she displays her profoundest understanding of what it takes to achieve 'a complete blending of words, music and action'. The sound quality of the recording, understandably never anywhere near that of a studio version, undergoes a decline towards the end of the piece, but it cannot hide the fact that this was truly a performance to justify Callas's reputation as the

---

* Ettore Bastianini, possessor of probably the richest baritone voice I ever heard, maintains too relentless a forte. A friend of mine recently referred to his singing of this scene as being reminiscent of Queen Victoria's complaint about Mr Gladstone – 'He addresses me as if I were a public meeting.'

greatest singing actress of the post-war period.

Perfectionism in a singer can be an uncomfortable quality for the rest of the cast. I remember asking a mezzo soprano of my acquaintance whether it was a fact that a certain celebrated dramatic tenor with whom she had frequently appeared had been a perfectionist, to which she replied, 'If by that you mean that everything had to be perfect for him, yes he was.' To be fair, this was not the form which Callas's perfectionism took. She was herself a total professional who was never late for a rehearsal and never turned up less than note perfect, and her perfectionism was channelled into an all-consuming desire to do the best that could possibly be done for the piece in hand. This inevitably led to conflict with those colleagues who took a more happy-go-lucky view of things. Giuseppe di Stefano, her Alfredo in the TRAVIATA première, became so fed up with what appeared to him to be an exercise in the glorification of Maria Callas that he left the stage before the curtain-calls were over and walked out of the production with three performances still to run.

Incidents like this provided fuel for the fire of those journalists who were busy building the picture of Callas the Tigress, and from time to time she could assuredly be faulted. She behaved inexcusably towards Richard Tucker when they recorded AIDA together,* behaviour which, as Serafin explained to the infuriated tenor, arose from her necessity to create an atmosphere of tension; while her well-documented rows with operatic managements throughout the world kept newspaper editors and their readers happy for many a day. The longest-running of these contests was with Rudolf Bing, manager of the Met in New York, who eventually cancelled her contract for twenty-six performances in 1959, the main bone of contention being that Callas would not agree to

---

* One of the leading musical patrons of the day, Frederic Mann (after whom the Mann auditorium in Tel Aviv is named), had asked Tucker if he and his wife could attend one of the recording sessions. Although they were sitting quietly in a box Callas claimed that Mr and Mrs Mann were distracting her and insisted that they should leave, or she would leave herself.

appear as Violetta in between two performances as Lady Macbeth. When it came to handling the press Bing was an opponent well worthy of Callas's mettle. 'I am not prepared to enter into a public argument with Mme Callas', his press statement began, 'because I fully realise how much more skill and experience she has than I do in such matters. Although her artistic qualifications are the subject of violent debate between her friends and her enemies, it is well known far and wide that she has the gift of bringing her undeniable histrionic talent into her business dealings.' To this Callas replied with such broadsides as, 'When I think of the lousy TRAVIATA performances he had me sing, without rehearsal and without knowing my partners . . . do you call that art? All those performances, each with a different tenor or baritone . . . do you call that art?' – remarks which may have brought her a momentary sense of gratification, but which mostly served to reveal how little she was able to accommodate herself to the imperfect facts of operatic life. No singer is bigger than the institutions which employ us, not even Callas; she felt the need to be, and it did her untold harm. You tangle at your peril with people like Rudolf Bing,* especially if you have already succeeded in making yourself *persona non grata*, as she had, in Milan, San Francisco, Vienna and several other leading international houses.

To set against the occasional flare-ups between Callas and her stage partners (as opposed to her employers), several of those who were themselves sufficiently professional to tolerate her relentless dedication have testified how agreeable a colleague she could be. The baritone George London once wrote: 'When I learned that I would sing Scarpia to Callas's Tosca I must admit that I had a few forebodings. So much had been printed about this "stormy" star that I was prepared for almost anything. My first rehearsal reassured me. Here was a trouper, a fanatic worker, a stickler for detail.' He went on to describe an entirely friendly bit of banter

---

* Not for nothing did the British actor and director Cyril Ritchard say of him, 'Don't be deceived – beneath that cold, strict and sober exterior there beats a heart of stone.'

during the televising of a scene from the second act, which led to reports in several papers that he and Callas had fallen out. 'I tried to tell my friends that this was just not so', he continued, 'but I finally gave up. For I realised that Callas, the prima donna reincarnate, fires not only the imagination of her audiences but also of the press. They want her to be "tempestuous" and "fiery", and that is the way it is going to be. And I believe this is a good thing. It brings back a long-lost atmosphere of operatic excitement. There is nothing that can fire opera-goers – and send them to opera box-offices – so surely as the desire to see a genuine member of that sublime species, the prima donna.'*

Further to the subject of Callas as a colleague, I was recently given an interesting insight by Sir John Tooley, for many years Director of the Royal Opera House, Covent Garden. When Callas made a come-back there in 1964 as Tosca, the young and comparatively inexperienced tenor Renato Cioni had been engaged as Cavaradossi. Far from being dismissive of a partner less celebrated than those with whom she was accustomed to appear, Callas went out of her way to assist and encourage him – she respected him as an artist anxious to give of his best. Jon Vickers, too, who was her Jason in a celebrated production of Cherubini's MEDEA in Dallas in 1958, has left an entirely sympathetic picture of what it was like to work with Callas. Initially he had to stand up to her and prove that he was her equal in stamina, but thereafter, as he himself put it, 'She was a superb colleague. She never tried to steal anyone's thunder or manipulate anyone. The enormous operatic revolution of the post-war era can be attributed to two artists, Wieland Wagner and Maria Callas, who put her gifts to

---

* Tempestuous prime donne have long possessed a talent for hogging the headlines. I recently came across the following description of an earlier member of 'that sublime species' in a nineteenth-century publication: 'At the age of forty-five Caterina Gabrielli, a coloratura vocalist who had secured the admiration of various continental sovereigns, made her appearance in London. The most dangerous syren of modern times, she was wonderfully capricious, and neither interest nor flattery, nor threats nor punishment had any power to control her.'

almost masochistic use for the purpose of serving her work and bringing out the meaning of an opera.' When I saw the two of them together in MEDEA a year or two later in Epidauros Vickers's vocal performance was greatly preferable to that of Callas, whose steam-whistle top notes struck me as being simply no longer acceptable. Her dramatic portrayal, on the other hand, was on the grandest of scales. It was not, perhaps, entirely conducive to verisimilitude that when she made her first entrance as the sinister stranger whose identity is known to no one, swathed in black and with her face concealed, the action was suspended while thousands of enthusiastic admirers put up a welcoming roar of recognition; nor, in that vast arena, was it possible for the subtler details of her portrayal to register as they evidently did whenever she sang the role in an opera house of normal proportions. When she played it at Covent Garden in 1959 Desmond Shawe-Taylor was moved to write in *The Sunday Times*: 'It will be long before we forget the awful fixity of her oblique gaze, the barbaric passion of her pacings to and fro before the palace, the play of her supplicating or accusing hands, the fierce animal caressings of the two children she is about to murder. Even those who felt Cherubini to be too mild were riveted by the truth and force of Mme Callas's impersonation.'

Apart from her rows with managements, another fertile source of journalistic copy concerning Callas during this period of her life was the celebrated feud between herself and Renata Tebaldi; a quarrel which was not, I fancy, of either lady's choosing, but which was foisted onto both of them by the public's delight in partisanship. A similar situation exists today with Pavarotti and Domingo. Again and again people have asked me which of the two I prefer, and it is noticeable that they do not wish to be fobbed off with any such reply as 'I admire both of them equally in different roles' – one is required to deify the one by denigrating the other. So it was, *mutatis mutandis*, during my student days in Vienna. It was almost obligatory to be a Callas man or a Tebaldi man – I, when cornered, adhered to the latter faction – but whereas in our case it was merely a matter for friendly debate, in Italy it reached the stage where performances were disrupted by rival groups of supporters. Journalists would needle the two prime donne into making derogatory remarks about each other, and one Italian magazine produced a scoop in the form of parallel interviews published on opposite pages. The first question put to them both was how did they feel about the so-called fact that Callas was known as 'The Devil' and Tebaldi as 'The Angel'. For several paragraphs both ladies fought off this mischief-making by being scrupulously polite about each other, until Tebaldi, when asked if she thought that the description of herself as 'having no backbone' might have originated with Callas, replied that to her regret she thought it did, but that she at least possessed something which Callas lacked, namely a heart. Whether it was this indiscretion which fanned the flames I do not know, but eventually a British newspaper was able to quote Callas as saying, 'My repertoire, by God's will and nature's blessing, is complete. If the time comes when my dear friend Renata Tebaldi will sing, among others, Norma or Lucia or Anna Bolena one night, then La Traviata or Gioconda or Medea the next – then, and only then will we be rivals. Otherwise it is like comparing champagne with cognac. No – champagne with coca-cola!'

Earlier in this chapter I mentioned my enthusiasm for Callas as Lucia di Lammermoor in the Vienna State Opera in 1956. This was in a production from La Scala under Herbert von Karajan which had been performed during the previous year in Berlin and recorded on that occasion by Berlin Radio. EMI have now brought out this recording as a two-CD set, *CMS 7 63631 2*, and while not being the exact performance that I heard it comes very close to it. The cast is the same, though the orchestra is not, and Callas's voice sounds much as I remember it from Vienna. I have been intrigued to read almost totally dismissive references to these performances and to the recording in one of the most recent Callas biographies,* a book written by a widely respected

---

* *Maria Meneghini Callas*, by Michael Scott. See bibliography.

authority on the history of singing, in which the author declares that her voice had aged considerably since she sang the role at La Scala eighteen months previously, and specifically that it had become 'thinner and paler'. I remember thinking in Vienna, and the recording confirms those feelings, that she had benefited by slimming down her voice in such a way that she could manage the pyrotechnics of the Mad Scene without any of those sudden lurches into what I have referred to above as the Brünnhilde timbre.* It seemed to me to be more 'all of a piece' than it had been at the time of the Covent Garden Norma, and ideal in timbre for the sad, deluded figure of Lucia. The accuracy of the coloratura was phenomenal, and, as with the live recording of LA TRAVIATA, it gained immeasurably in impact through the degree to which she used it for the expression of the character she was portraying, and not merely as a display of vocal acrobatics.

Any Lucia is bound to be judged first and foremost on her handling of the Mad Scene, and the skill with which Callas moulded her phrases around the text she was singing was something that one encounters rarely in this repertoire – echoes of the early 'Qui la voce'. To me, though, almost equally impressive was the delivery of her opening solo, 'Regnava nel silenzio'. In the Mad Scene the singer knows that once she has put that behind her she is home and dry – thereafter come only the curtain-calls. When she launches into 'Regnava nel silenzio', on the other hand, she still has it all in front of her; she goes into it cold, not having picked up the feeling of the house and not knowing yet whether it is one of those evenings when everything goes right, or one when it is all a bit of a struggle. Here the recording gives us Callas the magnificent risk-taker, not easing herself into the part but taking every hurdle full tilt. The soaring melody is given a majestic flow,

---

* Between the Covent Garden Norma and the Berlin Lucia the celebrated slimming blitz had taken place. Experts disagree on the effect that this had on the voice. Purely visually I found her rather magnificent as Norma, a statuesque earth-goddess figure with red hair hanging down to the backs of her knees, though of course the svelte look of post-1953–4 was far more suitable for most of her repertoire.

the hideous vision of the silent ghost comes chillingly to life, the trills are crisp and clean, the marvellous sense of rhythm comes instantly into play and if there is a hint of the Callas shriek on one or two early high notes it does not prevent her from holding them through immaculately controlled diminuendi, or following them with gracefully graded downward swoops. Desmond Shawe-Taylor, who reviewed the Berlin performance for *Opera* magazine, wrote: 'Miss Callas, I must say, was tremendous. No more than on other occasions was she a flawless vocalist; but when singing at her best she diffused a kind of rapturous pleasure now virtually inaccessible from any other source.'

One of the most successful of Callas's studio complete sets is the LUCIA which she had recorded with Serafin three and a half years before the Berlin performance (EMI *CMS 7 69980 2*). The sound quality and the balance are predictably far better than those on the live recording, but equally predictably the sense of occasion is missing. I would certainly recommend the Serafin version to anyone wanting to buy a set for the opera itself rather than as an example of La Divina in the white heat of action, but I can think of few other singers with whom the difference of voltage between a live performance and a studio recording is so marked. This is not surprising when one hears first-hand accounts of how much it used to cost Callas to get herself onto the stage at all. Sir John Tooley has told me that before her first entrance she was always desperate to have someone in the wings with her, whose task it was to lend not only moral but also physical support – she would cling to that unfortunate person's arm with a strength that was positively frenzied. Her faithful dresser once showed Sir John a mass of bruises running from her wrist to her elbow, and on one occasion Callas's finger-nails drew blood from the palm of someone's hand. Almost all of us in the opera business suffer from nerves, especially at a first night, but mercifully not on that sort of scale. There are, as Nicolai Gedda once succinctly expressed it to me in a radio interview, two sorts of nerves – positive nerves, which key you up, set the adrenalin running and put an edge on your work, and negative nerves, which will detract from your performance if you are feeling unwell, unsure of your voice, or perhaps unsure of your role. In Callas's case there was an additional ingredient. By the time she had reached the highest pinnacle of her fame she had antagonised so many people that in certain countries she used to go on stage knowing that a sizeable proportion of the audience was longing for her to fail. To be assailed by the kind of nerves which amount to a form of terror, as she clearly did, must be an appalling burden, but at the same time it was probably part of her secret. Bernard Levin wrote in *The Times* not long ago, 'We all tingled when she entered as though we had touched a live wire', and I do not believe that any singer could generate that much current without suffering in the process.

As I have already indicated, it is not my intention to attempt a review of Callas's entire recorded output – that would be a book on its own. Suffice it to say that some of the full sets are distinctly more successful than others – the first TOSCA with di Stefano and Gobbi under Victor de Sabata (EMI *CDS 7 471758*) still strikes me as being the last word on that much recorded opera; IL BARBIERE DI SIVIGLIA (EMI *CDS 7 47634 8*) and IL TURCO IN ITALIA (EMI *CDS 7 49344 2*) display her remarkable versatility by presenting her in the guise of a coloratura comedienne; and even those recordings which do not find her at her best, amongst which I would class her AIDA (EMI *CDS 7 49030 8*), invariably contain at least something which is special. Of the many single-recital discs I might feel inclined to recommend one entitled 'La Divina 2' (EMI *CDC 5 55016 2*), but the choice is vast; and however much I may find to criticise about Maria Callas one cannot argue with the fact that seventeen years after her death her recordings continue to outsell those of any other operatic soprano.

The last time I heard Maria Callas in the flesh was the occasion of her concert in London's Royal Festival Hall on 26 November 1973, and for virtually all the wrong reasons it was an occasion which I fear I shall never be able to forget. I had recently come back to live in England after seventeen years working mainly in the German-speaking countries, and I was asked by the proprietor of a Swiss illustrated magazine to attend the concert and write an article on the lines of a younger singer's homage to the greatest of all opera stars. I was not expecting to find Callas back at the peak of her form. She had been through all the traumas of the split-up from her elderly husband and manager, Giovanni Battista Meneghini, and her universally publicised love affair with, and devastating abandonment by, Aristotle Onassis, during which time she had become one of the most famous women in the world, but one more written about in the gossip columns than on the arts pages. She had not sung in public since her final Covent Garden Tosca on 5 July 1965 – it had followed a string of cancellations on grounds of illness, but it earned her fifteen curtain-calls – and apart from excursions such as her public masterclasses at the Juilliard School in New York in 1971–2,* she had virtually disappeared from operatic sight. I assumed, though, that if she was now prepared to undertake a gruelling world tour she must have recovered some degree of her formal vocal prowess, but alas I was wrong. Armed with our press tickets my wife and I settled ourselves in a box, the other two occupants of which were a lady of forty or so and her schoolgirl daughter, both in a high state of excitement. The lady explained to me how she worshipped Callas above all other singers and was determined that her daughter should have at least one chance to hear her. When Callas entered on the arm of her tenor partner, Giuseppe di Stefano, and progressed slowly round the stage, picking her way between banks of flowers and acknowledging the cheers which broke out from every corner of the packed auditorium, for all the world like an empress receiving

---

* Recordings of these sessions, together with illuminating notes by John Ardoin, are available as a three-CD set on EMI *CDS 7 49600 2*. I have always been sceptical about this style of public tuition – the students are generally little more than cannon-fodder for a celebrity who can no longer command an audience in his/her own right – but the scope of Callas's knowledge of the operatic repertoire is truly remarkable.

the homage of her subjects, no one was cheering more vociferously than my neighbour. By the interval her cheers had turned to boos.

It was a catastrophic occasion, indeed I would go so far as to say a disgraceful one. In return for some of the most expensive tickets ever charged for a London concert the public was offered scarcely forty minutes' music – the rest of the programme consisted of the two stars prancing about, bowing and curtseying to their admirers – and I am not exaggerating when I say that on that evening's evidence neither of them would have stood the remotest chance of being engaged for the chorus of a small provincial opera house. There was just one brief moment, I remember, when di Stefano, with the phrase 'Bada, Santuzza, schiavo non sono di questa vana tua gelosia' in the duet from CAVALLERIA RUSTICANA, evoked faint memories of that once refulgent voice, but apart from that it was an unequivocal disaster. I remember looking down from our box onto a row which contained Lord Harewood, Elisabeth Schwarzkopf and Victoria de los Angeles, and wondering what thoughts were running through their minds – the latter lady, exactly the same age as Callas, and the former, eight years older, were both still singing splendidly – and I wondered, too, what the veteran accompanist Ivor Newton, who had in his time played for just about every great singer of the century, must have thought about it. In the interval I encountered Harold Rosenthal, the editor of *Opera* magazine, looking inconsolable. 'I have to go straight from here to a television studio,' he told me; 'what *am* I going to say?' 'Tell them the truth,' I replied, and with a note almost of pleading in his voice Harold simply said, 'I *can't*.'

Several suggestions have been made as to why Maria Callas should have let herself be a party to this humiliating and long-drawn-out farrago – the concert I attended was one of dozens which took place throughout the world. Having never been special friends during their glory days she and di Stefano had become very close, and according to one version it was he, sensing that Callas without a public would simply fade away, who persuaded her to climb back into harness. Another version is that she did it entirely for him. He was in financial difficulties, because apart from his lifelong weakness for the gambling tables he was now in the tragic position of needing money for the treatment of a teenage daughter who was dying of cancer. Whatever the truth of the matter I would not dwell at such length on this distressing event were it not for one aspect which I found fascinating. Despite everything, not many of the ticket-holders in the Festival Hall seemed to feel that they had been in any way short-changed. I am happy to say that the lady in our box was one of the few who felt it necessary to boo – whatever the provocation I find it a loathsome habit – and hundreds of people appeared happy to go on clapping and cheering as long as Callas and di Stefano felt inclined to keep walking on and off the stage. In my unaccustomed role of reporter I made it my business to mingle with as many of the audience as possible during the interval, and it became evident to me that there were masses of people there who were hearing Callas for the first time and were bowled over by her. I saw one young man rush up to another with the words 'Isn't she *fabulous*? It would have been worth the money just to see her in that frock!' That, I think, says it all – hundreds of people were happy simply to be in the presence of a legend.

Perhaps it was inevitable that the end of Callas's life should assume the veil of tragedy. She withdrew to her rented apartment in Paris, and there lived virtually the life of a recluse. Sir John Tooley has told me how he used to ring up from time to time and if ever she was out he hoped it meant that she was with friends, having fun; but when she called back it would always turn out that she had been on her own in the shops or at the hairdresser's. The social life which had once meant so much to her had totally lost its appeal. Exactly how or why she died, on 16 September 1977, aged not quite fifty-four, nobody really seems to know. She had been taking pills to help her sleep and pills to wake her up again, and though some people believe that she took her own life it seems likely that she did not so much come to a conscious decision to do so at that specific moment as surrender to a general sensation of the pointlessness of survival. Without Onassis, who had overturned her life, and singing, which had been her life, the real Callas had anyway ceased to exist. In an interview some years before with *Life* magazine she had made a prophetic statement: 'Remember always that only a happy bird sings, while an unhappy one creeps into its nest and dies.' Ornithologically unsound; but it could serve as her epitaph.

FEODOR CHALIAPIN

RUSSIAN BASS

b. Kazan, 1 February (13 February Old Style) 1873
d. Paris, 12 April 1938

Few singers can be said to have a lasting influence on the world of opera. Some, such as Caruso and Ruffo, can accelerate changes of fashion by being the ideal interpreters for composers who introduce a new style of music, while others, such as Callas and Supervia, can by the same means be responsible for reviving the public's interest in a type of opera which has fallen from favour. On the whole, though, singers, however wonderful their voices, merely grace the scene for a number of years and then depart, leaving the art of opera much as they had found it – that is the normal function of the interpretative rather than the creative artist. There has, however, been one singer in the twentieth century whose impact exceeded these normal limitations, a man whose genius and originality became the catalyst for a widespread reappraisal of many aspects of opera, and whose influence did not die with him – Feodor Chaliapin.*

Many great opera singers have had to suffer the burden of poverty in their early days but I think it would be fair to say that none has had to survive as much hardship and even degradation as Chaliapin. His father, a member of the peasant class, had learned to read and write and worked as a clerk for the town council of Kazan, but he was an alcoholic and spent most of his money on drink. Chaliapin's memories of his early

---

* Fashions in the transliteration of Russian names are subject to constant change and recordings have been issued under the names Fyodor Shalyapin, Fedor Schaljapin and so on. As a pronunciation guide the emphasis should be on the penultimate syllable of Chaliapin and not, as one customarily hears in the English-speaking world, on the first and final ones.

life centred largely around beatings – beatings from his drunken father, beatings from his schoolmasters, beatings from the various people to whom he was apprenticed while he was still too small to hit back. He compounded his difficulties by taking refuge in the world of his own imagination and by being resolutely uninterested in anything except singing and the theatre. His love of singing was probably inherited from his mother, who was illiterate but hard-working and used to sing doleful Russian melodies as she cooked and cleaned,* while his passion for the theatre was originally ignited by the antics of a favourite clown at the local fairground. For six years he sang in the choir of a neighbouring church where he learnt to read music, and during this time he took every possible opportunity to lap up whatever form of public entertainment his miserable circumstances allowed.

At the age of seventeen Chaliapin took to singing with various wandering opera and operetta troupes and undertaking such tasks as loading and unloading steamships on the River Volga whenever his engagements fell through, which they regularly did. At one point he earned his keep by amusing a colony of thieves and murderers with his songs, but had to escape when they tried to involve him in one of their professional operations. Penniless and starving, he spotted the body of someone who had died in the current cholera epidemic, and was fascinated by the fact that the dead man had a handkerchief clutched in one of his hands. As he himself described the incident many years later: 'I looked at this handkerchief as if in a nightmare and, crawling close to it, I finally pulled this dreadful scrap of fabric from the peeling hand. And when I opened it, Lord of all the Icons, I found in it four kopecks, do you hear, four kopecks, which made me happier than all the hundreds of thousands of francs I have earned since. I was able to eat, and leave for another town where there was no

---

* She died before Chaliapin's career had taken off, spending the end of her life as a beggar and being buried in a pauper's grave.

cholera, only the plague.'*

Chaliapin's travails eventually brought him to the verge of suicide, but one man succeeded in reversing this ghastly story and transforming his life. This was Dimitri Andreevich Usatov, who had had a distinguished career as a tenor in Moscow and who later devoted himself to teaching in the city of Tiflis, now known as Tbilisi. He not only took on Chaliapin as a pupil free of charge but also secured him a small grant, and furthermore made it his business to feed him up, clothe him and teach him the rudiments of civilised behaviour. Chaliapin was only with him for a year, as his voice was one which presented few problems, but Usatov was a teacher who went beyond the basics of vocal technique. He was evidently one of those people who possess the gift of firing their pupils with enthusiasm and Chaliapin never forgot his debt of gratitude – after Usatov's death Chaliapin supported his widow financially until the end of her life.

What one can reasonably regard as Chaliapin's real career began with a five-month season as soloist with the Tiflis Opera in 1893–4, during which he sang sixty-two performances in fourteen different roles. How he managed to master so many I cannot imagine, but he must have acquitted himself with credit because at the end of the season he was granted a benefit performance and was presented with a gold watch, a silver cup and 300 roubles in cash. He also persuaded the management to stage not one opera that evening, but two – PAGLIACCI, in which he took the high baritone role of Tonio, and FAUST – an arrangement which I would have expected to stretch the goodwill of his colleagues as well as the audience's ability to stay awake. In any case he had made such strides that he was able to secure an engagement with the Imperial Opera in the Mariinsky Theatre, St Petersburg, where he remained as a company member for the next two years.

---

* This quotation from an interview with a French journalist is published in Victor Borovsky's book *Chaliapin* (see bibliography), one of the finest biographies I know of any singer.

During this period Chaliapin was, on the surface, nothing more than an up-and-coming young bass who was attracting attention with the beauty of his voice, but who was regularly hauled over the coals by the critics for the ineptitude of his acting – not an unusual situation for someone who had received no dramatic training and was learning the job as he went along. Beneath the surface, however, the mental process was already fermenting which was to transform him into the greatest singing actor of his time, an unprecedented breaker of conventional moulds and probably the most widely discussed figure in the world of international theatre. The more he sang the more discontented he became with the artificiality of opera. Simply to sing as impressively as one could while going through the standardised motions of pretending to be a king, a high priest, a beggar or whatever else that particular evening may have thrown up was not enough for him; unless every vocal phrase told the audience something about the psychological state of the character he was playing, and unless every movement and every gesture contributed to this embodiment, he was dissatisfied with the results. He was beginning, though, to fall between two stools – it was all very well to be disenchanted with conventional operatic acting but he was in danger of making a fool of himself because he had not yet fully worked out what to offer in its stead.

He took to spending much of his time with straight actors, and especially with one of the outstanding personalities of the Russian stage, Mamont Dalsky. Chaliapin referred to Dalsky as 'a Russian Kean because of his talent and his dissipated way of life', and when the two friends were not hard at work on their theories of stage technique drink and women came high on the list of their leisure pursuits. Dalsky taught Chaliapin all he could about the importance of mental preparation for a new role, how to transpose yourself into both the mind and the body of the character you have to portray so that you end up thinking as he would have thought and moving as he would have moved. He also taught him that much of this is a matter of repetitive hard work – the uncanny effects which Chaliapin used to achieve with the

cloaks that he wore did not slip into place of their own accord –
and that it is no good on stage to deceive yourself into thinking
that you have *become* the character you are playing. It is fine if
the public or the critics go away saying 'Chaliapin *was* Boris',
but the real Boris did not prance around singing, and a singer's
job while playing Boris is to play and sing Boris as convincingly
as he knows how, not to *be* Boris. The question of how far it is
safe to lose yourself in a role that you are playing is a fascinating
one, and almost every colleague with whom I have spoken on the
subject agrees that however deeply 'in character' you may be there
is nothing more dangerous than allowing your own emotions to
take control. It is less likely to happen in opera than in straight
theatre, because in opera we can never afford to let our attention
wander too far from the conductor and the consideration of how
many beats there are in the next bar; but it is all too easy, especially if you are young and inexperienced, to shout while singing
a quarrel scene, for instance, or to become lachrymose over a
death or a parting. Neither shouting nor weeping will do your
voice production any good, and the more you allow yourself to
be carried away the less likely you are to carry your public with
you.

Chaliapin's opportunity to work out his newly devised theories
came when he moved from the Imperial Opera in St Petersburg
to a private company in Moscow run by a wealthy entrepre-
neur and patron of the arts named Savva Ivanovich Mamontov.
After Usatov, Mamontov emerges as the most essential figure in
Chaliapin's formative years because he gave him virtually *carte
blanche* to develop his roles as he himself wished. In the state-run
opera houses the word that counted was that of some bureaucrat
in the administrative office, whereas in Mamontov's company the
overriding considerations were always artistic, and if Chaliapin
could convince Mamontov that what he wanted to do had an
effective artistic purpose he would be allowed to do it. The
most influential members of Mamontov's creative team were the
designers: decisions about a singer's stance and movements would

grow out of their plans for the sets and costumes to the extent that the designers were almost functioning as stage directors. In the state-run theatres, by contrast, the scenery often had nothing whatever to do with the action of the piece being performed – it merely provided a back-drop for what was virtually a concert performance in costumes, and very predictable costumes at that.

Chaliapin became more and more fascinated by the visual arts, and in his determination to make his operatic characters as convincing as possible in every respect he developed uncanny skill as a make-up artist. He possessed by nature considerable talent as a draughtsman and sculptor and these he put to use in the transformation of his own appearance. He was an impressive figure of a man, six feet two inches tall and strongly built,* and he treated his face, which was basically a bland and open one, like a blank canvas onto which any likeness he chose could be superimposed. It is an extraordinary experience to compare photographs of Chaliapin in his many different roles; it is virtually impossible to detect a resemblance between any two of them, and none of them looks the slightest bit like the real Chaliapin. Anyone who is halfway competent with make-up can make himself more or less unrecognisable by hiding his features under a huge beard and sticking an outlandish wig on his head, but Chaliapin used to transform the actual shape of his physiognomy without recourse to any such obvious methods. As Don Quixote, for instance, the essential roundness of his countenance has been removed as if by surgery; this is a man of elongated features, the sturdy neck has become scraggy and the whole effect is one of emaciation, with the skull rising to a wispy, quizzical point. Then we turn to his Viking guest in SADKO and we are confronted by a totally different human specimen, a creature hewn out of granite with a lowering gaze and a massive, brooding brow. As Boito's Mefistofele he is not a human form at all, but some creature out of the darkest

---

* Though one regularly reads descriptions of his 'gigantic stature' they are exaggerated; it was the power of his personality which made him appear to dwarf those around him.

world of phantasies and nightmares, cruel, sardonic, like a massive serpent coiled to strike – and so the roll-call continues. As one of Chaliapin's colleagues in Moscow put it: 'Really, the term "making-up" does not do justice to the result of two hours' work in front of the mirror. Chaliapin was able to make the external aspect of the personage he was portraying reflect its true, inner character.'

If photographs give us some idea of the purely visual side of Chaliapin's characterisations, for the intensity of the life which he breathed into them we who never saw him obviously have to rely on the accounts handed down by those who did. To quote one of a thousand possible examples of this mesmeric power, at a dress rehearsal of BORIS GODUNOV in Paris in 1908, although Chaliapin, displeased as he frequently was by various imperfections in the circumstances of the rehearsal, had refused to wear costume or make-up, and although he was singing in Russian which the invited audience did not understand, when the terrified Tsar addressed the imaginary spectre of the murdered child in the Clock Scene those members of the audience who could not see the corner of the stage into which Chaliapin was gazing stood up in order to spot what it was that had filled him with such horror.

This spell of Chaliapin's could affect colleagues as well as audiences. Lotte Lehmann has left a vivid description of a performance of FAUST in which she sang Marguerite and he Méphistophélès:

> The impression he made was indescribable. After the scene where Méphistophélès challenges nature to help him in corrupting the innocent Marguerite, he stood like a tree, perfectly still against the background. He gave the impression of *being* a tree, and then, quite suddenly, he had disappeared, as if blown away. I did not see him sneak off, and I have no idea how he managed it, but it was black magic. At the end of the act . . . a tall figure appeared above me that twisted its way along the window like some frightful spider, seeming to encircle Faust and me. An indefinable terror made me go cold. This was no longer opera, this had turned into some terrible reality. And when the curtain

came down, and Méphistophélès changed back into Chaliapin,
I breathed a sigh of relief. So great was this man's magic.

The rest of the evidence left to us when we attempt to imagine the
effect of Chaliapin in performance – apart from the film of *Don
Quixote* which he made in 1933 with music by Ibert, and a silent
film of 1915 entitled *Tsar Ivan the Terrible* – lies in his recordings, and here one should not be too put off by Neville Cardus's
oft-quoted verdict: 'You can get no more idea of Chaliapin from
a gramophone record than you get of a pterodactyl by looking
at a skeleton preserved in a museum – because he was such an
enormous, abounding personality on the stage.' True up to a
point, no doubt, but the skeleton in the museum *is* better than
nothing at all, and in any case several of the Chaliapin reissues
on CD are considerably more than skeletal in their effectiveness.
On *Lebendige Vergangenheit 89030*** we have sixteen tracks from
the earlier years of Chaliapin's recording career, 1907–12, and they
provide incontrovertible evidence that taken purely as a singer he
was a very remarkable performer indeed. His voice was probably
at its absolute best during this period, the sound wonderfully
rounded and, despite the many dramatic effects to which it is put,
essentially soft-grained in quality. It is not the inky-hued bass of
a Kipnis or a Ghiaurov; although all the bottom notes are there
with no trouble it is the amplitude of the middle register and the
ease of the top which really impress. One of the most beautiful
pieces of singing on the disc is the aria in which Nilakantha,
the Brahmin priest in LAKME, gives tender expression to his
feelings of love for his daughter, and Nilakantha is classified as
a bass-baritone role. The ease of a high F attack in 'Ave Signor'
from Boito's MEFISTOFELE and the steadiness with which this
regal note is sustained give further confirmation that the voice was
by nature more of a basso cantante in the Italian mould than what

---

* Readers should not be put off by this mouthful of a title. It simply means
'Living Past' in German and is the name of an excellent Viennese company which
specialises in the reissuing of old recordings.

we normally think of as a 'black Russian bass'.

Mefistofele was the role which launched Chaliapin's international career when he sang it at La Scala, Milan, in 1901.
The engagement of this totally unheard-of Russian was an act
of considerable daring by the director of La Scala, Giulio Gatti-
Casazza; he was determined to bring Boito's opera back into the
repertoire, but was consistently discouraged from doing so by
the composer himself, who felt that no Italian bass of the day
possessed the theatrical ability to give the title-role that special
something which it required. Chaliapin was recommended to Gatti
by a Russian Count who was involved in the administration of the
Imperial Theatres and who happened to be in Milan on a visit.
This gentleman described Chaliapin as an artist whose voice was
no better than that of several chorus singers – how remarkable
the bass sections of Russian choruses must have sounded! – but
whose personality would make him ideal for Mefistofele. On the
Count's say-so Chaliapin was engaged, which provoked a furore
in Milanese artistic circles and widespread accusations that Gatti
had betrayed his country. This may seem an excessive reaction,
but in those days the vocal traffic between Italy and Russia
flowed exclusively in the other direction. The stars of Italian
opera travelled regularly to St Petersburg, where they were lavishly
received and munificently rewarded, but it had never happened
before that a performer from the mysterious and, in the eyes of
many Westerners, barbaric land beyond the Carpathians had paid
a return visit. When Chaliapin arrived at La Scala everyone took a
liking to him – Gatti wrote in his memoirs of his 'simplicity and
joyousness of temperament', a side of his personality which was
not always on parade – but as he gave hardly any voice at the first
musical rehearsal Boito and the conductor, Toscanini, began to
fear that a terrible mistake had been made. At the second rehearsal
Toscanini asked him to sing out; Chaliapin obliged, and instantly
all worries evaporated. 'He prepared his role', Gatti wrote, 'with
that attention and diligence which characterises the few members
of that select company of artists who look after everything, think

of everything, with perfect conscientiousness. His Mefistofele turned out to be something new, without precedent, breaking all traditions. His make-up and costume have since been copied by everyone, but above all were his great authority, mobility of countenance, richness of expression and incredible acting.' As Boito put it: 'Only now do I realise that up to this time I never had any but poor devils.' As a further indication of the extent of Chaliapin's triumph he almost succeeded in stealing the notices from Caruso in the role of Faust. Although, according to the *Gazzetta dei teatri*, Caruso was in such glorious voice that applause broke out every time he stopped singing, the lion's share of the critics' praise was lavished on the new phenomenon. Indeed, during the course of his long career this star quality of Chaliapin's was to raise the whole status of bass singers, who so often have to content themselves with a supporting role while the soprano and tenor bask in the limelight.

Strangely enough, the very qualities which brought Chaliapin such success as Mefistofele in Milan led to an utterly different reception from several of the most influential critics when he made his New York début in the same role six years later. Where his appearance in the Prologue, as naked as contemporary stage conventions would allow, had caused a thrill at La Scala it caused shudders at the Met. Henry Krehbiel of the *New York Tribune* wrote of his performance, 'It calls to mind more than anything else the vulgarity of conduct which his countryman Gorky presents with such disgusting frankness in his pictures of Russian low life', while W. J. Henderson of the *New York Sun* complained: 'He is continually snarling and barking. He strides and gestures, grimaces and roars. All this appears to superficial observers to be tremendously dramatic. The present writer much prefers a devil who is a gentleman.' To add to Chaliapin's chagrin when he was shown such notices as these there appeared to be a plot afoot to prevent him from seeing the favourable ones. Of his Basilio in IL BARBIERE DI SIVIGLIA the critic of the *Evening World* wrote: 'Thanks primarily to Chaliapin, the best performance within memory of Rossini's opera was given last night . . . The audience, which was a large one, bubbled over all the time that he was on stage. Peal after peal of laughter followed his utterances' – but nobody translated this to Chaliapin. In some quarters it was felt that the director of the Met, Heinrich Conried, had come under pressure for engaging a mere bass at $1600* a performance, more than he was paying anyone except Caruso, and that he himself was hoping to see the back of this extravagant acquisition. In any case Chaliapin left the United States feeling less than enchanted by his experiences and did not return to the Met until 1921, when his fee as Boris Godunov had risen to $3000 a performance, more than anyone was destined to receive there until the late 1960s.

The *Lebendige Vergangenheit* disc includes several interesting recordings of Chaliapin in the Italian *bel canto* repertoire, one in which he was seldom heard in the years of his international fame. The gentle cantilena of Count Rodolfo's greeting to the scenes of his childhood in LA SONNAMBULA flows smoothly on a tide of warmly human nostalgia, and in the great bass arias from Verdi's ERNANI and DON CARLOS there is much to be admired and enjoyed. Here and there, however, in his desire to extract the maximum effect from the text, Chaliapin does undeniable violence to the legato line, as well as paying scant heed to the difference between dotted and undotted notes. When Verdi appended the direction *parlato a mezza voce* (spoken in half voice) to King Philip's sinister utterance of 'Se dorme il prence, veglia il traditore' ('If the prince sleeps the traitor awakes'), I doubt if he imagined quite such distortions of the notes as this particular monarch allows himself.

Chaliapin, however, was clearly more than happy with the histrionic effect of these idiosyncracies of his because when he re-recorded the same aria in 1922 he went even further in the same direction. This later version forms one of thirty-six tracks on a Nimbus two-disc selection (*NI 7823/4*) which gives a splendid

---

*   Approximately the equivalent of £12,500 or $19,000 at the time of writing.

summary of Chaliapin's recorded output, extending from 1911 to 1936, and including plenty of songs as well as numerous examples from the repertoire with which his name will always be most closely associated, that of Russian opera. The song of the Viking guest from SADKO exactly matches the picture of him in the role which I have already described – monolithic, uncompromising and self-contained; while his account of Prince Galitzky's outbursts from PRINCE IGOR, in which that dissolute figure lauds the delights of wine, women and song, is one of the most compellingly extrovert pieces of singing I know, the sort of performance which picks an audience up and carries it along on the tide of the singer's own jubilation. In the title-hero's lament for his lost love in Rachmaninov's ALEKO the vocal colour changes to one of bleak despair, and this ability of Chaliapin's to transform the timbre of his voice almost as radically as he did his appearance led to an interesting comparison being made by a colleague of his, the baritone Sergei Levik, between the skills of Chaliapin and Titta Ruffo. 'Titta Ruffo', he wrote, 'found colours for each given section of the role and adroitly superimposed them on the foundation of his voice, and we always said "What a voice Titta had in such and such a passage!" When we talked of Chaliapin, however, we would say: "What a voice Chaliapin had as Boris (or the Miller, Méphistophélès, Basilio)." '

There can be little doubt that the voice which Chaliapin used for Aleko was just the one the composer wanted because Chaliapin's friendship with Rachmaninov was one of the deepest he ever formed and it was a relationship strengthened by immense mutual respect. They first met when Rachmaninov was engaged by Mamontov as assistant conductor for his opera company, and he coached Chaliapin in three of his most important roles, including Boris Godunov. He gave Chaliapin the musical education which he had never had the chance to acquire elsewhere and Chaliapin in turn taught Rachmaninov a great deal about the art of writing music for the human voice. In personality the two of them offered a perfect example of complementary opposites, Rachmaninov introspective, nervous, easily depressed, and Chaliapin gusty, inexhaustible, the matchless raconteur whose charm, when he chose to switch it on, could melt an iceberg. Rachmaninov used to call Chaliapin 'a big difficult child', adding that to accompany him was the greatest joy of his life, while Chaliapin regarded Rachmaninov as the ultimate authority on all matters musical.

One of the most extraordinary aspects of Chaliapin's career, it always seems to me, is the extent to which he, the rough, crude product of a hideously deprived childhood, was able to become a central figure in the cultural life of his country, enjoying the friendship and respect of leading personalities in virtually every branch of the arts. It was not only musicians such as Rachmaninov who sought his company but painters and writers too, Maxim Gorky perhaps the most prominent amongst them, and no less a figure than the great director Konstantin Stanislavsky was known to seek his advice. When Diaghilev organised the first of his series of Russian concerts in Paris in 1907, thereby raising the curtain as far as Western Europe was concerned on the glittering diversity of riches which Russian art had to offer, it was Chaliapin who really captured the public's imagination. At the opening concert the power of his performance and his personality roused the audience to such a frenzy that the conductor, the great Artur Nikisch, had to abandon the last orchestral number on the programme; he was driven from the platform by persistent cries from the gallery of 'Chaliapin, Chaliapin!'

Needless to say, personal success on such a scale as this can make a performer less than popular with his colleagues, and there were times when Chaliapin's unprecedented prominence led to resentment. Rimsky-Korsakov declined to rewrite the baritone role in one of his operas for Chaliapin because he was afraid that the singer's inevitable triumph would obliterate interest in the opera itself, and when Chaliapin's single-minded pursuit of perfection in the visual presentation of his own roles overflowed into a demand that the rest of the cast should present themselves in a compatible manner he met with predictable resistance. Nevertheless, when he was wooed away from the Mamontov Company and joined the Bolshoi Theatre he was in a position to present the director with an astonishing document headed 'Conditions under which I, Chaliapin, am prepared to work at the Imperial Theatres'. Its seven clauses included demands that only conductors of his choosing should be in charge of his performances, that a fully authorised member of the management should be present at all times when Chaliapin was rehearsing or performing so that any requirements of his could be instantly met, that the rest of the company should submit to his professional demands as though he were the principal director, that the theatre's lighting equipment should be totally overhauled – and so on. Whenever Chaliapin was crossed in his artistic demands, or if ever he encountered sloppiness of effort, he would fall into a rage that was fearful to behold. It was a favourite theory of his that the Russian character admits of no moderation, and in his bewildering switches of mood from boisterous good humour to uncontrollable wrath it was a theory which he himself did nothing to disprove.

The stage role in which Chaliapin introduced himself with sensational impact to the opera public first of Paris (1908) and then of London (1913) was Mussorgsky's Boris Godunov. It had been not the least of Usatov's services to Chaliapin that he had introduced him to the music of Mussorgsky, music whose essential Russian-ness stirred the young singer to the depths of his being. 'How I revere and love Mussorgsky,' he once said while he was preparing the role. 'In my opinion this great man was created on the same mighty scale as one of Michelangelo's statues.' In his determination to find out everything he could about the character and the times of Godunov he travelled from Moscow to the distant country home of the most eminent Russian historian of the day, Vasili Kliuchevsky, a man who possessed the knack of describing the figures of the past in a manner which brought them vividly back to life for his listeners. The music, the text (adapted by the composer from a tragedy by Pushkin), the rest of the characters in the cast, all so familiarly Russian, and the central figure of the Tsar himself combined in Chaliapin's imagination to form a unified artistic whole in which his own instincts and aspirations could reach their completest fulfilment. When he first sang the role with Mamontov's company in 1898, to quote a contemporary critic, Edward Rozanov, 'Chaliapin rose to new heights of musical and dramatic interpretation rarely seen on the operatic stage' – and at that time he was still only twenty-five years old. By the time his Boris reached London it had matured into a performance of astonishing theatrical power, and, surprisingly perhaps for those who have attempted over the years to denigrate Chaliapin as something of a 'ham', it was the restraint of his acting which most deeply impressed the critics. In an article entitled 'The Art of Chaliapin; the secret of his appeal' the *Times* correspondent wrote '. . . his way of standing, of eating and drinking, of doing the commonest things, all express character so eloquently because they are the outcome of the character which is his for the moment. His acting comes out of him, and is not superimposed upon him.'

The last of these London performances – they were at Drury Lane, not Covent Garden – gave rise to the kind of incident in which no other singer but the combustible Chaliapin could possibly have figured, and which is hilariously described in the memoirs of Sir Thomas Beecham. It was an extra performance, mounted at the request of the British Royal Family, and there had been some talk of it being a benefit performance for the Russian chorus, to whom Chaliapin was thought to be donating his fee. Things went badly wrong, however, when Chaliapin entered for the Coronation Scene and found that the only members of the chorus to have come on stage were the British supernumeraries. There followed an unholy row during which the Russian chor-isters' spokesman so inflamed Chaliapin that he floored the man with a single mighty blow; whereupon, in the words of Sir Thomas, 'Like a pack of wolves the rest of the chorus flung themselves upon him, brandishing the tall staves they were to use in the next scene; the small English group rushed to his assistance and the stage-door keeper telephoned for aid to the police station, which luckily was hardly a stone's throw from the theatre. The struggle was still raging when a few minutes later Drury Lane beheld the invasion of about a dozen familiar figures in blue, and very soon something like order was re-established, but not before my own manager had intercepted with his head a blow intended for Chaliapin, which raised a lump as big as a fair-sized plum.' When Chaliapin emerged from his dressing-room for Act II he took the precaution of stowing a brace of loaded pistols into the pockets of his sumptuous gown, and after the performance was safely over the altercation continued until well after five a.m. 'But the following morning', Sir Thomas concludes, 'they all turned up punctually for rehearsal, as blithe and unconcerned as if nothing unusual had happened, and as if wrath and violence had no part in the Slav temperament.'

Chaliapin appeared in an extensive repertoire of Russian operas – the Drury Lane season also introduced Mussorgsky's KHOVAN-SHCHINA and Rimsky-Korsakov's THE MAID OF PSKOV* to British audiences – but Boris was the role with which, particularly in Western countries, he was most closely identified; as the critic of the *Daily Graphic* wrote after one of his performances at Covent Garden in 1928: 'In the mind of the public Chaliapin and Boris are so intertwined that many people find it difficult to think of one without the other.' It was also the role which led to a reconciliation between Chaliapin and the United States, a country which he had vowed never to revisit after his début season at the Met. In the winter of 1921–2 Gatti-Casazza, who had moved from La Scala to the Met, was desperate to provide the public with as many attractions as possible to compensate for the loss of Caruso, who had died the previous August; Maria Jeritza and Titta Ruffo were both signed up, and Chaliapin was brought back as Boris. This time the critics sang a very different tune, and Henry Krehbiel, who had been so dismissive fourteen years before, was amongst the most enthusiastic. 'Last night', he

---

* Also known as IVAN THE TERRIBLE.

wrote, 'nobility of acting was paired with a beautiful nobility of voice and vocal style, and his Boris stood out of the dramatic picture like one of the old-time heroes of tragedy. He sang in Russian;* and though it was possible even for those unfamiliar with the language to feel some of that intimacy which must exist between the original text and the music, the effect on the Russians in the audience was akin to frenzy. All that we have heard of the greatness of his impersonation of the character of Boris was made plain. It was heart-breaking in its pathos, terrible in its vehemence and agony.'

Between 1910 and 1931 Chaliapin made numerous recordings from BORIS GODUNOV, including Pimen's Narration and Varlaam's aria, as well as different versions of the principal scenes for Boris himself. On the Nimbus disc quoted above we find two studio recordings of the great monologue 'I have attained the highest power', one made acoustically in 1923 and the other electrically in 1931. The earlier is perhaps vocally more ingratiating – Rosa Ponselle, who sang with Chaliapin during this period of his career at the Met, described his voice as one of the 'warmest there ever was' – but it seems that he felt better able to let rip dramatically when faced with a microphone than with an acoustic horn. In his search for the perfect marriage between text and music he appears to me to have developed a technique of his own, a delivery which never ceases to be sung and never quite overflows into the realms of *Sprechgesang*, but in which each syllable, no matter in which register of the voice it is pitched, is articulated with such eloquence and depth of feeling that the overall effect is almost that of a heightened form of speech. When, in the Clock Scene, Chaliapin intensifies this theatrically gripping style of delivery with the gasps of a man stifling with pent-up horror he releases a merciless assault on the nerves of the listener, and had I been at that dress rehearsal in Paris I feel sure I would have been on my feet with the rest of them. As for the final scene, recorded

---

* The rest of the cast sang in Italian, as was customary at that time.

in London during a live performance of 1928, it lends credence to Neville Cardus's words, 'I have watched people in the stalls at Covent Garden when he was in the throes of the death scene and I could see their hair bristling.' Whether muted to the merest whisper,* or hurled into the auditorium in a final cry of defiance, Chaliapin's voice is an instrument of staggering theatrical potency.

In my chapter on Maria Callas I have referred to a certain dichotomy which lay at the heart of her search for perfection, and in the case of Chaliapin this characteristic becomes even more evident. At one of the BORIS performances at Covent Garden in 1928 he suddenly strode off the stage during a scene in which Prince Shuisky was imparting vital information to him and launched into a fierce altercation in the wings with the chief electrician, who, in the words of one contemporary account, 'resented it'. So much for *being* Boris. In the same season, as Méphistophélès in Gounod's FAUST, he became dissatisfied with the tempi chosen by the conductor, Eugène Goossens, and strode down to the footlights hissing *'plus vite, plus vite'*. Goossens, who had already complained to the management that at the piano rehearsal Chaliapin had been 'as usual very shaky in the matter of both words and music', refused to budge, much to the admiration of the *Times* critic who wrote of the dramatic potential of having 'a live wire in the pit, and a high explosive on the stage'. On another occasion, when the company of the Met was appearing in the Eastman Theater at Rochester, New York, Chaliapin had a vested interest in the performance not running over time, as he was catching a boat for Europe early the following morning. When the stage-hands seemed to him to be dilatory in the setting up of scenery for the last act they suddenly found Méphistophélès in their midst, and, as one eyewitness has recalled, he was 'lashing at them, ordering this to be put there,

---

* Rosa Ponselle once gave a nice description, too, of Chaliapin's soft singing. 'His pianissimos were like honey – when the last little bit leaves the spoon, a little thread that gets thinner and thinner until you almost can't see it, but it's still there.'

and that to pulled here, shouting "Idiots! Move! Faster! Faster!", his arms whirling, his voice cracking with rage'.

Sometimes Chaliapin's determination to involve himself in aspects of a performance which are not normally considered the singer's legitimate business could produce startlingly beneficial results. The leading Chicago critic, Edward Moore, described one such occasion in the following terms:

> Having come on for a rehearsal of the opera MEFISTOFELE Chaliapin pronounced himself dissatisfied with it, took it all apart and put it together again. Will those who saw the performance ever forget it, not only for Chaliapin himself, but those surrounding him? Who can forget the Brocken scene, where, after some instruction from the star, the customarily placid chorus was suddenly converted into a whirling, shrieking, frenzied crew of minor devils on a diabolical spree? And over them all sat the giant himself, half nude, gloating, dominating his followers, deriding the world, blazing out in his voice of golden trombone, sweeping back the stageful with a wave of the arm. It was one of the most magnificent scenes in all the history of the Chicago Opera.*

Amongst the many other Chaliapin reissues on CD I would like to recommend EMI's *CDH 7610092*, a single disc dedicated exclusively to Russian opera and including the Coronation Scene from BORIS as well as the Monologue, the Clock Scene and the Death Scene; also Pearl's contribution, amounting to four CDs in all. Two of them appear as a set (GEMM *CDS 9920*), which is of particular interest as it extends from a hitherto unpublished recording from 1910 of the genial aria 'In olden days our forefathers lived a merrier life' from ASKOLD'S TOMB by Verstovsky, the composer who is sometimes hailed as 'the father of Russian opera', to the version of Mussorgsky's 'The Song of the Flea' which Chaliapin

---

* In his book *Forty Years of Opera in Chicago* Moore tells a story of Chaliapin, curious to see how a major newspaper operates, coming to look for him in his office at the *Tribune*. Moore was out and on his return a member of the staff told him that 'a big Swede named Charley Apple' had been looking for him.

recorded in his very last session, on 6 February 1936 in Tokyo. This number was a virtual *sine qua non* at Chaliapin's concerts – audiences would not let him go until he had sung it – and it is evident that at the age of sixty-three he was still putting it over with the same malicious glee as he had twenty, thirty and forty years before, the chuckles still as spontaneous and the irony still as biting.

Chaliapin's recitals were quite unlike any other singer's. Instead of deciding in advance what songs he would be singing so that the audience could be provided with the usual printed programme he would make up his mind from one song to the next as to what best suited his own mood and that of his listeners. They would be armed with booklets containing the texts of a vast array of songs – at the Albert Hall in 1925 the booklets contained 104 songs and in 1937 seventy-seven – and Chaliapin would announce 'Number So-and-so' as the spirit moved him. There would then be a brief pause while the public read up the text of that particular song and the accompanist searched feverishly in his pile of music hoping that he had it with him. Chaliapin used to claim that these recitals were more of a strain to him than a stage performance, because by nature he could not help acting out every song he sang, which meant that during the course of an evening he would have to undertake dozens of different characterisations rather than only one; and where most recitalists will take up a position somewhere near the piano and then remain relatively still, Chaliapin would range freely around the platform giving rein to his dramatic instincts.

Several of Chaliapin's favourite concert numbers feature in the Nimbus set referred to above, and another *Lebendige Vergangen-heit* release, *89207* (two discs), offers no less than thirty-eight songs, all recorded electrically between 1926 and 1934. They include Schubert's 'Der Tod und das Mädchen' and 'Der Doppel-gänger' and Schumann's 'Die beiden Grenadiere', all sung in Russian with orchestral accompaniment, and to enjoy these it is essential to dismiss from one's mind any preconceived ideas about the singing of classical Lieder. As the accompanist Gerald Moore wrote in his memoirs:

> A song by Schubert or Schumann would be distorted out of all recognition by his wayward rhythm and his own personal interpretation of the poem. In 'Der Tod und das Mädchen', death would become a sinister threatening spectre, instead of the sublime comforter that Claudius's words and Schubert's music indicate. The Grenadier in Schumann's music and Heine's words, expiring to the sound of the Marseillaise became a conquering and resilient figure; and when I played the postlude which depicts the dying soldier's gradual collapse, the music was unheard, engulfed by the storm of applause which Chaliapin deliberately evoked. He was bowing to all sides of the Hall while I played and was walking off the platform before I had finished.

Moore feels obliged to add 'Yet there is no doubt in my mind that I was playing for a great singer, who could lift the audience out of their seats and thrill them as few basses before or since have been able to thrill. Certainly I have never been associated with a more exciting artist'; and therein lies the nub of the matter. Chaliapin would not have cared tuppence for a review which accused him of doing violence to Schubert. He interpreted everything as he himself felt it, and the songs he chose to sing were the songs which stirred his own emotions – an approach which trampled on many an accepted stylistic tenet but which invested everything he sang with his own elemental power of expression. When he interprets Death as seen by Mussorgsky in 'Trepak', the Death who invites a drunken old peasant to join him in a dance, Chaliapin is on territory where no Westerner would have dared to question his stylistic credentials, and if he chose to see Schubert's Death in much the same light – well, that was Death as he himself had witnessed it often enough.

The majority of the tracks in this selection are naturally

Russian songs, including such celebrated Chaliapin party pieces as Koenemann's 'The King Went Forth to War' and his own arrangement of 'The Song of the Volga Boatman', both marvellously vocalised, the former a theatrical *tour de force* and the latter an object lesson in how to create atmosphere by purely vocal means. They both end on just the kind of honeyed threads of sound which Ponselle so graphically evoked, but from an anecdote in the memoirs of the accompanist Ivor Newton we learn that this particular weapon in the Chaliapin armoury could occasionally misfire. They were recording Massenet's 'Elégie' – the final result features in the *Lebendige Vergangenheit* set – with Cedric Sharpe providing the cello obbligato, and for various reasons it seemed difficult to achieve a satisfactory version. 'As work went on,' Newton writes,

> Chaliapin took off his collar and tie, then opened his shirt to the waist, displaying a startlingly white, hairless torso. 'We shall get it right now,' he declared confidently, and all went well until the closing bar of the song, when his voice cracked on the penultimate pianissimo note. At this, Chaliapin flew into a rage and hit himself, with full force and clenched fist, on the side of the face, hard enough to make himself stagger. Cedric Sharpe hid behind his cello and I was prepared to dive under the piano, but the storm was momentary and ended with an apology. 'Forgive me, gentlemen,' he said mournfully, 'but you must admit that that was very disappointing.'

Newton also provides a graphic account of how that rollicking number 'Down the Petersky' (in which Chaliapin enacts an inebriated lady of easy virtue) came to be recorded. The accompaniment was provided by a balalaika group, whose conductor had little idea of how the music was supposed to go, and eventually Chaliapin asked with the utmost politeness if he himself could take the baton. Thereupon everything suddenly went right – everything, that is, except for the playing of the largest of the balalaikas, which was entrusted to the only woman in the group, a severely dressed lady, plain and of a certain age. 'In the mood of extreme graciousness which had so far prevailed,' as Newton puts it, 'he asked her permission to demonstrate how he wished her to play a certain glissando passage. She then played it perfectly and, when Chaliapin thanked her, he threw her a kiss, and for a moment she became positively beautiful. Then I began to realise the complete validity of the Chaliapin legend as I had known it.'

On that particular occasion Chaliapin had arrived late for the session because he had been detained at his tailor's – always an important event for him, as he was highly clothes-conscious – but as we learn from the reminiscences of that great pioneer of the recording industry Fred Gaisberg, in his early days in Russia it was impossible to predict whether Chaliapin would turn up in the studio at all. Sessions were usually arranged for the late evening, and Gaisberg would go round to Chaliapin's palatial residence to collect him, but if he was feeling less than entirely happy about the state of his voice Gaisberg would find him still in bed. On the occasion of Chaliapin's very first session, by the time Gaisberg had persuaded him to get up, get dressed and climb aboard the waiting sleigh the chorus and orchestra had been hanging around in the studio for several hours; and yet so great was their respect for the star that his arrival was greeted with enthusiastic cheering. That evening Chaliapin turned out to be tireless. Hour after hour he sang in resplendent voice, one recording was completed after another, and they worked until one o'clock in the morning. When they eventually finished Chaliapin invited Gaisberg and the entire chorus to join him for dinner in a restaurant which boasted gipsy entertainers, and there he carried on singing and conducting, pausing only to become involved in a brawl with a gentleman who was trying to conduct a choir of his own in another corner of the establishment, for several hours more. Gaisberg, after one of the wildest nights he had ever experienced, eventually returned to his hotel at eight a.m.

To return, though, from these bacchanalian goings-on to the *Lebendige Vergangenheit* CD, amongst the many other memorable performances in this particular set there are the four principal solos from the *Don Quixote* film, conducted by the composer, and the intensely evocative 'Twofold Litany' by Gretchaninov with the Choir of the Russian Metropolitan Church in Paris – a piece which, within six years of the recording, was to be sung at Chaliapin's funeral. There is also one other number which I would like to discuss in some detail, not because it is musically of special value – indeed it is one of the least distinguished compositions in the set – but because it is sung in English. I imagine that when listening to the vast majority of Chaliapin's recordings many of my readers will suffer from the same disadvantage as myself, namely that of not understanding the Russian language. If one follows the text with a translation alongside one can of course form a good impression of his interpretative powers; but I have always been of the opinion that when one listens to any great vocal actor it is impossible to appreciate the finest nuances unless one is thoroughly familiar with the language being sung. The song to which I am referring now is a sentimental ballad entitled 'The Blind Ploughman' and it opens with the words 'Set my hands upon the plough, my feet upon the soil'. It is not, in other words, a great poem any more than it is a great piece of music; and yet I am not ashamed to admit that when I first came across the recording a number of years ago so intense was the effect of hearing this extraordinary man speaking to me in his touchingly personal version of my own language, that by the time he had reached the final lines 'God has made his sun to shine on both you and me, God who took my eyes away that my soul might see' I was as deeply moved as if I had been listening to a tragic masterpiece. Trite though the song may be the passion of this performance eliminates any mental picture of Chaliapin in a recording studio or standing in his tail suit on a concert platform – the image he manages to evoke is one of him standing with his hands on the plough, his sightless eyes gazing at the sky.

Despite the triumphant manner in which Chaliapin had survived his early struggles and emerged as one of the most celebrated figures in his native land his troubles were not over. When the

Revolution broke out he was initially sympathetic – after all, no one knew better than he what life at the bottom of the pile could be like under Tsarist rule. In 1918 he returned to the Mariinsky Theatre as soloist and artistic director and for a while he was on friendly terms with Lenin and Trotsky. It soon became evident to him, however, that in the name of democracy these people were introducing a regime far more oppressive than that which they had replaced. Management of the theatres was passing into the hands of political commissars and associates of Chaliapin's started disappearing to the torture chambers. He was allowed to leave the country in 1921 to sing in England and America but neither his wife (he was married twice) nor his children, to whom he was deeply devoted, were allowed to join him, so he returned to Russia. In June 1922 he left again, supposedly for another limited period, but this time some of his family were given permission to leave as well and he never went back. He set up home in Paris and eventually all his family except for his eldest daughter joined him there. Although he had lost one fortune he was still able to build up another and they all lived in comfort, but from the soles of his feet to the hair on his head Chaliapin was a Russian and it was bitter for him to live the life of an exile. In 1936 Stalin sent him a message urging him to come home. Under the Soviets, Stalin assured him, Chaliapin would be given plenty of money, a large house in Moscow and another in the country. When he received the message Chaliapin muttered, 'And what about my soul? Can you give me back my soul?'

It was in his Paris apartment that Chaliapin died, aged sixty-five, of leukaemia; his last words, addressed to his wife, were 'Masha, why is it so dark in this theatre? Tell them to turn on the lights.' To quote Ivor Newton once again: 'Before the funeral it looked as though all the great men of France and of music had come to pay homage; the lying-in-state might have been that of a king.' The Afonsky Choir of the Russian Metropolitan Church, with whom Chaliapin had so often sung, contributed to the funeral what Fred Gaisberg was to describe as 'the most magnificent unaccompanied choral singing that I have ever heard in my life', and their ranks were swelled by many of the most prominent Russian opera stars then resident in Paris. Gaisberg, knowing that Chaliapin had not always been the easiest of colleagues, expressed to a certain Prince Zereteli his surprise at their devotion. 'With all his faults', the Prince replied, 'he was for them *their* Russia. A chapter is closed.'

Now that Chaliapin has been dead for nearly sixty years how can one define his artistic legacy? It is as big a mistake to call him the 'inventor' of operatic acting as to attribute the same distinction to Maria Callas; since opera began there have been singers whose histrionic style, odd as it might seem to us today, thrilled their own contemporaries. I believe, though, that the reforms introduced by Chaliapin, and his radical reappraisal of the task of the singing actor, have had a profound influence on the overall quality of operatic performance in the twentieth century, even reaching to the works of composers with whom he had no connection – Janáček, for instance, and Alban Berg. It is perhaps best summed up in the words of Stanislavsky: 'We cannot create a Chaliapin, but we must create a Chaliapin school ... The only correct approach to opera is Chaliapin's approach, which proceeds not from the external reality of the character being portrayed, but from its inner reality, its psychological depth.'

For the last word on Chaliapin the singer, as opposed to Chaliapin the theatrical reformer, I would like to turn to Rachmaninov, one of the last of his friends to visit him before his death. 'It is impossible to describe how he sang,' Rachmaninov declared. 'He sang as Tolstoy wrote.'

KATHLEEN FERRIER

ENGLISH CONTRALTO

b. Higher Walton, Lancashire, 22 April 1912
d. London, 8 October 1953

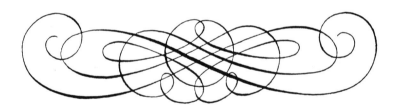

When a great artist dies young a special light tends to be cast in retrospect over his or her existence, and the notion of a dazzling talent cut off in its prime contains an element of the romantic as well as the tragic, sometimes to the exclusion of objective judgement. The death of Kathleen Ferrier at the age of forty-one after a professional career of little more than a decade resulted in a spate of tributes such as few other singers have ever received. Those who wrote them, however, men such as Benjamin Britten, Bruno Walter, John Barbirolli and Gerald Moore, were people who chose their words with care. From the deep sense of personal loss expressed by all of them in their different ways it is abundantly clear that this was not merely a case of saying nice things about a great singer who had died in mid-career. Apart from her remarkable qualities as an artist they all regarded Kathleen Ferrier as a quite exceptional human being, and they all truly loved her.

She was born on 22 April 1912 in the little Lancashire village of Higher Walton where her father was headmaster of the local school. He also undertook most of the musical instruction there and the Ferrier household included a piano, which from an early age was an object of fascination to Kathleen. By the time she was nine she had made such progress as a pianist that her mother felt she should have proper tuition. Kathleen was only fourteen when she passed the top grade of the Associated Board's examinations, a most unusual achievement, and at sixteen she won herself a brand new upright piano by coming top of her area in a national competition organised by the *Daily Express* newspaper. There had been 20,000 entrants from all over Great Britain, and although she was not among the six prize winners when she played in the finals in London's Wigmore Hall, up in Lancashire she had attracted considerable attention. There was, however, no question of her being allowed to attempt a career in music. Her family – she had an elder sister and brother – was dependent on her father's modest earnings, and they were brought up in the good old north-country traditions of industry and thrift. Despite her excellent all-round record at school Kathleen was obliged to end her education at fourteen and become a probationer in the Blackburn post office; that way lay financial security and the attainment of a pension.

Kathleen naturally started with the most repetitive routine jobs which the post office had to offer, and the reserve and self-discipline which she developed in order to cope with a situation not to her liking were to remain lifelong characteristics. When she was eighteen she was promoted to the rank of probationer telephonist at nineteen shillings a week, and four years later she was transferred to the larger and more important post office in Blackpool. Here she was chosen as one of the entrants in the Golden Voice competition to find the ideal speaker for TIM, the telephone system's first speaking clock, but she was not selected to represent Blackpool in the finals, having succumbed to nerves and inserted an extra aspirate in the reading test. It is a strange thought that the British public might otherwise have first become aware of the Ferrier voice via the familiar words 'At the third stroke it will be . . .'

Kathleen's free time was still largely devoted to music and she was in regular demand as accompanist to several of the singers and instrumentalists, both amateur and professional, who performed in the concerts and competitions which were a regular feature of musical life in the north of England at that time. She also indulged in music of a lighter vein by joining up with two other girls from the post office to form a trio of male impersonators. They assumed the names of Clarence, Cuthbert and Claude (Ferrier was Claude), and sang popular songs in close harmony at social gatherings, snappily attired in dinner jackets, stiff shirts, top hats and monocles. The act habitually opened with their signature tune, 'Three perfectly priceless old things', and the piano accompaniment was provided of course by Claude.

It was in fact as a solo pianist that Kathleen Ferrier made her first broadcast; this was from the BBC's Manchester studios at the age of eighteen, playing Brahms's Scherzo in E flat minor, with which she had just won the Gold Medal in the Liverpool Festival. She had, however, also joined a choir and her ambition veered more and more towards singing. She took some voice lessons from an organist and choir master named Thomas L. Duerdon and entered a competition in Blackpool for singers who performed to their own accompaniment. It was a major blow to her when she failed even to elicit a mention from the judges; her piano playing was beyond reproach, so it could only have been inadequate talent as a singer that had let her down. Soon after this Ferrier married a young man who worked in a local bank, left her job in the post office and set up as a piano teacher. Her husband was not destined to play a prominent role in her life, but he did make one vital contribution by betting her a shilling, when she entered the 1937 Carlisle Festival as a pianist, that she would not enrol for the singing cup as well. This time things went her way. She swept the board in both capacities, and soon afterwards she earned her first fee as a singer – one guinea, singing 'Thank God for a Garden' at a local harvest festival. The following year she attracted the attention of the BBC producer Cecil McGivern by appearing in a talent-spotting charity concert with the singularly uninspiring title 'Artists You May Not Have Heard'. Most of them Mr McGivern clearly regarded as 'Artists I Sincerely Hope I May Never Hear Again', but in Ferrier's case it led to her first broadcast as a singer. This was on 23 February 1939, from the BBC's Newcastle studios, and her programme consisted of 'Curly Headed Baby', 'Mighty Like a Rose' and 'The End of a Perfect Day'.

Encouraged by this heady turn of events Ferrier decided that it was time to go in for some serious voice training and applied to a distinguished musical figure in Newcastle named Dr J. E. Hutchinson, who had expressed himself in terms of unrestrained enthusiasm when judging her performance of Richard Strauss's 'All Saints' Day' ('Allerseelen') in the Carlisle Festival of 1938. They worked together over a period of three and a half years, during which time Ferrier also gained invaluable experience singing all over the north of England in concerts put on by a government-backed organisation known as CEMA (Council for the Encouragement of Music and the Arts). In May 1942 she was auditioned by Dr Malcolm Sargent, who predicted a great future for her but warned that it would be difficult to achieve unless she was prepared to base herself in London. At the end of that year she took the plunge, uprooted herself and moved south.

Before leaving this formative stage of Ferrier's career I would like to mention two more of the competitions which she had won back in 1938. Her sister Winifred was to write in her biography of Kathleen: 'In a lighthearted song she felt free to express her own feelings of gaiety and humour, but if the subject was serious she was not so confident. She had a north-country horror of showing emotion, and when she saw someone else "in a state" she felt unhappy and embarrassed.' Now this accords strangely with the fact that the songs she sang to win the two competitions I have in mind were Vaughan Williams's 'Silent Noon' and Wolf's 'Secrecy' ('Verborgenheit'); admittedly not songs to put anybody into 'a state', but at the same time certainly not songs marked by any gaiety or humour. They are compositions of great solemnity, the first rapt and serene, the second heavily introspective and laden with hidden grief. It so happens that both feature on the same CD, Decca *433 4732*,* 'Silent Noon' as part of a BBC

---

*   The situation with Ferrier's Decca recordings is complicated because the company has issued a ten-disc edition which includes the majority of her recordings, but differently grouped than in previous CD selections and under different numbers. To avoid confusion I am using as far as possible the numbers of the ten-disc edition, which can be bought separately or as a boxed set, but anyone buying Ferrier CDs is advised to take a good look at the Decca catalogue.

broadcast of 1952 and 'Verborgenheit' as part of a Norwegian broadcast of three years earlier. They demonstrate the totality with which Ferrier the mature artist could immerse herself in songs of this nature, but to judge from the success which she had had with them even in her amateur days (and indeed with 'Allerseelen', another song weighted with inner yearnings) she must always have possessed this capacity for communicating depth of feeling without herself indulging in any emotional display. Not for nothing was Bruno Walter to write of her, 'it was particularly music of spiritual meaning that seemed her most personal domain'.

Once Ferrier was installed in a flat in Hampstead, which she shared with Winifred, her reputation as a concert singer spread so quickly that within eighteen months she was invited to the EMI studios to make some test recordings. The first two titles to find their way into the catalogues were songs by Maurice Greene, an English contemporary of Handel's, shortly followed by two more of Handel's own, numbers from his opera OTTONE sung in the customary English translations, which fit the music very nicely despite having turned their backs entirely on the Italian originals. These recordings so clearly announced the arrival of a major new talent that EMI must surely have been anxious to keep Ferrier firmly tethered in their stable, but she was already displaying a healthy independence of mind. She did not care for EMI's star producer, Walter Legge, so decided to move to Decca, and not wanting to record any more important solo material for the company that she was about to leave she invited the soprano Isobel Baillie to help her complete her obligations to EMI by joining her in a set of duets. Three of these, two by Purcell and one by Mendelssohn, now appear, as do Ferrier's four solos, as part of EMI *CDH 7 61003 2*, and they enable us to sample two voices which represented the cream of contemporary English oratorio singing blissfully blending and harmonising together. One can almost see the smile on Gerald Moore's face as he accompanies such an immaculate display.

Several of Ferrier's first recordings for the Decca company are now to be found on their *CD 433 470–2*, and I fancy that to many of her British admirers this selection would represent the quintessential Ferrier. It includes 'What is life' ('Che farò') from Gluck's ORFEO ED EURIDICE, 'Art thou troubled?' from Handel's RODELINDA, and 'Have mercy, Lord, on me' from Bach's ST MATTHEW PASSION, all conducted by Dr Malcolm Sargent, and they reveal many of the qualities which, after the late start to Ferrier's career, endeared her so rapidly to the concert-going public. First there is the quality of the voice itself. It was a true contralto, not a mezzo soprano, and it was totally without the orotund hoot so beloved by our Victorian and Edwardian forebears but which now seems, dinosaur-like, to have receded into the mists of time. Although Ferrier's voice could descend without difficulty to the lowest depths of the female register it had a shine to it. All the warmth in the world is there, but without the plumminess which comes from trying to delve down into the sound – indeed, listening to Ferrier and the silvery voiced Isobel Baillie singing together on the EMI disc,* it is remarkable to hear how similarly the two contrasting voices are actually produced. Ferrier's tone is smooth and velvety – one can see why one of those north-country adjudicators should have said that he felt as if he were being stroked – and the phrasing is natural and uncontrived. There are one or two personal idiosyncracies, such as the consonant 'l' pronounced unusually far back, but it is wonderfully uncomplicated singing. The strength of Ferrier's breath control can be gauged by an exceptionally expansive 'Ombra mai fu' from Handel's SERSE – I could imagine many another singer being gripped by panic as Sargent unfolds the orchestral introduction – and the patent sincerity which shines through her singing of a piece such as 'O rest in the Lord' from Mendelssohn's ELIJAH indicates that here is a singer who is content to be the servant of

---

* In the brightness and purity of her tone I always think of Isobel Baillie as a kind of English equivalent to Elisabeth Schumann.

the music – nothing is done for show.

To add to the seven solo numbers on this disc there is also a complete version of Pergolesi's STABAT MATER conducted by Roy Henderson, who became Ferrier's teacher soon after she moved to London. It was from him that she learnt a great deal about how to present herself on the concert platform; never, for instance, to bury her head in her score as she had done the first time he encountered her, and always, while singing a song, to retain a mental picture of what she was singing about rather than concentrating her thoughts on herself and her voice. Although Ferrier was thirty years old by the time she began to make a real name for herself she often felt shy amongst the famous figures with whom she suddenly found herself consorting. The first recital she was booked to sing with Gerald Moore was in the Sussex town of Lewes, and having recognised him on the train she hid herself in another compartment and carefully kept her distance behind him as they both walked to the concert hall, so much in awe was she of the celebrated accompanist. When she was invited to Benjamin Britten's London flat to discuss the possibility of creating the role of Lucretia in his new opera the first impression recalled by the librettist, Ronald Duncan, was of 'a woman dressed rather like a country schoolteacher creeping shyly into the room'. Too nervous to make conversation she sight-read Lucretia's Flower Song from the manuscript which Britten handed her and the role was hers. Duncan ended his account of this first meeting with the words, 'I could see tears not far behind the eyes. They never were.'

THE RAPE OF LUCRETIA, which had its première at Glyndebourne in 1946, provided Ferrier with her first taste of the operatic stage. She was keenly aware that she had new skills to master, and despite an outstanding personal success she was never entirely convinced that people who told her how good she was were not merely being polite. It is an odd thought that when the production was subsequently taken over to Holland, Ferrier, at the age of thirty-four, was making her very first trip abroad. During the war, of course, foreign travel had been impossible and even moving about within Britain had not been without its problems. The life of a concert singer tends to consist largely of 'one night stands', and many are the expressions of disgruntlement in Ferrier's letters home about the woes of living out of a suitcase and existing on a diet of sandwiches and buns. When she was asked to return to Glyndebourne in 1947 to sing Gluck's Orfeo the prospect of six weeks in one place was not the least of the engagement's attractions.

People often said of Ferrier's Orfeo that the part appeared to have been written for her, but in fact that Glyndebourne production was not an entirely smooth ride. To start with she had to learn the role in Italian, and having done so with her customary thoroughness she arrived to find that much of the text had been changed; with the result, so she claimed in a letter to a friend, that she 'cried for the first three days'. Nowadays, when British singers regularly appear in the great opera houses of the world, it is hard to imagine a star performer being thrown by the very normal circumstance of having to cope with a foreign language, but when Ferrier entered upon the scene a British singer with anything more than a purely British career was virtually a contradiction in terms. Furthermore not having been brought up in the rough-and-tumble of international opera Ferrier had not grown a thick enough skin to be able to cope with the acid tongue of the Austrian-born conductor Fritz Stiedry, whose jibes about her lack of stage experience cut her to the quick. Ultimately, of course, she emerged triumphant – 'I wasn't given this chin for nothing' she would occasionally remark – and as an abridged studio recording was made of the production (Decca *433 468–2*) most of her role has been preserved. From the first heart-broken cry of 'Eurydice', through the eloquence of her appeal to the Furies and on to the gently floated wonderment of her arrival in the Elysian Fields, Ferrier gives a performance which is vocally never less than exquisite and musically never less than immaculate. Dramatically, however, there is a certain amount missing. Apart from the fact that Stiedry seems to me to take 'Che farò' at an inappropriately jaunty lick (possibly owing to the exigencies of the time factor on a 78 r.p.m. record) Ferrier's Italian contains several very English inflections. It sounds careful, not like a lived-in language, leaving the listener inevitably aware that this is a British concert singer who has strayed onto the operatic stage.

This becomes even more apparent when one hears excerpts from a live performance which she gave four years later in Holland. They are included in the EMI disc *CDH 7 61003 2* to which I have already referred, and this time we are listening to a vocal actress who has left her inhibitions in the dressing-room. To give but one example, in the earlier recording that magical phrase 'Che puro ciel! Che chiaro sol!' ('How clear the sky! How bright the sun!') which breaks from Orfeo's lips at his first glimpse of the Elysian Fields is as serene as the orchestral playing which has preceded it – a lovely piece of vocalisation. In the live recording, however, marred though that inevitably is by variable sound quality and the bumps and whisperings inherent in a stage performance, it is much more than this. The phrase has an impact which makes the heart lurch as one hears it – these are no longer foreign words that have been carefully memorised, they are an expression of something infinitely beautiful, a vision of the sublime. Ferrier has unlocked the door to the role's dramatic and tragic possibilities, she is using her voice with a new fearlessness, and it represents a most remarkable leap forward in artistic self-confidence.

In fact, with the exception of ORFEO and LUCRETIA opera was never to become a field of interest to Ferrier; indeed in a letter written late in her life she expressed the opinion that 'the more I see of opera the less I want to take part in it'. After tackling the role of Carmen in a local concert performance back in 1944 she had decided that that kind of thing was not her cup of tea, and when the eminent director Carl Ebert tried to talk her into doing it at Glyndebourne some years later she wisely stuck to her guns. When she attended a performance of DER ROSENKAVALIER given in Holland by the company of the Vienna State Opera any chance there might have been of interesting her in the title-role of *that* was rapidly annihilated. 'Phew!' she wrote in a letter the following day, 'it goes on for hours, and though the production was wonderful I'm completely unimpressed, unmoved and rather bored.'

Ferrier was extremely critical of her own recordings and she often found it hard in the impersonal confines of a studio to kindle the spark which came so naturally to her when faced with a live audience. One recording with which she did express satisfaction, however, was that of Brahms's 'Alto Rhapsody' – or 'Alto Raspberry', as she liked to call it. This has always been a personal favourite of mine as it happened to be the first Ferrier record which I ever possessed, and it now forms part of Decca *433 477–2*. After a chillingly atmospheric evocation of Goethe's lost soul wandering amongst the inhospitable wastelands of the wintry Harz mountains her voice soars with radiant beneficence over the carpet of sound provided by the male section of the London Philharmonic Choir in the concluding prayer. The conductor was that charismatic figure Clemens Krauss and by this time (December 1947) Ferrier was quite accustomed to collaborating with the pick of the world's conductors.

The one who exercised the most profound influence on her artistic life was Bruno Walter. She had met him earlier in this same year when he was looking for a contralto to sing in Mahler's DAS LIED VON DER ERDE in the first Edinburgh Festival, and after she had sung him some Lieder by Schubert and Brahms he asked her to try a few lines of Mahler's totally unfamiliar music. 'She overcame their great difficulties', he was later to write, 'with the ease of the born musician, and I recognised with great delight that here was potentially one of the great singers of our day . . . From this hour began a musical association which resulted in some of the happiest experiences of my life as a musician.'

One of those experiences has been preserved with fascinating immediacy on Decca *433 476–2*, a Lieder recital given during the Edinburgh Festival of 1949, with Ferrier singing Schubert, Brahms and Schumann to Walter's piano accompaniment. The disc actually opens with something of a curiosity, a brief radio talk given by

Ferrier under the title 'What the Edinburgh Festival means to me', and it compares interestingly with a similar introductory chat recorded by her fellow Lancastrian Dame Eva Turner on one of her CDs.* Whereas Dame Eva's speaking voice brings her straight into the room just as her friends remember her, Ferrier sounds muted and ill at ease, almost as if this were another reading test and another extra aspirate might intrude. Her artistic humility is made evident by the generosity of her tribute to Dr Walter, but it is a strangely careful little talk from one whose spontaneity has so often been commented on.† As soon as the recital itself begins we are faced with a very different Kathleen Ferrier. The programme opens with Schubert's 'Die junge Nonne', a song of wide emotional scope, and Ferrier commands every nuance and every gradation of vocal colouring which it requires of her. The balance between voice and piano is not ideal and as an accompanist Walter, at the age of seventy-three, was in any case no Gerald Moore or Benjamin Britten – out of respect for the great man critics used to employ expressions such as 'highly individual' or 'richly idiosyncratic' to describe his playing – but in interpretation singer and accompanist are *ein Herz und eine Seele* (one heart and one soul). Ferrier says in her talk that to study the Lieder repertoire with Walter was 'to feel that one is gaining knowledge and inspiration from the composer himself' and there was certainly no trace of self-doubt about the songs she sang that day. The occasional British inflection is to be heard in the text, and even the occasional small mistake, but that has become immaterial

---

* See *Legendary Voices*, p.260.

---

† One typical instance of Ferrier's usual spontaneity has been provided by a journalist on the *News Chronicle* named Philip Sked. Describing the regular press conferences during the Edinburgh Festival at which 'a very mixed bag of press people' would be let loose on whatever stars of the musical, theatrical and art worlds happened to be in the city he wrote: 'There never was anyone at those conferences to hold a candle to Miss Ferrier for sheer charm and gaiety. She always seemed to be bubbling over with laughter at us, at our questions and at herself. Even if she hadn't been able to sing a note, she would have been a grand person to have around.'

– the foreign language is no longer any sort of stumbling block in the gaining of access to the music. For my personal taste it is the Brahms group which is the crowning glory of the recital. The sumptuousness of the lower register in the opening of 'Der Tod, das ist die kühle Nacht'; the inherent shade of melancholy which suffuses 'Immer leise wird mein Schlummer'; the burnished gleam of 'Denn du, Holde, denkst an ihn!' at the conclusion of 'Botschaft' – these are things which seem to me to make the Ferrier voice an ideal instrument for Brahms, a veritable cello amongst voices. As for her rendering of that grand old favourite 'Von ewiger Liebe' which closes the group, it is a glorious, triumphant piece of singing, with Walter coming as close as a pianist can to unleashing the full orchestra in her support.

However out of place it may be – and, as I have indicated in my opening paragraph, I know that it *is* out of place – I find it hard to listen to Ferrier now in live performance without a certain feeling of eeriness. When she gave this recital she was still in perfect health, but with hindsight the lurking presence of death behind at least two of the Brahms songs acquires an extra, albeit quite spurious poignancy; while it is simply not possible to hear her as Schubert's Maiden addressing Death with the words 'Do not touch me, I am still young' without being mindful of what was to come in only four years' time. Another song which resonates with a sorrowful irony is Schumann's 'An meinem Herzen' from the FRAUENLIEBE UND -LEBEN cycle, in which the young married woman exults over the pinnacle of happiness achieved through the joys of motherhood. Ferrier's own marriage had been a sad story, culminating in annulment after eleven and a half years, the grounds being non-consummation of the union. Had she had a family to raise during those wartime years I suppose it is possible that she might never have launched herself into a singing career, though it is hard to imagine a talent such as hers being indefinitely suppressed. One incident related in her sister's book, however, does seem to tell a story of its own. When Ferrier visited the infant school at which Winifred taught, and was treated by the children to a 'concert', she had to turn her head away to hide her tears, and subsequently told a friend, 'I sat in the bus afterwards and cried all the way to Baker Street at the thought of their little flower faces.'

Home for Ferrier was still the London flat where she and Winifred were joined after their mother's death by their elderly father, to whom Kathleen used to refer fondly as 'our father which art in Hampstead'. For all the solemnity of so much of her sung repertoire she was a convivial person who loved to let her hair down, and often ended an evening sitting at the piano and treating her friends to hilarious performances of *risqué* cabaret numbers – none of which, unfortunately, ever found their way onto tape. Some of the eulogies written after her death created an image of unremitting saintliness, but, as the critic Neville Cardus put it, 'she would tell a ribald tale with all the taste and refinement of a fine lady in a Restoration comedy', and her letters contain many a touch of the down-to-earth. As a signature she liked to use the nickname Klever Kaff, sometimes abbreviated to K. K., which had stuck to her after a little boy of three had come out with it to express his admiration for the stylishness with which she snapped the cotton after sewing on a button. If the letter in question contained an account of a concert in which she did not feel that she had given of her best, or which had been followed by lukewarm reviews, her soubriquet would occasionally be adapted to 'Not So K. K.' or 'Klever Question Mark Kaff', and the degree to which her head had not been turned by her meteoric rise to fame is neatly caught in an anecdote told by the Decca producer John Culshaw in his memoirs. 'She had been the guest of honour', Culshaw wrote, 'at a dinner at the Savoy, to which I also had been invited. The room was packed with distinguished musicians, socialites and politicians, and there were some rather boring speeches until Kathleen got to her feet and replied with a north-country directness and simplicity that changed the atmosphere in a second. When it was over the Rolls-Royces and the hire-cars and the taxis lined up to collect the guests. Kathleen took me on one side. "Can you lend me two-and-six, luv?" she said. "I'm going back on the tube and I've come out without any money." She was like that.'

Despite the cosmopolitan existence of her last few years Ferrier remained one hundred per cent British, and she habitually ended her mixed recitals with a group of songs in English. Twenty-one of these have been collected on Decca *433 475–2*, and they extend in style from Quilter's classic setting of the Herrick poem 'To Daisies' (with which Ferrier had won her husband's shilling and the Rose Bowl in Carlisle) to a comical folk song called 'The stuttering lovers'. In what one might loosely classify as the 'serious' numbers in this selection Ferrier touches the heart as unerringly as she does with more exalted music. She does not overload them with excessive 'interpretation', but by grafting her own sincerity onto their simplicity she imbues several of them with a devastating emotional directness; I would rate 'The lover's curse', for instance, an Irish folk song arranged by Herbert Hughes, alongside the most moving of her Brahms or Mahler recordings. Occasionally some of the other songs on this disc can sound dated. Fashions change in singing as they do in most things and certain aspects of Ferrier's enunciation – the rolled 'r' at the end of words like 'for' and 'or', for instance – come across today as a gilding of the lily. In dialect songs the immaculate enunciation can sound a trifle prim, but of course when Ferrier had a live audience she used to put these numbers across with tremendous gusto – by this stage in the evening the public was always eating out of her hand – and it is probably the absence of that give and take between singer and audience that leaves one or two of the songs a trifle high and dry. In any case, nothing can alter the fact that the unaccompanied folk song 'Blow the wind southerly' became for many British radio listeners virtually Ferrier's signature tune, and that very few other singers have attempted to sing it since.

When Ferrier made her first appearance in New York in 1948 singing DAS LIED VON DER ERDE with Bruno Walter she was disappointed to meet with a mixed reception from the press,* but she soon established the same degree of personal popularity in the United States as she had in Britain. When she returned to the New York Town Hall on her second American tour in 1949 she was greeted with almost overwhelming enthusiasm. The audience, which included Elisabeth Schumann and Bruno Walter, greeted her first appearance with such extended applause that she found herself wishing that they would stop and let her start; and at the end she had to sing no less than five of her British and Irish folk songs as encores. She had already signed contracts for US tours in each of the next two years (only one of which she was able to undertake) and so great was her following in the States that in 1952 Ian Hunter, the director of the Edinburgh Festival, claimed that Ferrier's participation there was 'sufficient to bring Americans over the Atlantic to attend it'.

Obviously it is not possible to discuss every one of Ferrier's CDs in detail; they are happily too numerous, and apart from the releases by major companies one or two smaller ones have managed to lay their hands on tapes of performances discovered by radio stations here and there. I would, however, like to mention three other composers with whom Ferrier's name was particularly associated – Bach, Handel and Mahler. As a Bach singer Ferrier enjoyed one of her most inspiring experiences, and one of her greatest public triumphs, when she was engaged for the ST MATTHEW PASSION, the B MINOR MASS and the MAGNIFICAT in the Vienna Bach Festival of 1950, all conducted by Herbert von Karajan. Her fellow soloists were the not inconsiderable *crème de la crème* of the Vienna State Opera – Seefried, Schwarzkopf and Schoeffler to name but three – and when the festival was over she received a letter from the president of the *Gesellschaft der Musikfreunde in Wien* (Association of the Friends of Music in Vienna) thanking her for having

---

* Like every other singer Ferrier had her share of bad notices, including one in the *New Statesman* referring to her as 'this goitrous singer with the contralto hoot' – words which I hope the critic lived to regret!

sung Bach's alto parts to a standard 'not heard for many years'. Perhaps an even greater tribute to Ferrier's special quality as a singer of religious music was the fact, subsequently attested to by Elisabeth Schwarzkopf, that as Ferrier started the 'Agnus Dei' in the last performance of the B MINOR MASS Karajan was seen to be weeping – not an everyday event.* Three years earlier Ferrier had recorded an almost complete ST MATTHEW PASSION in English and her contributions to this set, together with several of the choruses, are now to be found on Decca *433 469-2*. The massed forces include the Bach Choir, the Jacques Orchestra under their founder Dr Reginald Jacques, and two other splendidly evocative names – Dr Osborne Peasgood on the organ and Dr Thornton Lofthouse on the harpsichord. This may be a less imposing line-up than Karajan and company in Vienna, but as a portrait of Ferrier the rising star of British oratorio singing it remains a valuable issue. The purity of her tone and the clarity of her attack give her singing that air of the seraphic which is normally the territory of the soprano voice – there is a luminous quality to Ferrier's singing, with all thickening of the tone scrupulously avoided.

By the time Ferrier returned to the Decca studios in October 1952 to record a Bach–Handel recital with the London Philharmonic Orchestra under Sir Adrian Boult she had already undergone one cancer operation and was having treatment for a recurrence of the disease. During the recording sessions she was accompanied by a nurse who sat by the telephone awaiting the results of the hospital's latest tests. John Culshaw was the producer in charge of the sessions, and to quote once again from his memoirs, 'Nothing happened on the first day; but on the second I came down the stairs to say something to Kathleen between takes,

---

* Various tapes, complete and incomplete, of broadcasts and rehearsals from this festival have become available in varying degrees of technical adequacy on two Foyer CDs, two Verona CDs and three EMI CDs. The best explanation of this complicated state of affairs is to be found in Paul Campion's book *Ferrier, a Career Recorded* (see bibliography).

and she faced me with an expression of indescribable happiness. She just said, "I'm all right, luv. They've just phoned to say I'm all right." '

It is indeed extraordinary the extent to which, whenever at this stage of her life she was well enough to sing at all, Ferrier's actual voice remained unaffected. Comparing the two versions of the aria 'Grief for sin' from the ST MATTHEW PASSION, for instance, one recorded at the beginning of the short time that she enjoyed as a Decca artist and the other at the end – these final sessions are now released on Decca *433 474–2* – it is the second which more fully emphasises the lustrous quality of what she used to call 'the fat of my voice'. The assurance which she had gained during those five years of singing in the most elevated of company and in so many parts of the world gives this recital a stamp of greater authority than is to be heard in her earlier recordings. The selection of arias is on the whole a solemn one, but when an extract from Handel's MESSIAH, 'O thou that tellest good tidings from Sion', gives Ferrier a message of joy to deliver she does so with infectious panache; indeed the words 'lift up thy voice with strength, lift it up, be not afraid' come across as something of a personal battle-cry. Culshaw does not relate whether this was recorded before or after the receipt of the telephone call.

It was Bruno Walter who introduced Ferrier to the music of Mahler with that first DAS LIED VON DER ERDE in the original Edinburgh Festival. In his young days Walter had been an ardent disciple of Mahler's, working under him in the opera houses of both Hamburg and Vienna, and it was he who conducted the first performance of DAS LIED a few months after Mahler's death. He delighted in guiding Ferrier's footsteps into the unexplored territory of Mahler's musical world, and it was an experience which seemed to stir within her many of the emotions which she had learnt throughout her life to keep under wraps. Walter was later to recall that whenever they worked together on the final song 'Abschied' ('Farewell'), they would regularly have to take a break as the acuteness of her responses began to overcome her. 'Tears streamed down her cheeks,' he wrote. 'With all her will-power and vigour she could not help it, and only by and by did she learn to control her feelings.' One anecdote told by Winifred Ferrier seems to me to sum up the distance which her sister had travelled between the solid British restraint of her family background and the exotic emotional realm of Mahler's music. When Bruno Walter met their old father in the Hampstead flat he congratulated him on his wonderfully gifted daughter, and prophesied that within a short time she would be famous throughout the world. 'Yes,' Mr Ferrier replied, 'Kath's not doing badly.'

The first Mahler recording which Ferrier and Walter made together was of the KINDERTOTENLIEDER and this completes the EMI disc, *CDH 7 61003 2*, to which I have already made two other references. As I have written elsewhere* I cannot imagine how Mahler could have undertaken the task of setting these agonising poems to music. The possibility of losing a child is, I feel sure, every parent's deepest dread, and the poet Rückert had lost two of his within a few days of one another. When Mahler composed the songs he was the devoted father of two happy, healthy children, one of whom was to die tragically only three years later, and as he subsequently wrote in a letter to a friend: 'If I had already lost my own daughter at that time I would not have been able to write these songs.' Be that as it may, the poems on their own are enough to wring the flintiest of hearts, and with Mahler's masterly settings repeatedly turning the knife I must confess that I never choose of my own free will to listen to this particular cycle. That said, however, I have to add that in my opinion no other music shows off the sheer beauty of Ferrier's voice more startlingly than this. The songs call for a subtle variety of colouring, and from the tenderness of her upper register in the opening 'Nun seh' ich wohl', making her sound

---

* See *Legendary Voices*, p.88.

momentarily almost like a soprano, to the deceptively nursery-rhyme-like 'Wenn dein Mütterlein', for which she reserves the full richness of her lower tones, the instrument is gorgeously displayed. Despite the ever-present depth of sympathy this is an interpretation of great dignity; it never spills over into self-pity, and is all the more heart-rending as a result.

This studio recording with the Vienna Philharmonic Orchestra under the sensitive and eloquent Bruno Walter compares interestingly with a live performance under that other dedicated but temperamentally very different Mahler disciple Otto Klemperer. This took place nearly two years later as part of the Holland Festival – the orchestra is the Concertgebouw – and it can be heard, thanks to a reasonably good recording taken from the broadcast, as part of Decca *425 995–2*. Klemperer's approach is more dramatic, more theatrical, and Ferrier's performance, heightened perhaps by the presence of an audience, is entirely faithful to his interpretation, but she pulled no punches on the subject of which of the two Mahlerian champions she preferred. 'I hate to work with Klemperer,' she wrote after the concert, 'I find he shouts like a madman . . . just to impress – though why he should think it impresses I can't think. Perhaps his Mahler comes off sometimes, because he wastes no time nor sentiment – but oh!!! Whattaman.'

Uncongenial though Ferrier's association with Klemperer may have been, there is no doubt about the happiness with which she joined in the other broadcast performance which completes this particular disc. It is of Brahms's irresistible LIEBESLIEDER-WALZER, which she sang in her final Edinburgh Festival, that of 1952, with Irmgard Seefried, Julius Patzak and Horst Günter as the other three members of the vocal quartet, and Hans Gal and Clifford Curzon, no less, as the piano duettists. It was clearly one of those occasions when it is hard to tell whether audience or performers are enjoying themselves the more, and in case the first half of the disc has put its listeners' emotions too mercilessly through the mangle this second half provides the perfect antidote.

It was in May 1952 that Ferrier and Bruno Walter met in Vienna for their last collaboration – two public performances and a studio recording of DAS LIED VON DER ERDE, with three of Mahler's Rückert songs to complete the fourth side of what started life as a set of two long-playing records; the orchestra was the Vienna Philharmonic, and these sessions resulted in what many of Ferrier's admirers, myself amongst them, have always considered the peak of her achievement as a recording artist. Ferrier's doctors had not wanted her to undertake the trip but at that time she was confident that her current treatment was going to effect a cure, so perhaps once again one should not allow too many fanciful notions to colour one's enjoyment of these performances. It would, however, be scarcely possible to hear the other-worldly resignation of Ferrier's 'Ich bin der Welt abhanden gekommen' (the three Rückert songs are now to be heard on Decca *433 477–2*, along with the 'Alto Rhapsody' and other Brahms songs) without feeling that this is a singer who has faced certain grim realities and come to terms with them; and the intensity of feeling in 'Um Mitternacht' would represent a miracle of the imagination if she herself had never been forced to explore at least comparable depths of introspection. Certainly Walter felt that a new spirit had entered Ferrier's singing of the three alto solos in DAS LIED VON DER ERDE (Decca *414 194–2*). 'What tragic similarity of destinies is here revealed!' he wrote. 'It was in the shadow of death that Mahler conceived and wrote his SONG OF THE EARTH – and Kathleen Ferrier was approaching that same dark region when she sang it that last time in Vienna ... She and this symphony of farewell – for not only the last song but the whole work has the meaning of a farewell – for ever they will belong together for me.' Mahler had confided to Walter that he regarded DAS LIED as his most personal work, and both Walter's conducting of it and Ferrier's singing carry the hallmarks of an intense and dedicated commitment. From the moment Walter first introduced her to the piece Ferrier had sur-rendered to its emotional impact, to the extent indeed that in her first public performance of it, back in the Edinburgh Festival of 1949, she was prevented by her own tears from enunciating the final word 'ewig' ('for ever'), and felt impelled to apologise afterwards to Walter for such lack of professionalism. In the recording studio the tears may not have been flowing, but she was certainly singing with the vocal floodgates fully open. There is an almost desperate urgency to the cry 'Ich komm' zu dir, traute Ruhestätte!' ('I come to thee, familiar place of rest!'), and an unbridled passion such as I can think of nowhere else in Ferrier's recorded singing surges through the passage 'Sonne der Liebe willst du nie mehr scheinen?' ('O sun of love, wilt thou shine no more?').

After Bruno Walter, the conductor who exercised the greatest influence on Ferrier was probably her fellow Lancastrian Sir John Barbirolli. She appeared under his baton for many memorable performances, not the least of them being her rendering of 'Land of Hope and Glory' at the Royal Gala opening of Manchester's new Free Trade Hall, and he regarded her Angel in THE DREAM OF GERONTIUS (alas never recorded) as one of the pinnacles of her artistic achievement. It was he, too, who dragooned her into tackling a work way outside the rest of her repertoire, Chausson's 'Poème de l'amour et de la mer', as he felt that it would help her to keep her voice light and bright and to explore new possibilities of vocal colouring far removed from the sombre tones of so much of the alto oratorio literature. The success of this experiment can be judged on Decca *433 472–2* (coupled with various English songs and Sargent's orchestral arrangement of Brahms's 'Four Serious Songs') and although this is another issue with a peculiar history, nowhere near the technical standard of a studio recording, it cannot but leave the listener sad indeed that Ferrier was never able to explore the world of French music more extensively.

Another area of collaboration between Ferrier and Barbirolli, albeit a private one, was that of chamber music. Barbirolli was a fine cellist, and with his wife, the distinguished oboist Evelyn Rothwell, he used to visit Ferrier in the Hampstead flat where they would play trios together and sample her expertise as a cook. 'She was', Barbirolli attested, 'an expert in that delectable but difficult art of fish and chips.'

It was Sir John who, in 1952, suggested to David Webster, the general manager at Covent Garden, that as Britain's greatest singer Ferrier should not be indefinitely ignored by the Royal Opera House.* Aware that time might be short Webster decreed with commendable despatch that a new production of Gluck's ORPHEUS AND EURIDICE (everything was sung in English in those days) should be mounted for her in February 1953. I was lucky enough to be in the audience at the first night, and it was an occasion which I imagine that nobody present could possibly forget. I have witnessed many emotional operatic occasions from both sides of the footlights and I know what an atmosphere can be engendered when in a mounting fever of enthusiasm the public bids farewell to a beloved artist. Usually, though, the audience is wishing the artist in question a long and happy retirement, whereas in Ferrier's case it had become common knowledge that she was grievously ill and we all knew that it was a different sort of goodbye. She knew it, we knew it, she knew that we knew it. It was a strange, deeply moving occasion, mournful but at the same time curiously uplifting. She was due to sing four performances, by the end of the second her colleagues had to help her stay on her feet for the curtain-calls, and she never appeared in public again.

One extraordinary thing that must be emphasised, though, about this last great performance of Ferrier's is that it *was* a great performance. Neither in her singing of the role of Orpheus nor in her acting of it was it necessary to make any concession whatsoever to the fact that she was mortally ill. It is not just in the glow of hindsight that I write this, nor was it at the time some kind of self-delusion, a conspiracy by the public to pretend that she had sung magnificently simply because we so much wanted her to have done so. Perhaps it will bring home the incredible

---

* Her only two appearances there had been back in 1947 as part of the English Opera Group's tour of THE RAPE OF LUCRETIA.

degree to which Ferrier rose above her sufferings when I say that I recently asked the British soprano Adèle Leigh, who sang the role of Amor in that production, what were her memories of working with Ferrier. I was expecting some harrowing account of her grimly fighting her way through the rehearsals, her face etched with pain, but the answer I received speaks volumes. 'She was hilarious,' Miss Leigh replied. 'She had an endless supply of amazingly funny stories and she had us all in stitches.' If you want the unvarnished truth about one prima donna, ask another. About Ferrier as singer, actress, musician and colleague Adèle Leigh only expressed herself in superlatives.

I have one further memory of that first night of ORPHEUS because for me it had an unexpected postscript. When I left the opera house I went back to the London flat where I was staying at the time and to my surprise after half an hour or so I heard the bell ring. I went down and opened the street door (in those days one could risk such a thing late at night in London) and there to my amazement, leaning against the doorpost in a state of self-evident exhaustion, was Kathleen Ferrier. It turned out that one of the other flats belonged to a friend of David Webster's, he was giving a supper party for Ferrier, and she had rung the wrong bell. I managed to stammer out something on the lines of 'Miss Ferrier, you were wonderful tonight', and although I cannot pretend to remember her exact reply (I think it was something equally original such as 'I'm so glad you liked it'), I do vividly recall that as I showed her into the lift I became for just once in my life a recipient of that famous smile.

The story of Ferrier's heroism during the remaining six months of her life has been frequently told and has brought inspiration to many. I remember the British critic and broadcaster John Amis telling me that when he and his wife went to visit her in hospital they wondered what on earth they could say to cheer her up. 'We needn't have worried,' he went on; 'she cheered us up.' To me she seems to represent the very antithesis of Shakespeare's 'The evil that men do lives after them; the good is oft interrèd with their bones'. If Ferrier had ever been guilty of anything evil I would be surprised, and the good she did lives on not only in her recordings but also in several invaluable charities which have been set up to celebrate her memory; the Kathleen Ferrier Scholarship, for instance, granted each year to help launch the career of a young British singer, and above all the Kathleen Ferrier Cancer Research Fund and the Kathleen Ferrier Chair of Clinical Research. Through the glow of her personality, the splendour of her artistry and the dignity with which she accepted suffering Kathleen Ferrier captured the imagination of the general public to a degree that no other British singer ever has. No question marks – K. K.

BENIAMINO
GIGLI

ITALIAN TENOR

b. Recanati, 20 March 1890
d. Rome, 30 November 1957

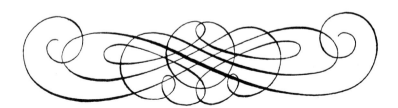

I have at home a Japanese print of a small bird sitting on a twig. The bird appears to have filled itself so full of air that if it does not sing it will surely burst and I can never look at the picture without thinking of Beniamino Gigli. This was a man put into the world to sing and if some malignant fate had prevented him from doing so I cannot imagine that he would have survived for long.

He was born on 20 March 1890 in the country town of Recanati in the province of Italy called Le Marche, probably best known as the home of Verdicchio wine. He was the youngest of six children and his father was a cobbler, not making fashionable shoes for the well-off, but stout ones for the peasantry. From early childhood Gigli enjoyed a local reputation as a vocalist, singing for sweets and small coins to the people who sat around the café tables, and when he was not quite seven he was enrolled in the choir of Recanati's modest little cathedral, where his father had meanwhile secured the position of bell-ringer. The organist, Maestro Lazzarini, devoted a great deal of time and attention to his new recruit and within a short time Gigli was entrusted with important solos. By now he was besotted with singing. He sang as he walked to school, he sang again as he walked back, and he used to climb to the top of the cathedral tower and sing at the top of his lungs to anyone below who might feel inclined to listen. This uninhibited delight in the act of singing out loud is a very Italian characteristic, as anyone will know who has walked past a building site in Italy on a sunny day. It is something neatly caught by E. M. Forster in his novel *Where Angels Fear to Tread*, when he describes an Italian walking down the street 'singing fearlessly from his expanded lungs, like a professional. Herein he differed from Englishmen, who always have a little feeling against music, and sing only from the throat, apologetically.'

When Gigli was twelve he finished his schooling and was given a job helping the owner of the local chemist's shop; he also made his first acquaintance with operatic music by playing the saxophone in the town's junior band, whose repertoire included selections from the works of several famous composers. When he was fifteen his voice had still not broken and he was impressed, much against his parents' will, into a student production of an operetta called LA FUGA DI ANGELICA, or ANGELICA'S ELOPEMENT, in the province's capital city, Macerata. No suitable young lady had been found for the role of the flighty Angelica, but one of the organisers of the event had heard Gigli singing a solo in Recanati cathedral; and so in a floor-length white dress and a huge black hat, with a parasol clutched stiffly in his hand, our hero took his first bow on any public stage. The applause which greeted his principal solo confirmed him in his belief that he would never be happy unless he could devote himself to singing – which for a penniless boy in Recanati was more easily said than done.

When he was seventeen, however, and his voice had settled into the tenor register, he was persuaded by a chance acquaintance named Giovanni Zerri, who was a cook and had worked for the great tenor Alessandro Bonci, that if he wanted to get anywhere he would have to take the plunge and try his luck in Rome. There he shared an attic with one of his brothers, who was already in the capital with a scholarship to study sculpture, and who had found a job for Gigli in a chemist's shop in the Via Cavour. Their life-style was that of Rodolfo and Marcello in LA BOHEME, and they were frequently weak with hunger. Gigli's singing lessons were costing most of the pittance that he earned, and the brothers were heavily dependent on scraps smuggled by Giovanni Zerri from his current place of work, the kitchens of the Portuguese theological seminary.

After several months of this dismal existence Gigli's fortunes improved. He left the chemist's shop and was taken on as the humblest of many servants in the household of a lady named Countess Spannocchi. Although his wages were still miserly he was housed and fed, and at the same time he was accepted by a new singing teacher who expressed herself willing to train him without charge. Her name was Agnese Bonucci, and the Countess, who took a close interest in Gigli's progress, allowed him free time every afternoon to practise or to attend Signora Bonucci's lessons. After a year of this routine Gigli was called up for his two years' military service, which could have involved being sent to all sorts of faraway places, spelling disaster to his vocal development. Fortunately, however, as in Caruso's case twenty years earlier,* the Italian army showed a proper sense of priorities. Countess Spannocchi sent Gigli to a friend of hers called Colonel Delfino, the Colonel asked Gigli to sing him an aria, Gigli sang 'La donna è mobile', and the Colonel decreed that he should do his soldiering as a telephone operator in Rome.

When Gigli's two years were up Colonel Delfino persuaded him to try his luck with an audition for the Academy of Santa Cecilia and although officially no student could be accepted without taking the obligatory piano exam Gigli was awarded the top scholarship on the strength of his singing alone. He studied with two of the Academy's most distinguished teachers, Antonio Cotogni and Enrico Rosati, and at the end of two years he passed out with the highest honours. Shortly afterwards he won a widely publicised international competition in the city of Parma; there were 105 contestants, and many years later, when a friend of Gigli's presented him with the judges' original report, he found that one of them had written at the bottom in block capitals ABBIAMO FINALMENTE TROVATO *IL TENORE!* (At last we have found *the tenor!*).

After such a triumph Gigli was in a position to pick and

---

* See *Legendary Voices*, p.29.

choose in which role and in which of Italy's many provincial theatres he should make his début. He settled for Enzo in LA GIOCONDA in the city of Rovigo, and on 15 October 1914 his career was launched. Straight away he learnt a lesson which he was never to forget. As with many another Italian role the hero of LA GIOCONDA is largely judged by the public on his success with one familiar number, in this case the aria 'Cielo e mar'. In the score the final note is a high G, but the public is accustomed to hearing the tenor go up to a B flat instead. At the dress rehearsal Gigli went for the B flat and fluffed it, so in the first two performances he made a virtue of necessity and sang the aria as the composer had written it. His début was a success and Gigli was welcomed by the press as a revelation but there was no denying that the aria, beautifully though he had sung it, had not brought the house down. At the third performance he screwed up his courage and took the high B flat. The audience went mad. People leapt to their feet, stamped, shouted and flung their programmes in the air. In a role containing notes by the thousand one single note had made that much difference, because it was a note which the public wanted to hear.

Gigli's climb up the ladder of the Italian opera houses was a rapid one; within two years of his début he had appeared in Genoa, Palermo, Bologna, Turin and Naples. In December 1916 came the evening to which he had been looking forward with the keenest anticipation of all – in the Teatro Costanzi in Rome he sang the role of Faust in Boito's MEFISTOFELE to an audience which included Countess Spannocchi, Colonel Delfino and Maestro Rosati, as well as various members of the Gigli family feeling very conspicuous decked out in evening dress. In between his operatic engagements Gigli sang countless concerts for the troops; then, when the war was over, Mr Fred Gaisberg of His Master's Voice came over to Milan to set up a new studio and Gigli's recording career began.

One of the first arias which Gigli chose to record was 'Cielo e mar', which features on a Nimbus CD of his acoustic recordings,

NI 7807, and when one listens to it now it is easy to imagine what effect this new tenor must have had on people hearing him for the first time. It is an intensely poetical aria, sung by the hero of the opera as he stands in the prow of his ship gazing out at the tranquillity of night-time on the Venetian lagoon, and it gradually mounts to a passionate climax as his thoughts turn to his beloved, whose arrival he awaits with growing impatience. Both in the honeyed mezza voce with which Gigli opens the aria and in the outpouring of emotion with which he ends it the vocal quality is one of captivating beauty. It is the archetypal glorious Italian sound; there is a sweetness to it, a glowing, soft-grained caressing quality which quite simply seduces the ear, and which never hardens or coarsens when the voice comes under dramatic pressure. The technical control with which the head and chest registers are blended is flawless – the phrase 'Vi conquide, o sogni d'or', which takes the vocal line from a low F to a high A flat, could serve as an object lesson in how to handle the 'break in the voice' – and it allows Gigli to ride these sweeping phrases as if the singing of opera were the most natural function in the world.

I remember working in Rome with an accompanist who had played frequently for Gigli in his later years, and he described him to me as *'furbo'* – 'cunning' or 'crafty', not in a pejorative sense but in the sense of knowing every trick of the vocal trade. He told me that before a concert Gigli never tried out his top register at all. He would sing through the opening section of the aria 'Dalla sua pace' from DON GIOVANNI, which lies right in the 'break', and if that was in place he knew that nothing else could go wrong. As a young man Gigli had taken his time and trained for six long years, though his poverty must have tempted him to do otherwise. He was already twenty-four when he made his début – Caruso made his at twenty-two, Schipa at twenty-one and Björling at only nineteen – and by the time he made this recording, at the age of twenty-eight, the combination of thorough preparation and practical experience had matured him into a vocal master.

The impact of Gigli's singing, however, is not only due to the beauty of the voice and the soundness of the technique; the additional factor lies in the passion with which he goes about it, whether he is singing grand opera or the humblest little song. The other track on the Nimbus CD which dates from 1918 is a popular ditty in march-time about a soldier and his girlfriend, and Gigli flings himself at it in a positive frenzy of emotion. This whole-heartedness in his singing was something which he never lost throughout his long career and the impression created by the great tenor in action was well described by Richard Capell, the critic of *The Daily Telegraph*, when Gigli made his British concert début at the Albert Hall in 1933:

> Gigli is a superb singer. He is a little man, a bantam fighting cock. He sings with the whole force of his body, as naturally as a game cock fights. And there was not an ugly note all evening. He began by singing 'God Save the King' at 8.15 then sang on for two hours with only one break, for which he had to plead. By ten o'clock the audience was making a noise like a football crowd. Those who wanted 'Quest' o quella' were trying to shout down the partisans of 'Celeste Aida' or whatever their fancy was.

This instinct of Gigli's for pouring out his soul with every phrase he sang was precisely what certain people disliked about him, because the truth of the matter is (as he himself always happily admitted) that his soul was a simple one. The one cautionary observation in Richard Capell's review came right at the end – 'But next time Mr Gigli must leave Mr Gihigli in the dressing-room'; while Capell's opposite number on *The Times* protested rather pompously that Gigli 'broke the legato phrases with a distracting amount of noisy exhalation', and Ernest Newman came up with the famous gibe about Gigli 'so-howing his wild notes'. In other words, Gigli did not display stylistic fastidiousness, but then fastidiousness had not brought home the bacon in those first two performances of 'Cielo e mar'. Mr Gihigli never *was* going to be left in the dressing-room, because it is a pleasant feeling to run aspirates through your throat while you sing and for Mr Gigli singing was one huge pleasant feeling.

Passing on to the various recordings on the Nimbus disc which date from 1921–4 one can again and again find fault on stylistic points if one feels inclined to do so. Why, for instance, in his first aria from TOSCA, should Cavaradossi sound as if he is about to burst into tears when he sings his matter-of-fact phrase about contrasting forms of beauty being blended through the mystery of art? This after all is Act I and he does not yet know that he is going to be shot in Act III. Why should Faust in Boito's MEFISTOFELE, after an immaculately taken rising phrase on 'in un sogno supremo', slither down to the next note a full octave below on a totally superfluous portamento? You can either condemn these things and condemn Gigli with them, or you can shrug your shoulders and let the little bantam cock bathe your day in golden Mediterranean sunshine.

Different people will have different favourites amongst the twenty-two tracks on the Nimbus disc, but all of them show this heaven-sent voice in the first flush of its youthful beauty. There is a marvellously poised account of the FAUST aria, and a performance of the less familiar 'Nel verde Maggio' from Catalani's LORELEY which I could not imagine being bettered by any other tenor than Caruso. There is also an 'Improvviso' from ANDREA CHENIER which demonstrates with what an impact this essentially lyrical voice could be employed; the perfect focus of the vocal emission and the incisiveness of the diction make this a declamatory outburst of which many a dramatic tenor would be proud. Six months before recording this aria Gigli had made his début at the Met* as Andrea Chénier in a production which had been

---

* In his memoirs Gigli describes how he spent the last few moments before going on stage – 'I stood in the wings drinking black coffee and thinking of my mother.'

intended for Caruso, and as he started his career very much in the great man's shadow comparisons between the two of them were, and remain, inevitable. Gigli, however, was much too *furbo* to present himself to the world as the second Caruso; nobody could have succeeded in that ambition, and to be the first Gigli was distinction enough. His was a lighter voice than Caruso's, without that 'chiaroscuro', that gleaming darkness of timbre, which made the Caruso sound uniquely magnificent. In its place there was a liquid quality which I always think of as the essence of Gigli's singing. I know that the image of a singer 'pouring out' the voice is an overworked one, but in Gigli's case it is hard to avoid; in passages such as Cavaradossi's 'O dolci mani', in the aria 'Spirto gentil' from Donizetti's LA FAVORITA, or in a Neapolitan song such as 'Notturno d'amore' one can almost see the lips lovingly wrapped around the language as the labial softness of the Italian consonants, the mellifluous contours of the Italian melody and the gentle sentimentality of the Italian spirit combine in a flood of effortless sound. Gigli was indisputably Caruso's successor as the world's most popular Italian tenor and by the end of his career he had sung most of Caruso's repertoire, but in drawing attention to these parallels it is worth noting that he postponed his first Radamès in AIDA until he was forty-seven, his first Don José in CARMEN until he was fifty-one and his first Canio in PAGLIACCI until he was fifty-two, whereas all of these roles were central to Caruso's repertoire before he had reached the age of thirty.

Another CD issue which concentrates on Gigli's early output is a two-disc set from Pearl, GEMM *CDS 9423*, which offers every one of his acoustic opera recordings, plus one song. Amongst the delights which were not included in the Nimbus selection are the Cherry Duet from Mascagni's L'AMICO FRITZ (a piece which Gigli felt suited his voice better than the more popular CAVALLERIA RUSTICANA), a remarkably restrained and intimate 'Amor ti vieta' from FEDORA and two duets from his début role of Enzo to add to the 'Cielo e mar'. Two other tracks of particular charm are the duets from the first and second acts of Gounod's ROMEO ET JULIETTE, sung with Lucrezia Bori; and thereby hangs a tale. Lavish as were the vocal gifts which had been bestowed on Beniamino Gigli, physically he was less blessed. He was short in stature and with increasing prosperity came a swelling waistline. He clung to the theory that for glandular reasons tenors were inevitably rotund, indeed he referred to this in print as 'an established biological fact', but this did not prevent certain critics from making cutting references to his unromantic appearance. He began to feel self-conscious about his shape when he found himself cast opposite the tall and hand-some Claudia Muzio for his transatlantic début – TOSCA in the Teatro Colón in 1919 – but it was the prospect of singing Romeo during his second season at the Met which really concentrated his mind. Having already engaged the services of a private secretary as well as persuading his old mentor Maestro Rosati to move to New York as his personal accompanist and coach, he now added to his entourage a certain Mr H. J. Reilly as his physical trainer. Whenever Gigli was in the States, whether in New York itself or on tour, he was subjected by Mr Reilly to a daily dose of what the tenor called 'his ingenious tortures', designed to build up beneficial muscle and reduce superfluous flab; and though even Mr Reilly could not turn Gigli into an Adonis, I can well believe that the work put in on his chest and back muscles helped to support the growing robustness of his voice.

Unlike Caruso, Gigli was not without rivals in the tenor field. At the lighter end of his repertoire there was Tito Schipa,* and at the heavier end Giovanni Martinelli. It was Gigli's physical appearance which lost him the Italian première of Puccini's LA RONDINE to Aureliano Pertile in 1917 – Schipa had sung the world première in Monte Carlo – and it was widely assumed that the same reason lay behind the choice of Miguel Fleta as creator of the role of Calaf in TURANDOT nine years later although Puccini had gone so far as to offer it to Gigli. Giacomo

* See *Legendary Voices*, pp.215–27.

Lauri-Volpi, too, he of the clarion top notes, was widely admired, but Gigli emerged from amongst this starry bunch as the man the public most wanted to hear – the proof of which lies in the fact that he was able to charge a higher fee than any of his rivals. He was undoubtedly the least talented actor of them all, but he possessed the ultimate weapon – by far the most beautiful voice.

There are so many reissues of Gigli's electrical recordings on the market today that it would make tedious reading were I to discuss them all, but let us consider just one of the countless arias now available, 'Una furtiva lagrima' from L'ELISIR D'AMORE, which is to be found on EMI's *CDH 761051 2*, Pearl's GEMM *CD 9367* and Nimbus's *NI 7817*. The role of the country bumpkin Nemorino was one which allowed Gigli to shed all inhibitions about his unaristocratic appearance and simply revel in the lyrical riches of the vocal line. His performance of the aria is not etched with original genius, as is that of Caruso in his incomparable recording of 1904, but leaving that aside Gigli's version is quite simply as beautifully sung as one has the right to expect from any singer who is less than superhuman. He positively juggles with the creaminess and pliancy of the tone. The phrases swell to a passionate forte or taper into a wistful piano as the spirit moves him, and the whole effect is rendered vital and compelling by Gigli's priceless gift of sounding as if his very life depends on every note that he sings.

Fortunately for us we are not dependent for the assessment of Gigli's artistry on his recordings of individual bits and pieces, impressive though most of them are. Back in those days complete recordings of operas were rare events, but in 1934 Gigli embarked on the first of what was to become a series of nine full sets, eight operas and the Verdi REQUIEM, all of which have been reissued on CD by EMI. The first of these recordings was PAGLIACCI, produced by the indefatigable Fred Gaisberg in Milan with the chorus and orchestra of La Scala under the conductor Franco Ghione, and it now reappears on a single disc, *CDH 763309 2*. It was to be nearly eight years before Gigli undertook the role of Canio on stage, but listening to the recording one would not guess it. Nowadays it is frequently apparent that the starry casts assembled in the recording studios have familiarised themselves with the notes and not much more, but Gigli is in the part heart and soul. He has a nice light touch with the jocular passages at the beginning, his 'Vesti la giubba' is delivered with a dignity which adds considerably to its power, and his final breakdown is a vocal and histrionic *tour de force*.

The second of the series came three and a half years later. This was LA BOHEME, again with the forces of La Scala, this time under the baton of Umberto Berretoni, and with the twenty-four-year-old Licia Albanese as Mimi. In its new guise as *CHS 7 63335 2* (apart from PAGLIACCI all the operas are two-disc sets) it comes up as bright as a new pin, obviously not able to compete in spaciousness with modern stereophonic versions, but clear and immediate, and above all wonderfully lively in the singing. Rodolfo was one of Gigli's most regular roles – he sang it forty-three times at the Met alone, more often than anything else – and so this time it is no surprise that he should be right inside the skin of the character. For the badinage with the other bohemians he gives the voice an infectious little chuckle and during his first encounter with Mimi his manner is so relaxed and natural that when she sings 'grazie' to thank him for his kindness he can't help answering with a spoken 'prego'; it is not in the score, but it would be any Italian's reaction. 'Che gelida manina' is a gem. The high C is perhaps not quite the triumphant note that it is on his individual recording of the aria made seven years earlier, and not everyone will be happy with the breath which he takes before the very last note in order to achieve his immaculately sustained pianissimo on the word 'dir'; the great thing, however, is that we are not merely listening to the delivery of a famous set piece but to a continuous revelation of the character of Rodolfo. The opening is playful, even a little teasing, and as the melody expands so does the warmth of Gigli's tone. We do not feel, though, that at this stage of the proceedings Rodolfo is taking himself or anything else seriously. That comes later, in Act III, and here once again we find that Gigli, however bad a physical actor he may have been, was a considerable vocal one. As he tries to persuade Marcello that Mimi is nothing better than a heartless flirt his voice takes on just the edge of forced sarcasm that the passage demands – the instrument is not capable of ugliness, but he pushes it as far in that direction as it will go – and when he admits the truth, namely that he is fearful for Mimi's life, Puccini's direction of *con la massima espressione* is obeyed to the letter.

Gigli's range runs to a splendid brashness, too, as Pinkerton in MADAMA BUTTERFLY (*CHS 7 69990 2*). His attack on 'Vinto si tuffa' carries exactly the heedless arrogance of the young naval officer with a bride in every port, and I particularly enjoy his gurgle of approval when the consul sensibly chooses whisky in preference to milk punch. Gigli's method of characterisation lies partly in singing Puccini's vocal line as if it had been written for him, and partly in the vivid projection of the Italian language; today, when the outstanding vocal qualities of so many non-Italian singers have brought them to international eminence, this is something which we encounter increasingly seldom. With Gigli it is almost super-fluous to mention that the love duet and 'Addio fiorito asil' call forth a cascade of emotion expressed in twenty-four carat curren-cy, and this is the principal characteristic, too, of his participation in TOSCA (*CHS 7 63338 2*). Mario Cavaradossi is a gentleman who requires less characterisation than either Pinkerton or Rodolfo, but, at least in the opinion of *The Times*'s critic, rather more than Gigli gave him when he first sang the role at Covent Garden in 1930. 'Signor Gigli now and again showed an appreciation of the role's dramatic possibilities,' we read, 'but these glimpses of spontaneity were spasmodic, and when he was apostrophising his picture he seemed more concerned with the back of the gallery than with the supposed object of his address.' Gigli's concern with the gallery was something for which he was regularly hauled over the coals by critics both in London and in New York, but that was where most of his compatriots used to be sitting and he was determined that they should have their money's worth. In any case the same critic was gracious enough to express gratitude for Gigli's 'fine ringing tone, and still more for his beautiful singing of the quieter passages', and anyone listening to this recording is likely to say amen to that. As it was made in Rome in the course of four afternoons when Gigli was singing the role in the Baths of Caracalla during the evening, it says a great deal for his stamina even when deprived of the services of Mr H. J. Reilly.

I remember an old friend of mine in the Covent Garden chorus telling me that when Gigli first came to the Royal Opera the company all took it for granted that they would be bowled over by his forte singing, but that none of them had dreamt how beautiful his mezza voce would be. One typical example of its ravishing quality is to be found in the 'Hostias' section of the Verdi REQUIEM recording (*CDH 7 63341 2*). I have heard people dismiss this soft singing of Gigli's as 'crooning', but he had no difficulty in projecting it to the back of the largest opera houses of the world without recourse to a microphone – a claim which would not have been made, I think, by Bing Crosby in his heyday. In this recording Gigli's style came in for more criticism than usual, particularly from British reviewers, on the grounds that he introduced too strong a dash of operatic sentiment into religious music, but in their attitude to religion as to so many other things the Italians do differ from us Britons. I recently came across an article in an old Italian newspaper which may serve to illustrate my point. According to the writer Gigli told him in an interview that on 23 September 1930, shortly before going on stage for the last act of LUCIA DI LAMMERMOOR, he received a telegram telling him that his dearly loved mother had died. He went back on stage to sing 'Tu che a Dio spiegasti l'ali' ('Thou who hast spread thy wings towards God'), and was quoted as saying 'I sang the aria with deep intensity. Perhaps even as I was singing my mother with her spotless soul was winging her way towards the throne of the Almighty.' It slightly spoils the effect that in his memoirs Gigli says that it happened on 24

September and that the opera in question was MIGNON, but even granted that the 'interview' was pure invention I doubt whether the most imaginative British journalist would have put those particular words into any compatriot's mouth. Be that as it may, this version of the REQUIEM with Caniglia, Stignani and Pinza as the other soloists and with the chorus and orchestra of the Rome Opera under Tullio Serafin is a thorough-going Italian affair, and none the worse for that.

For his Covent Garden début in 1930 Gigli chose the role with which he had been introduced to the New York public ten years earlier, Andrea Chénier. It is one which tenors do greatly enjoy – I remember my old teacher Alfred Piccaver, who sang it frequently in Vienna, referring to it as 'good straight singing' – and there was no doubting the impact which Gigli's Chénier had on the opera-goers of London. It was probably his compatriots in the gallery who led the tempest of applause as Gigli sang the final note of the 'Improvviso' in Act I – wherever and whenever Gigli sang the local Italian colony always turned out in force – but where they led the rest of the audience followed and each of his solo numbers brought the proceedings to a total halt. The critics, too, were ecstatic and Francis Toye of the *Morning Post*, one of the most respected of their ranks, opened a lengthy eulogy with the words: 'The audience went mad over Beniamino Gigli and well they might, for he is undoubtedly the best tenor we have heard here since the war.' The full recording of ANDREA CHENIER (*CHS 7 69996 2*), once again with the forces of La Scala, was made in 1942 and it is remarkable how little Gigli's voice had changed since the acoustic recordings made twenty years earlier of the arias from Acts I and IV.

The list of Gigli's verismo full recordings is completed by CAVALLERIA RUSTICANA (*CHS 7 69987 2*), conducted by the seventy-six-year-old Pietro Mascagni, who opens the proceedings with a splendidly vigorous spoken introduction. His tempi are occasionally rather less than fiery, but none the less Gigli gives us an all-stops-out rendering of the youthful and impetuous Turiddu.

Further interest is added to this particular issue in that the second disc is completed by six recordings of individual Mascagni numbers including two from L'AMICO FRITZ – the 1919 version of the Cherry Duet, which we have already met, and the 1948 version of Fritz's aria 'O amore, o bella luce del cor', thus spanning in the one role three decades of Gigli's recording career. Verdi once declared that the libretto of L'AMICO FRITZ was 'the worst he had ever seen'. This is a pity, because much of the music, characterised as it is by a certain wistful sentimentality, strikes me as the most attractive Mascagni wrote.

Besides the verismo composers, to whose operas Gigli's voice and style were so ideally suited, Verdi's is naturally the name which crops up most frequently in the catalogue of his repertoire, and in 1943 he recorded the role of Riccardo in UN BALLO IN MASCHERA (*CHS 7 69993 2*). I have already written in my chapter on Tito Gobbi* about the complications which this piece can lead to because of the censors compelling Verdi to transplant historical goings-on in Sweden to a British colony in America. Nowadays in Britain we usually restore the action to its original setting but in Italy this has never been the practice, and on this recording, made in the middle of the war, the plot thickens yet further as it was not felt appropriate to have mention made of England or America. What remains intact, however, is one of Verdi's most compelling scores and of all the Verdian roles the one which probably suited Gigli's voice the best, even at the age of fifty-three. With the exhilaration of the opening aria 'La rivedrà nell'estasi' he announces straight away that all his old bounce is still intact, an impression which is confirmed by the agility of 'Di' tu se fedele' and the virtuoso jauntiness of 'È scherzo od è follia'. The Act II duet with Amelia finds him as ardent as ever he was, and he responds to the electrifying intensity of Maestro Tullio Serafin with a really gripping performance of his big solo in Act III. As to the death scene, it is the kind of performance which explains

---

* See *Legendary Voices*, p.101.

how one singer can achieve a position of pre-eminence amongst his contemporaries; anyone wanting guidance in the matter of dying on a high B flat need seek no further.

The last of the Gigli full sets was AIDA (*CHS 7 63331 2*), recorded when he was fifty-six, and it is remarkable how few concessions need to be made to the fact that his voice at this point had done thirty-two years' hard labour.* The top still has a triumphant ring to it, the enthusiasm for the task in hand has in no whit abated, and the final duet is despatched with an exemplary smoothness of legato as well as almost all the old suavity of tone. Gigli had first sung Radamès in Rome in 1937 and it was his last role at Covent Garden before the war, when he astonished even his most enthusiastic admirers with the new element of heroism which his singing displayed. I remember one venerable opera-goer telling me that it was 'as if he had thickened his vocal cords specially for the part', and although as early as 1930 several of the London critics had commented on the baritonal quality which Gigli was able to introduce into his middle register when he felt inclined, none of them had been prepared for his mastery of a role so much more dramatic than any in which they had heard him previously. 'He captivated his hearers with "Celeste Aida" at the outset,' wrote *The Times*, 'and showed himself throughout the tenor of the grand manner possessing unlimited sustaining power and resilience'; and though Scott Goddard of the *News Chronicle* 'longed for a more dignified stage presence to match such vocal ability', to the rest of the press as well as to the public the glory achieved by Gigli's singing heavily outweighed the unlikeliness of his ever having achieved comparable distinction on the field of Mars. Visually, in any case, the audience was offered one compensation – the

---

* For obvious reasons I have not gone into detail about the rest of the casts of these full recordings. Suffice it to say that almost every role is taken by a singer who was at that time at the top of the tree in Italian opera, with names such as Maria Caniglia, Ebe Stignani, Gino Bechi and Tancredi Pasero making regular appearances.

première danseuse of the production was a talented twenty-year-old named Margot Fonteyn.

Radamès was also Gigli's last new role at the Met when he went back there in 1939 after a gap of seven years, and the reason for his long absence from New York has to be regarded, I think, as the most regrettable episode in his career. The bare bones of the matter were as follows. In 1932, when the Depression was endangering the survival of the Met, the general manager, Giulio Gatti-Casazza, called upon everyone in the company to accept a ten per cent cut in salary. Everyone complied except Gigli and the upshot was that he was presented with the alternatives of resigning or being dismissed. As is usual with such cases, however, there were two sides to the story. Gigli was on a long-term contract extending to 1935 and he was advised by his lawyer that an acceptance of the salary cut would render the remainder of the contract null and void. He himself offered a solution, namely that he should retain his performance fee, but sing a certain number of evenings gratis. This Gatti turned down, and it is difficult not to form the impression that he was wanting to relieve the Met of one of its most expensive commitments. On the other hand one cannot overlook the fact that thirty-two members of the company, including Maestro Serafin, Ponselle, de Luca, Pinza, Melchior, Bori, Rethberg and other famous names, signed a joint letter to Gatti virtually demanding Gigli's removal, using such phrases as '. . . we all feel it our duty to protest against a colleague whose conduct is inexcusable. He disturbs the harmony and endangers the safety of our institution and is a challenge to the sentiment of every one.' This is strange because Gigli was generally regarded as a friendly and well-liked colleague, and there is an ironical contrast between this letter and one signed only a year before by 106 members of the company when he was presented with a gold medal by the chorus of the Met on completion of his first ten years amongst them.

It is possible, I suppose, that at some point his eminence and his wealth may have gone to his head.* As early as 1927 he had bought an estate of some 7000 acres outside Recanati and had had a villa of staggering magnificence built upon it. As he himself testifies in his memoirs he could not quite see why the architect found it necessary to incorporate twenty-three bathrooms and a refrigerator large enough to contain food for twenty people for a whole year, but he had had no difficulty in paying for it. Despite all this he was certainly not considered arrogant at Covent Garden. Dame Eva Turner, who was his last Aida there, spoke to me once or twice about him with great affection, and even more significantly he was extremely popular with the chorus; knowing that his name was hard for Englishmen to pronounce convincingly he used to introduce himself to one and all as 'Mr Giggly'.

Unfortunately for Gigli this was not his last fall from grace as far as America was concerned. After his return to Italy in 1939 extraordinary stories appeared in the Roman press, which were quickly picked up in New York, about Gigli launching a violent attack against the United States in general and the Metropolitan Opera in particular. He was reported to have said that the States were in the grip of 'nervousness and disorientation, and an air of extortion and corruption'. 'There are those who see in the not far future something like civil war,' he was quoted as stating, with most of the trouble apparently stemming from the unions, which were in the hands of the Jews. As for the Met, it was reduced to using cut-price American singers more talented as publicity-seekers than as artists; which produced reactions such as a statement from the tenor Richard Crooks that Gigli 'should have learnt by now to use his mouth for singing only. It sounds

---

* It was certainly Covent Garden's attempts to cut down on fees which kept Gigli away from there in the mid-1930s. In 1933 the management's representative in Italy was instructed to approach Gigli with an offer of £300 per performance, or failing him Lauri-Volpi at £150. He cabled in reply: 'Gigli indignantly refuses, and Lauri-Volpi will never recover from insult of my offer. Returning to London immediately.' These sums should be multiplied by approximately twenty-five to reach their modern equivalent, and there are tenors in the world today who would react similarly to an offer of £7500.

better.' To me it seems incredible that Gigli would have been so short-sighted as to alienate a country in which, apart from anything else, the greatest number of his gramophone records were habitually bought. Like many another singer he was politically naïve and it is easy to imagine the fascist press putting any amount of rubbish into his mouth; they must have been rubbing their hands with glee that such a world-famous artist should have chosen to come home, while others such as Pinza and Toscanini preferred to remain in America. Gigli could never fathom the political stand which Toscanini made; to him Italy was Italy whoever was in charge. When the company of La Scala went to Berlin in 1937 they were fêted by Goebbels, Gigli not least of all, and when Hitler paid a state visit to Rome in 1938 Gigli and Caniglia were the two artists chosen to sing for him. The following month, though, Gigli was performing in London – as far as he was concerned no political statements were involved.

During the war Gigli naturally sang on in Italy, only to find that in the political chaos which obtained in Rome as one side pulled out and the other moved in he was in trouble with certain of his own countrymen for having sung when Germans were in the audience. In June 1944 he was barred by the military governor of Rome, Major Harry H. Johnson, from singing in a concert for Allied troops because of his allegedly pro-Nazi sympathies, but early in 1945 the Council of the Musicians' Syndicate ruled that charges against him were 'exaggerated, non-existent or brought by rival singers'. On 12 March he made his first public appearance since his temporary disgrace, singing in a benefit concert for war refugees in the Teatro Adriano and, as the *New York Herald Tribune* promptly reported, he received a 'wild ovation' from the entire public, Romans and Allied troops alike.

When it was announced the following year that Gigli would be appearing at Covent Garden with the company of the San Carlo Opera from Naples the news caused, as Harold Rosenthal puts it in his history of the Royal Opera, 'chaos, both inside and outside the box-office'. There were to be four performances only, but 'thousands of people were unable to obtain tickets . . . and the house could have been sold out at least twenty times'. Of Gigli's Rodolfo *The Times* wrote: 'He walked casually through the part with no more than an occasional caper to signify that this was a stage performance, not a concert, and he rarely vouchsafed more than indifferent glances at his Mimi. But he still can sing; he opens his mouth and a stream of golden tone emerges.'*

Gigli's unflagging stamina was vouchsafed by the fact that for the two CAV & PAG nights he was only announced as Turiddu, but actually sang Canio as well, complete with an encore of 'Vesti la giubba'. Indeed his energy during the final decade of his career was truly remarkable. When he returned to the Teatro Colón for two strenuous seasons in 1947 and 1948 the public and the press were still as enthusiastic as they had ever been, and one of his greatest successes was the exceptionally taxing role of Don Alvaro in LA FORZA DEL DESTINO. The critic of *L'Italia del Popolo* complimented him not only on the 'unconquerable state of his voice' but also on 'his huge effectiveness on stage', which must have been particularly gratifying for Gigli, because the last time he had sung the role there, back in 1933, he had fallen victim to one of those mishaps which seem to be an inevitable feature of operatic life. One of the stretcher-bearers who brought him on stage in Act III, when Don Alvaro is apparently dying from a wound sustained in battle, tripped and fell, unloading his patient onto the floor. Unfortunately on these occasions there is never any time to be lost as the orchestra keeps on playing, so Gigli had nothing for it but to clamber back onto the stretcher as fast as he could and carry on dying.

After his final performances at Covent Garden Gigli kept in touch with his British public via regular concert tours and it would be hard to exaggerate the delight with which they were

---

* The Mimi was his own daughter Rina, a moderate soprano. Some observers charitably felt that Gigli was attempting to minimise the potentially incestuous effect of indulging in an excess of passion.

received. In 1946 the publicity leaflet was able to announce with justifiable pride that 'No other artiste *ever* sold out *four* Albert Hall concerts', and it was on one of these occasions two years later that I myself first heard Gigli in the flesh. It was an unforgettable experience. Gigli was by then that old cliché 'a legend in his own lifetime' and the sense of expectation amongst the audience as we awaited his appearance was almost tangible. Then on he came, that utterly undistinguished elderly figure in a baggy tail suit, and for the rest of the evening time stood still. He opened, I remember, with the aria 'O paradiso' from L'AFRICANA,* and from the very first phrase, 'Mi batte il cor', sung in the caressing mezza voce so familiar from his recordings, he held that gigantic auditorium in the palm of his hand. This is the aria sung by the explorer Vasco da Gama as he first sets foot on African soil and it was a favourite number of Gigli's for starting the ball rolling. With the contemplative recitative he would ease himself into the acoustics of the hall, with the opening of the aria he would allow the tone to expand up to the first high B flat of the evening, and with the final 'tu m'appartieni a me', which conveniently happens to mean 'you belong to me', he would trigger off a frenzied volley of applause. When he used to sing the role of Vasco at the Met he was regularly pilloried by the critics for the shamelessness with which he would step out of the role, stroll down to the footlights and sell the aria to the cash customers; but at the Albert Hall it had the effect of reducing that daunting cavern to a cosy spot in which we could all sit and enjoy Gigli for as long as he felt inclined to entertain us. The evening would end exactly as Richard Capell had described it back in 1933, with the audience yelling for their favourite arias, Gigli giving the matter a moment's thought, and then turning to his accompanist, usually Ivor Newton, whose job it was to conjure up whatever had been selected from the vast

---

* Gigli's 1923 recording of this aria is to be found in the Nimbus and Pearl acoustic selections discussed above, and his 1928 version on Pearl GEMM *CD 9361*.

pile of music at his side. The moment the opening bars of the accompaniment had been recognised there would be a ripple of welcoming applause which would cease as if cut off with a knife as Gigli began to sing.

Gigli had a characteristic stance on these occasions, with one thumb hitched into his trouser pocket, and as he grew older a noticeable tendency to lower his head as he went for a high note, like an elderly bull entering the fray. The last time I heard him – it must have been in the early 1950s – his voice had noticeably declined. It appeared to have lost some of its essential core of sound and there were far more little songs on the programme than of yore. During the applause after one of these songs I muttered to my companion 'I'm afraid this means he can't manage the big stuff any more', whereupon, as if in response to this blasphemy, Gigli hitched his thumb a little tighter into his pocket, lowered his head another couple of degrees and gave us the 'Nessun dorma'. He may have taken it down a semi-tone – not having perfect pitch I would not have known – but for those few minutes he summoned up much of the old glory once again and the effect was inspirational.

In any case Gigli was an irresistible singer of little songs, especially of the Neapolitan numbers written by de Curtis, de Crescenzo, Denza and others, as well as of the various sentimental ditties which featured in his films.* Most of the Gigli CD selections have at least a few of his humbler recordings hidden amongst the arias and one, Pearl's GEMM *CD 9915*, is exclusively devoted to Gigli in song. A number entitled 'Marta' by a composer named Simons has long been one of my favourite Gigli recordings – it was one of the first that I ever acquired – and under the alchemy of Gigli's vocalisation songs such as 'Musica proibita' or 'Canta pe' me' can improve one's mood in an instant. We are even treated to two examples of Gigli singing in 'English'. Despite his many

---

* Gigli made no less than fifteen films, none of them aspiring to high cinematographic art, but all of them packed with singing and extremely lucrative.

seasons in New York he never learnt the language, living there virtually in a Little Italy, and though stretches of de Curtis's 'Goodbye Mari' are in some strange way partially intelligible, the opening of Carnevali's 'Come love with me' would baffle Professor Higgins. Of course British audiences adored it when Gigli did venture into our native tongue, and he learnt 'Annie Laurie' for his Scottish public as he had 'Mother Machree' for the Irish community in New York.

Having fallen under the spell of Gigli and his Albert Hall concerts I once asked Sandor Gorlinsky, the impresario who first brought him back to England after the war and subsequently managed all his British tours, what he was like as a person. I rather dreaded hearing that he was temperamental and tiresome but Gorlinsky described him as not only the greatest singer he had ever represented but also the least difficult. When Gorlinsky went to his hotel to fetch him for a concert he would be sitting happily in the lobby playing cards, and he only had one particular quirk which had initially struck Gorlinsky as peculiar – he liked to be paid before a concert and in cash. When Gorlinsky asked him the reason for this he explained that after certain experiences in various other countries he liked to put his fee in his back pocket so that he could pat it between arias and know that it was still there.

For an impression of Gigli's status within Italy itself during his later years I would like to turn to the memoirs of Tito Gobbi.* In return for a favour which Gobbi had done him Gigli offered to sing a charity concert in Gobbi's home town of Bassano del Grappa, not far from Venice, and this is how Gobbi describes the event:

We put heart and soul into making all the arrangements perfect, but we soon found that it would have to be a concert without seats. It was going to be 'standing room only' with

* See bibliography.

loudspeakers fixed up everywhere . . . The next day the great trek began. Throughout the afternoon and into the evening there came winding down from the hills hundreds and then thousands of people from the countryside. Every square, every street was packed with waiting people. Then Gigli walked from the hotel to the square and began to sing. He sang and he sang and he sang – every aria they asked for, every favourite song. Finally, when the time came to rescue him and take him back to his hotel crowds stood outside calling for him as though he were a king. I went out onto the balcony and explained that they really must let him go, that he was tired and needed rest. But they pleaded for him to come out and show himself. 'I understand, I understand,' the old tenor said, getting slowly to his feet, and he climbed the two steps to the balcony and went outside . . . It was a sight none of us will ever forget. The people stood so close together that you could only see their raised faces – thousands of them – white in the moonlight. Then he flung out his arms to them and began to sing again, the voice as perfect and seemingly as untired as ever.

Gigli himself used to say 'Apart from my voice I am a very ordinary person'; but singers differ from instrumentalists in that where they go their voice goes too, and Gigli never was 'apart from his voice'. With him it was a case of 'I sing therefore I am' and on his visits to Britain he would sing to one group of reporters as he disembarked from the boat at Dover and to another when he arrived at Victoria station. It was on one of these occasions that a woman in the crowd was heard to say, 'I told you so, it *is* Tetrazzini.'

The last occasion on which Gigli appeared in public was a concert in Washington on 25 May 1955, after forty-one years in harness. He spent most of his brief retirement at home in Recanati and died in Rome on 30 November 1957. It had always been his avowed ambition to be regarded as 'The people's singer of Italy' – it was one which he fulfilled.

MARIA JERITZA

MORAVIAN SOPRANO

b. Brno, 6 October 1887
d. Orange, New Jersey, 10 July 1982

If opera-goers of the inter-war years had been asked which contemporary soprano was the greatest, they would have been unlikely to give a decisive reply. Ponselle, Muzio, Lehmann, Schumann, Rethberg, Flagstad, Leider – they and doubtless several others would all have had their adherents, but how can you compare a Norma with a Brünnhilde, a Sophie with a Tosca or a Mimi with a Marschallin? Asked, though, who was the greatest prima donna in the popularly accepted sense of that expression they would have answered in a flash. One person embodied everything that the story-book prima donna ought to be; she was glamorous, temperamental, controversial, a lady who could make her own rules, never out of the headlines, frequently in the law courts, adored by thousands of opera-lovers and dreaded by several famous tenors. Maria Jeritza would have won hands down.

She was born Marie (known as Mizzi) Jedlizková in the city of Brno, or Brünn as it is called in German, which would nowadays make her a Czech, but at that time made her a citizen of the Austro-Hungarian Empire. She was the sort of person around whom so many myths grew up, several of them stoked by her own volubility in newspaper interviews, that when dealing with her early life it is hard to sift fact from fiction. One tale which she told often enough to invest it with an aura of credibility was that she was sent as a child into a convent, not merely for her education, but because her mother had vowed that if one of her sisters should be saved from some sickness that had smitten her Mizzi would take the veil. Mizzi was not apparently too worried by this until she learnt that in due course her long blonde tresses would be cut short. Her hair, which was to become a focal point in many of her most famous stage creations, was of paramount importance to her, so she decided to avail herself of the hard-and-fast rule that any novice who incurred three reprimands from the Mother Superior would be summarily dismissed. The first she achieved by sewing together the habits of two other novices while they were at prayer, the second by climbing into the next-door garden to steal fruit, and the third by losing her temper while playing dominoes with a fellow inmate and crashing the board down on her head.

Be all of this as it may, it was certainly opera which Maria Jeritza embraced (she selected the name as being more pronounceable than her own) rather than the Church, though here again the exact circumstances of her entry into the profession have become clouded by conflicting accounts. According to one she was in the chorus of the Brno Opera and let fly with a high C so much more imposing than that of the soprano guesting as Aida that she was plucked from the ranks and given immediate promotion. This version, I think, can be discounted in favour of that whereby her teacher, Professor Auspitzer, secretly invited the director of the Municipal Opera of Olomouc (Olmütz) to sit in the next room during one of Maria's lessons, as she was too shy to submit to a formal audition. One thing at least is certain – it was in Olomouc that she made her professional début as Elsa in LOHENGRIN in 1910, and from then onwards her doings were more reliably chronicled. Within less than a year of her début she had successfully auditioned for Rainer Simons, the director of the Vienna Volksoper, another event which took an unusual course. She sang Micaëla's aria from CARMEN and halfway through it Simons shouted 'Stop, that's enough!' Jeritza had by now sufficiently overcome her shyness to storm into his office and berate him for not at least letting her finish one song, when he looked up in surprise and said, 'I didn't need any more – I'm engaging you.' Once again it was a Wagner role with which she introduced herself to her new public, this time Elisabeth in TANNHÄUSER.

Jeritza was not destined to remain with the Volksoper much

longer than she had with the Municipal Opera of Olomouc. In the summer of 1912 she combined a vacation in Bad Ischl with appearances in the town's operetta theatre as Rosalinde in DIE FLEDERMAUS. Now it so happened that the Emperor Franz Josef used to take his summer holidays in Ischl and one evening he attended a performance. He was no opera-lover – he once wrote to his mistress, the actress Katherina Schratt, 'I go to the opera as a sacrifice for my country. After all, I function only as an advertisement for the sale of tickets' – but he was greatly taken with Maria Jeritza. He demanded to know why this ravishing creature with the heavenly voice was never to be heard in his own Court Opera in Vienna, asking the director rather pointedly '*Müssen unsere Sängerinnen immer alt und hässlich sein?*' ('Do our lady singers always have to be old and ugly?'). Not surprisingly a contract for Fräulein Jeritza was rapidly forthcoming and before the year was out she had made her début in Vienna's premier house, creating the title-role in Max Oberleitner's opera APHRODITE.

1912 was something of an *annus mirabilis* for Jeritza. She had also been spotted by the great director Max Reinhardt; he was planning a lavish new production of Offenbach's LA BELLE HELENE for the Künstler Theater in Munich and he engaged her as the heroine, Helen of Troy. Another of Reinhardt's assignments for 1912 was to direct the world première of Richard Strauss's ARIADNE AUF NAXOS, and yet again the title-role went to Jeritza. Strauss was the most eminent German opera composer of the day, and ARIADNE was his first new piece since the immensely successful DER ROSENKAVALIER, so it was natural that the première, on 25 October in the Court Theatre, Stuttgart, should be attended by a host of prominent figures in the world of international opera. The piece itself was adjudged a disappointment, but Maria Jeritza was not, and Strauss in particular was delighted with her.

As if it were not enough to have won the admiration of so influential a figure, within a few more months Jeritza had endeared herself to the one composer who could perhaps be said to have enjoyed an even more prestigious position in the operatic firmament than Strauss himself, namely Giacomo Puccini. In the German-language première of his LA FANCIULLA DEL WEST in the Vienna Hofoper yet another title-role came her way, and she succeeded in capping the classical trio of Aphrodite, Ariadne and Helen with a rip-roaring embodiment of the pistol-toting, horseback-riding Minnie, proprietress of California's Polka Saloon. It was still only three years since she had been too scared to audition in Olomouc; she had come a long way.

It was soon after her success as Minnie that Jeritza began her recording career, and three of the titles which she sang for the Odeon company in 1914 are included in an interestingly chosen selection on *Lebendige Vergangenheit CD 89079*. Two of them are from DAS HEIMCHEN AM HERD, an opera by the Hungarian composer Carl Goldmark, based on Dickens's *The Cricket on the Hearth*, and both are pleasantly folksy in style. In the first the heroine conducts a dialogue with a cricket, whose representation in the orchestra does not quite survive the odd-sounding instrumental effects of an old acoustic recording, but who is charmingly imitated by the heroine; while the second develops into a spiritedly rendered rustic waltz, or Ländler. The voice which had been at least partly responsible for bringing Jeritza such rapid fame is revealed as one of great brilliance rather than warmth of tone, with the upper register particularly thrilling in quality, right up to an effortless high C. It is a powerful instrument, as one would expect from a soprano who had cut her teeth on Wagner, but flexible too, and even capable of a very acceptable trill.

It is, however, the third of these 1914 recordings which is the most significant, because it is her earliest version of the aria which, more than any other passage in her extensive repertoire, became identified with the name of Maria Jeritza – 'Vissi d'arte' from TOSCA. Here again, the story of how she first came to sing it in the manner which became her personal patent was told by her on many occasions and with numerous variations of detail. The broad outline was as follows. In 1913 Jeritza was rehearsing Tosca in the Vienna Opera under the personal supervision of Puccini. At the moment in Act II when Scarpia advances on Tosca with the threatening words 'Al tuo Mario, per tuo voler, non resta che un'ora di vita' ('It is by your will that your Mario has but an hour to live'), the stage direction printed in the score indicates that Tosca 'shattered by grief, falls back onto a sofa'. On this particular occasion, however, Jeritza slipped and fell (subsequently she would arrange to be pushed by whoever was singing Scarpia) landing on her face on the floor. In one version of the legend she bumped her nose and, fearing that it was bleeding, did not want to lift her head, while in another she was simply dazed and did not have time to rise to her feet before launching into the aria. In any case the upshot was that she sang it as she was, lying on her front, flat out on the floor. When the aria was over, Puccini, who had never been happy to have such a static number hold up the drama at this moment of emotional red heat, leapt up from the stalls and called out 'Brava, Maria! This was an idea from God! Never sing it any other way!' – nor did she, thereby earning herself the nickname of 'La prima donna prostrata'. During her opening season with the Metropolitan Opera in 1921 Tosca was the second role that she sang, and as the Met's general manager, Giulio Gatti-Casazza, expressed it in his memoirs: 'After the "Vissi d'arte" . . . the theatre broke out in a demonstration the equal of which I can scarcely recall. The American public was completely conquered.' This was echoed by Henry Krehbiel, critic of the *New York Tribune*, who wrote 'We cannot recall a similar scene in all the history of the opera house, which has witnessed many a great artistic triumph. It was not applause; it was an emotional tumult; a tempest.'

There was, of course, a great deal more behind Jeritza's triumph as Tosca than this one sublime gimmick, just as there had always been a great deal more behind her meteoric rise to fame than the mere possession of a voice. First there was her physical appearance. She was tall and athletic in figure, with long, elegant limbs. Her beautiful face was wreathed in hair of dazzling blonde (never mind the fact that at several points in TOSCA the story revolves around the heroine being a brunette) and, as the crowning glory of all this feminine loveliness, there were her eyes of cerulean blue, now flashing with dramatic fire, now tugging at the heartstrings with their depth of innocence and vulnerability – two qualities which in real life were seldom ascribed to this particular diva. Then there was her extraordinary flair as an actress. As the critic Deems Taylor wrote in the *New York World*: 'She gave a performance of thrilling beauty and intensity, every tone and gesture of which was instinct with authority and imagination ... One would have to forsake the opera stage and go back to Sarah Bernhardt to find a Tosca that could hold an audience so spellbound.'

The season in which Jeritza made her Met début was the first after the premature death of Caruso, and Gatti-Casazza was anxious to reassure the public that the house would not go into a decline. He brought back Chaliapin, and he lost as little time as possible in securing the services of Titta Ruffo, but the biggest favour he did himself was the engagement of Maria Jeritza. So great was the impact of her arrival upon the scene that one of the New York newspapers dubbed her 'the Viennese thunderbolt', and she remained a powerful box-office attraction for the next twelve years, frequently opening the season, a privilege which had been Caruso's as if by right, and causing certain other stars such as Geraldine Farrar and Claudia Muzio to feel that the time had come to move elsewhere. There were some, of course, who did not subscribe to the vogue of Jeritza-mania, and at her treatment of the 'Vissi d'arte' in particular a certain amount of fun was poked. One critic admitted that his lady companion had turned to him at the première and whispered 'I wish she had stayed on the sofa and sung it better'; while Geraldine Farrar, scarcely an unbiased witness as she had been the Met's Tosca on over fifty occasions, referred in her memoirs to 'a pose of unashamed abandon', and went on to say: 'From my seat I obtained no view of any expressive pantomime on her pretty face, while I was surprised by the questionable flaunting of a well-cushioned and obvious posterior.'

Part of Jeritza's fascination lay without doubt in her 'strange harmony of contrasts'. Enthusiasts raved about her spontaneous and instinctive theatricality, yet I remember an old colleague of hers at the Met, the soprano Nanette Guilford, telling me that every single thing Jeritza did on stage was the result of meticulous calculation; indeed Antonio Scotti, Jeritza's frequent partner in the role of Scarpia, told Miss Guilford that he knew exactly on which note Jeritza would accidentally release the pin which brought her golden tresses tumbling around her shoulders.*

Musically, too, Jeritza presents a confusing case. Puccini thought so highly of her that he wrote to Gatti-Casazza asking that LA FANCIULLA DEL WEST should be revived at the Met especially for her, and it was his intention that she should create the role of Turandot;† and yet her singing of the Tosca track on the *Lebendige Vergangenheit* CD, however beautiful the vocalisation may be, is so unrhythmical that it is hard to imagine any composer not tearing his hair in frustration. I have it on the best authority that during performances of TURANDOT a member of the Met's music staff, Wilfrid Pelletier, used to mingle with the chorus in costume and make-up to give her certain of her cues on a pitch-pipe; and when she was rehearsing the title-role in Suppé's operetta BOCCACCIO in 1931 her musical inaccuracy led to such violent clashes with the conductor, Artur Bodanzky, that at one point she walked off the stage during a full company call and refused to come back for fifteen minutes. To those unfamiliar

---

*   It is also interesting to note that one of the leading directors of the day, Wilhelm von Wymetal, claimed that Jeritza's horizontal rendering of 'Vissi d'arte' had been his idea, and that he and Jeritza had carefully rehearsed it.

---

†   She did create it at the Met, but the world première, for various reasons, went to Rosa Raisa.

with life in an opera house this may not sound hugely significant, but fifteen minutes of the chorus and orchestra's time costs a large sum of money and during the Depression that was not a commodity which grew on trees. Nevertheless, when the first night came, one of the most exacting critics, Olin Downes of the *New York Times*, not only heaped her with praise for her brilliance as a comic actress but also for the 'special care for tone, phrase and nuance' with which she had delivered the music.

Perhaps Jeritza's special gift for bending the rules is best illustrated by something which I was once told by Kurt Herbert Adler, the Viennese conductor who was for many years artistic director of the San Francisco Opera. When he was a young man he attended a performance of Richard Strauss's SALOME in Vienna, conducted by the composer and with Jeritza in the title-role. He was astonished by her musical sloppiness and at a party afterwards he asked Strauss if he himself had been pleased with the performance. 'I know why you're asking me,' Strauss replied with a smile. 'You mean Jeritza, don't you? Yes, she was all over the place – but wasn't she fabulous?' He certainly expressed his confidence in her in the most convincing possible manner, not only retaining her when the revised version of ARIADNE was unveiled in 1916, but also entrusting her with the creation of the Kaiserin in DIE FRAU OHNE SCHATTEN – his *'Frosch'* (Frog) as he liked to call it – and of the title-role in DIE AEGYPTISCHE HELENA. Furthermore it was discovered after Jeritza's death that he had presented her with the very last piece of music that he ever wrote. It was called 'Malven' (German for 'Mallows', a species of flower) and hardly anyone knew of its existence. The manuscript was inscribed *'Der geliebten Maria, diese letzte Rose'* ('To the beloved Maria, this last rose').

Another composer who was unstinting in his admiration for Jeritza was Erich Korngold, also born in Brno, but her junior by a decade. He was twenty years old when he wrote his masterpiece DIE TOTE STADT, and the dual role of Marie/Marietta was yet another which it fell to Jeritza to create.* The musical number which, more than any other passage in the score, was responsible for the opera's worldwide success was the duet for soprano and tenor 'Glück, das mir verblieb', and this is to be found on the *Lebendige Vergangenheit* CD adapted as a soprano solo. The melody is one of haunting potency, evocative and gently sentimental, and Jeritza's singing of it makes this perhaps my favourite of all her recordings. The voice in this performance has a more moving quality than usual, there is a greater depth of sincerity, of identification with the character, and the sweep up to the climactic high B flat is gloriously taken. This was the opera chosen for Jeritza's actual début at the Met and by introducing an unknown singer in an unknown piece Gatti-Casazza was taking a risk. Deems Taylor wrote a graphic account of how well that risk paid off ending with the words: 'New York had found the thing dearest to its heart – a new personality.'

One anecdote which I think speaks volumes about Jeritza's personality was told me some years ago by the distinguished American coloratura soprano Beverly Sills. Sills had been an infant prodigy vocalist, and Jeritza was extremely kind to her. On one occasion Sills sang at a party, and when she had finished she was presented by Jeritza with a gold toothpick. 'You must become a character,' Jeritza said. 'You must make people talk about you. After we have all eaten you pick your teeth with this gold toothpick, and you'll see – everybody will be talking about you.' She clearly felt that if you were not born flamboyant you must have flamboyance thrust upon you, and it was a quality which she herself vividly embodied.

In Vienna it was usually Jeritza's running battle with the

---

* It is probably no coincidence that the unusually detailed description of Marietta published as a stage direction in the original score could almost read as a pen portrait of Jeritza: 'She enters with an air of artless gaiety, with the pleasing demeanour and dignity of a woman who is conscious of her own beauty, and with the grace of a dancer. Later she often drops from her ladylike poise into the more relaxed manner of the backstage world. A mildly immoral, egotistical but always kindly creature; a passionately erotic temperament repeatedly breaks through.'

British-born tenor Alfred Piccaver which inflamed the opera public's curiosity and kept her name in the headlines. One of the many productions in which they were cast together was the FANCIULLA in 1913, and as they rode off-stage at the end of the opera, both on the same horse, elbows were known to make inadvertent contact with ribs before the fortissimo high B natural.* It was, however, an incident during a performance of CAVALLERIA RUSTICANA which brought the Jeritza–Piccaver feud to boiling point. The high spot of her performance used to be the culmination of the Quarrel Duet, when she would stand at the top of the church steps, Turiddu would give her a violent shove and she would fall headlong, eliciting gasps of horror and admiration from everyone present. On one occasion, though, Piccaver, thoroughly fed up with her endless shenanigans, merely crossed his arms and stood there, leaving her to take her dramatic tumble for no very evident reason – a discourtesy which resulted in Jeritza refusing ever to go on stage with him again. In that instance oil was eventually poured on the troubled waters; a few years later, though, she was to deliver the same ultimatum to the management of the Met with reference to Beniamino Gigli and this time her word was obeyed. There were the inevitable conflicting reports about how that quarrel arose. Some people said that it started when Gigli was rougher with her than she appreciated in a performance of Giordano's FEDORA, but in view of Gigli's easy-going personality and the phlegmatic nature of his stage deportment this scarcely seems likely – there was also the point, as one American journalist put it, that Jeritza 'can examine the crown of Gigli's hat without any effort whatever'. In any event it culminated in a disagreement about acknowledging applause at the end of TOSCA on 11 February 1925, when Jeritza stepped in front of the curtain, called for silence, held a handkerchief to her

---

* I happen to possess the score which Piccaver used during this production. He marked the spots where they had agreed to take their breaths, but there were occasions when interference prevented them from being adhered to.

tear-stained face, and announced to the public, 'Mr Gigli not kind to me.' By a happy coincidence it was a broadcast performance.

Newspaper coverage was by no means limited to Jeritza's on-stage activities, and while she was married to the second of her four husbands, the Austro-Hungarian Baron Leopold von Popper-Podhragy, she gave the Viennese gossip columnists one particular field-day. A scurrilous novel was written by the brother-in-law of Jeritza's recently sacked confidential secretary, the plot of which concerned the energetic love life of an international prima donna and the dubious business dealings of her aristocratic husband. The von Poppers sued to prevent publication, citing no fewer than sixty-two examples in the book of thinly disguised references to themselves. They won the case, but at a rather obvious price. In 1928 Jeritza announced to the world that she would never sing in Vienna again because when the company of the State Opera (as the Court Opera had become) gave a guest season in Paris she was only rewarded with the French decoration known as the Palme d'Officier d'Instruction Publique rather than the more exalted Légion d'Honneur. Six years later, she withdrew in a blaze of publicity from a State Opera benefit performance after coming under fire in the Austrian press because of her complicated marital situation. This revolved around the fact that she had married her third husband, a Hollywood producer named Winfield Sheehan, before her Arkansas divorce from von Popper had been legalised in Europe. 'If that's the way my countrymen feel about it,' she announced from her chalet in Unterach on the Attersee, 'I will not embarrass them by singing.' Instead she donated $6000 to charity.

All of this, however, was as nothing compared with the press campaign covering her first appearances at Covent Garden, which occurred in the wake of the Great Vienna Spitting Incident in 1925. This took place in the State Opera during a performance of DIE WALKÜRE, while Wotan and his wife Fricka were conducting their rather extended discussion on the subject of marital fidelity. It so happened that the Fricka, Maria Olczewska, was engaged

to the Wotan, Emil Schipper, and she suspected that there had
been some hanky-panky between her fiancé and the gorgeous
Miss Jeritza. During the duet Jeritza was in the wings waiting to
come on as Sieglinde, and according to Olczewska she was making
audibly derogatory remarks. Several times Olczewska hissed at her
to keep quiet, but Jeritza did not oblige, so Olczewska worked her
way to the side of the stage and spat at her. It is, of course, typical
that when great powers engage in combat, it is the little folk in the
middle who suffer; Jeritza ducked and the offending saliva struck
an innocent bystander, the mezzo Ermine Kittel. I personally dis-
count newspaper reports that Miss Kittel fainted from the shock –
she was fully accoutred as a Valkyrie, and I hardly think that one
expectoration could have done her that much harm – but in any
case Olczewska was dismissed from the Vienna Opera for conduct
likely to bring that institution into disrepute, while Jeritza survived
the incident without reprimand. This was all the more remarkable
because, according to a statement issued by Olczewska's lawyer,
during an altercation in the dressing-room afterwards Jeritza had
added insult to injury by calling Olczewska a bolshevik.

It was further reported in the press that the next encounter of
the two combatants would take place at Covent Garden, where
Jeritza was about to make her début as Tosca, and as her last
words to Olczewska had allegedly been 'All right, we shall meet
in London!' newspapermen were rubbing their hands in anticipation of fireworks. In fact I hardly see how such a meeting could
have been possible, as Olczewska was engaged for the German
season which ended before the Italian one began, and there was
no suggestion that Jeritza should inconvenience herself by arriving
in London in time to do anything much in the way of rehearsal.
Robbed of their sensation, the press started a 'Where is Maria
Jeritza?' story, and on the same day in mid-May she was reported to be 'living quietly with friends in St John's Wood', 'living
quietly with Madame Blanche Marchesi [her then mother-in-law]
in London W1', 'with Mme Marchesi in Paris', 'in New York',
'on her way to London from New York' and 'living quietly with

friends in Chelsea'. In fact she arrived two days before her début, which took place on 16 June. As Harold Rosenthal records in his book *Two Centuries of Opera at Covent Garden*, 'All seats for her TOSCA performance were sold out within a few hours of the box-office opening. Ten pounds was offered for twenty-five shilling seats and an all-night queue formed outside the gallery the night before.' The outcome was her customary triumph. The *Evening Standard* wrote of her: 'She is incomparably the finest dramatic soprano Covent Garden has seen for twenty-five years. Her tone is beautiful, her power is staggering and she is always dead on the note. Even her screams have a musical quality.' The representative of the *Manchester Guardian*, whose contempt for TOSCA as an opera ran to describing Act II as being usually reminiscent of 'Mme Tussaud's chamber of horrors animated by some ingenious machinery', was moved to write that on this occasion 'Sardou [the author of the original play], plus Puccini, multiplied by Jeritza, make a dramatic sum total of crushing effect. Tosca panted round the room like a tigress in a paroxysm of terror and fury, and there were distinct signs of hysterics among the audience.' Even Ernest Newman, who could be very grouchy about such over-publicised stars, was won over by her singing. 'Her voice', he wrote, 'was beautiful, powerful and delicate in turns and admirably under control,' but it is interesting to note that he alone did not join in the chorus of praise for Jeritza's skills as an actress – 'she did not get within hailing distance of the first class,' he found.

Jeritza's success was such that within four days of that first Tosca she had been summoned to Windsor Castle to perform for the King and Queen. If her second role at Covent Garden, that of the heroine in Giordano's FEDORA, caused slightly less of a sensation it was generally attributed to the weakness of the opera itself rather than any inadequacy on Jeritza's part. This time Ernest Newman pulled even fewer punches. 'Why the wretched operas of a mediocrity like Giordano should be given at all at Covent Garden in these days', he wrote in the

Glasgow Herald, 'is, from the point of view of art pure and simple, a mystery. The explanation, however, is pretty obvious. We have probably had to endure FEDORA because Jeritza likes it,' a diagnosis which was indubitably correct. It is not hard, though, to understand her predilection for the role. It offered her a splendid opportunity to exercise both her glamour and her temperament, and it is perhaps the ultimate test of the true star to be able to rise above the limitations of a disappointing score and still notch up a personal triumph. In the words of the *Manchester Guardian*, 'Her impersonation will remain stored in the memory. Small wonder that the house rose at her at the fall of the curtain and roared its enthusiasm in vast waves for many minutes.' *The Times*, too, was full of admiration for 'the beauty of Mme Jeritza's voice and stage presence, the adroitness with which she faints into the arms of the right gentleman at the right moment, and her skill in making a properly dramatic death without loss of dignity or grace'. It was also a typical Jeritza touch that for the role of Fedora she insisted on wearing her own jewellery. As it was valued at a sum which would nowadays amount to around a million pounds, several of the gentlemen on stage during the crowd scenes were not operatic extras in the normal sense, but detectives employed by her insurance company.

While it is difficult not to agree with Newman's opinion about the musical value of FEDORA (though I am one of those who have a distinctly soft spot for the same composer's ANDREA CHENIER), the heroine's two principal solos are welcome inclusions in the *Lebendige Vergangenheit* selection. They were amongst the last of her acoustic recordings, and I am assured by people who heard her in person that they offer a particularly faithful reproduction of her voice in its prime. The same can be said of two other tracks recorded in the same year (1923), the doom-laden aria 'Suicidio!' from LA GIOCONDA and Santuzza's heart-broken 'Voi lo sapete' from CAVALLERIA RUSTICANA. In the latter Jeritza's attack on a top A in the phrase 'Ah! l'amai' brings to mind a vivid expression of Kurt

Herbert Adler's: 'Her high notes were thrilling to the last.' I am also reminded of another remark of Nanette Guilford's, delivered with an affectionate chuckle – 'As far as Maria was concerned the only thing wrong with the role of Santuzza was that a Sicilian peasant girl simply *can't* be a blonde!'

Two further roles contributed to Jeritza's conquest of the London public. They were Maliella in Wolf-Ferrari's I GIOIELLI DELLA MADONNA, in which, amongst other exotic activities, she danced on a table-top; and Thaïs, the heroine of Massenet's opera of that name. At the time of writing, Massenet, after an over-long fallow period, seems to be re-establishing himself in the public's favour, and it is another interesting feature of the *Lebendige Vergangenheit* CD that it includes four Massenet titles, with two THAIS tracks amongst them – a swirling, urgent account of 'Dis-moi que je suis belle', and a perhaps unexpectedly thought-ful one of 'L'amour est une vertu rare'. That Jeritza should bring the house down as this particular character – Thaïs is a ravishing Alexandrian courtesan whom a sexually repressed monk converts to the path of Christian saintliness – was, of course, to be taken for granted. There was, however, one role in her Covent Gar-den repertoire with which she met some resistance – London's knowledgeable Wagnerians were not convinced by her Sieglinde in DIE WALKÜRE. The general trend of the criticisms was that she was too much the Hollywood vamp unaccountably stranded in a prehistoric Rhineland, and in an article entitled 'Arms and the Diva' Ernest Newman slated her unmercifully for the excessive waving around of her long and lissom limbs. He was, he assured his readers, not averse to watching a soprano play the role of Thaïs, but he preferred her to be doing so to the music of M. Massenet rather than that of Herr Wagner.

One of the main problems with Jeritza's Sieglinde was that she was trespassing on the private territory of her greatest rival, Lotte Lehmann. Lehmann's Sieglinde displayed both vocally and dramatically a greater warmth, a more submissive femininity than Jeritza's. Jeritza's recording of Sieglinde's passionate outburst 'Du bist der Lenz' is one of five Wagner tracks on the *Lebendige Vergangenheit* CD, and, radiantly as it is sung, particularly in the upper register, it does not carry the psychological conviction of either of Lehmann's two recordings of the same passage. It would perhaps be a permissible generalisation to say that it was Lehmann's forte to arouse the audience's sympathy for the characters she played, whilst it was Jeritza's to arouse the audience's admiration for Jeritza. In any case, between these two ladies very little love was lost, and it was without doubt Jeritza's influence which was responsible for keeping Lehmann out of the Met until 1934, when she was already forty-five years old.

Some thirty years later, when Jeritza and Lehmann were both in their mid-seventies, they were brought together for a marvellously entertaining radio interview in New York,* during which they reminisced about Richard Strauss, about the original production of ARIADNE and about the strange circumstances leading up to the first performance of DIE FRAU OHNE SCHATTEN in Vienna in 1919. Strauss had promised the central role of the Dyer's Wife to Jeritza, but then he made Lehmann's acquaintance and realised that she would be even better suited to the part. This left him with the tricky task of selling to Jeritza the idea that the more rewarding role was really that of the Empress. In the interview Jeritza relates how Strauss explained to her that as the Empress she would have virtually nothing to do in Acts I and II, but that in Act III she would come into her own, thus having the last word. 'Just right for Jeritza!' chortles Lehmann. The interview is punctuated by much happy cackling and many interjections of 'Lotte darling, don't forget . . .' and 'Yes, but Maria you must remember . . .', but despite the surface jollity the listener is always aware how sharp the claws are which are being kept just beneath the table. Shortly after this event Lehmann wrote an article about Jeritza which included the following passage: 'There is a lot that

---

* This conversation is now available on CD as part of a two-disc set on Eklipse *EKRCD20*, entitled 'Lotte Lehmann in Concert 1943–1950'.

I could tell about Jeritza, but so many years have passed that I will place the mantle of oblivion over all that took place between her and myself. A Primadonna Assoluta allows no one near her who might bar her way, even if unintentionally . . . I may say of her voice that there was something erotically exciting about it. It seemed to come out of the depths of her being . . . And from that source, too, came her laughter, rounded and full, and somehow provocative . . . She did not speak to the soul, she spoke to the sense. She was – and I mean this purely as a compliment – like one of the great courtesans of the past. In some other age she might have unseated a Madame Pompadour from her throne.'

The unseating of Jeritza herself from her throne at the Met came with brutal suddenness. It was often rumoured that she enjoyed a particularly close relationship with the chairman of the board, Mr Otto Kahn, and when he retired in 1932 Gatti-Casazza simply wired to her in Vienna that the executive committee of the Metropolitan had instructed him not to re-engage her. Her performance fee had risen by then to $2500, which was equal to Caruso's and almost the highest the company had ever paid, but her box-office appeal was beginning to wane, and in the financial circumstances of the early 1930s she had become an excessively expensive luxury. It seems evident, though, that there was more to it than this. The committee could have softened the blow by offering her at least a few performances at a lower fee, and reading between the lines I cannot help feeling that they must have grown weary of her shenanigans. In any case she was cut to the quick, and although she continued to sing in other leading American houses and in Europe, as well as undertaking a US tour in Rudolf Friml's operetta MUSIC HATH CHARMS, the end of her reign at the Met also marked the end of her true days of glory.

This did not mean, however, that Maria Jeritza vanished from the public eye. Her main home by then was a luxurious ranch in Hidden Valley, California, where, amongst much other livestock, she kept twelve magnificent Lippizaner horses, but the Met had by no means seen the last of her. At every opening night of the season until she was at least ninety her presence was a *sine qua non*, and it would have been scarcely thinkable that the performance could begin until she had made her regal progress to her seat in the front row of the stalls, swathed from neck to ankle in white mink. In 1951 she even gave a comeback performance, as Rosalinde in DIE FLEDERMAUS. She did so at the invitation of the then general manager, Rudolf Bing, who once told me that it had in fact been a ghastly mistake. Meeting her one day in the building he said, 'Ah, Madame Jeritza, would you like to come back and sing for us?', never dreaming that she would say yes. She did, however, and Bing chose DIE FLEDERMAUS for the occasion, on the grounds that as Rosalinde she could do the least harm. The resulting performance was, in his own words, 'pretty dreadful', a verdict confirmed years later in a radio interview by the soprano Patrice Munsel, who sang the role of Adele. 'It was a cruel, cruel evening,' she said. 'She just couldn't do it. I ended up in tears; I could barely get through it. It was almost painful to be on stage with her, and of course she had to learn it in English. She had always done it in German, and didn't really have time enough to learn it, so that she was a nervous wreck and forgot tons of things.' To Miss Munsel's distress Bing stood in the wings 'laughing hysterically and eating his usual banana', but as the outcome of the evening was a sold-out house at greatly inflated prices he did at least have one valid reason for feeling cheerful. The following month Lotte Lehmann wrote in a letter to her friend Elisabeth Schumann: 'Jeritza sang Rosalinde at the Metropolitan and made herself ridiculous. Why she does that, only the gods know. She surely has enough money to say goodbye.'

In this supposition Lehmann was correct. Unlike so many of the European singers who had been compelled in mid-career to start a fresh life as émigrés, Jeritza had no financial problems; she not only earned money, she also married it. After the death of Winfield Sheehan a wealthy umbrella manufacturer named

Pat Seery became her fourth and final husband,* and it was without doubt her love of the bright lights rather than any financial necessity which prompted her to keep on coming back. There was never any shortage of admirers to support her; for a Carnegie Hall recital in 1946 the stage was so stacked with flowers that she and her pianist had to pick their way between them. According to one Austrian-born friend of mine who was in the audience, a passionate admirer of Jeritza's in her heyday, she sang so appallingly that he was expecting people to leave in droves at the intermission. Nobody did, however, and when he looked around him during an excruciating rendering of Elisabeth's 'Dich, teure Halle' from TANNHÄUSER he was amazed to see that everyone was sitting entranced, so great was the spell of Maria Jeritza. This was also the occasion of one of her most endearing remarks to the press. When asked beforehand if she would be singing the 'Vissi d'arte' she replied that she would not, because of her promise to Puccini only ever to do so stretched out on the floor. 'Can you imagine?' she asked the interviewing journalist, 'brmph, brmph, Maria Jeritza goes flat on her nose in Carnegie Hall!'

When Jeritza returned to Vienna and sang Tosca there in 1950 to raise money for the rebuilding of the bombed Opera House it was much more than a mere operatic occasion, it was an event of national significance. She had been living in America as an American citizen for fifteen years, the other great stars of her era – Lehmann, Schumann, Piccaver, Tauber to name but a few – had all disappeared from Vienna during the time of Hitler, and there was little left of what the public had come to look back on as a golden age. Then, suddenly, there was Jeritza back amongst them and back to sing her most famous role. It was immaterial that the music was now vocally beyond her; the ovation accorded

---

* Jeritza veered between the Catholic and Protestant faiths according to the religious leanings of her successive husbands, and it is another indication of her talent for bending normally accepted rules that her fourth marriage took place in St Patrick's Cathedral, New York, attended by several high dignitaries of the Catholic church.

her at her first appearance had nothing to do with the quality of the performance which was to follow, it was a spontaneous outburst of pent-up longing for a world which had gone beyond recall, and of which she was a gleaming image. The shouting, the cheering, the stamping went on for minute after minute – and late that night Jeritza appeared on the balcony of her hotel room to throw down handfuls of autographed photographs on the crowd which had gathered to pay her homage.

A subsidiary reason for Jeritza wanting to make a come-back in Vienna was to show Mr Seery what it meant there to be Maria Jeritza, and he himself played a notable part in the staging of another of the roles she undertook, her old friend Minnie in LA FANCIULLA DEL WEST. The first scene takes place in the bar of the Polka Saloon, and Mr Seery, distressed at the rehearsal by the sight of papier-maché whisky bottles and cigarette packets all over the stage, had them replaced at the performance by the genuine articles, all of which were unobtainable to Viennese citizens so soon after the war. As one of the younger members of the cast, the tenor Waldemar Kmentt, once told me, by the end of Act I hardly anybody was bothering about the music, and there was not a 'prop' left on stage.

On Jeritza's eightieth birthday she was presented with the Golden Ring of Vienna, an award for outstanding artistic achievement, at a reception given by the Austrian Consul General in New York, and the critic Harold C. Schonberg reported the event in the *New York Times*. 'She is', he wrote, 'the peppiest eighty-year-old you ever saw. She shakes hands and you quietly retire into a corner to count your fingers, so bone-crushing is her grip. She talked and laughed and stood indomitably erect, and she wore a string of pearls each as big as a baseball, and a diamond brooch, each diamond as big as a basketball. This was the way a prima donna *should* look.' His words are reminiscent of another remark made to me by Beverly Sills: 'If her entrance onto the stage was anything like her entrance into her own drawing-room when she was receiving guests she must have been pretty terrific!'

In attempting to assess the career of a singer like Jeritza it is difficult to strip away the tomfoolery and evaluate the hard core of genuine achievement. For what is probably the neatest summing-up of her special quality as a performer I am indebted to that walking encyclopaedia of all things to do with opera in Vienna, Dr Marcel Prawy. 'Whenever she was on stage', he once told me, 'she generated incredible excitement.' She belonged to an era when there was always something new going on in the world of opera. Composers such as Strauss, Puccini, Korngold, Mascagni, Janáček and many others were constantly presenting the public with novelties. Jeritza created an extraordinary number of new roles, as well as being the first Jenufa both in Vienna and in New York. Some of the new operas established themselves in the popular repertoire, while others flourished only as long as there was a star of Jeritza's brilliance to carry them. Bruno Walter said of her that she and Chaliapin were exotics – you had to take them hook, line and sinker or not at all. Today that is not what is looked for in an opera singer; apart from anything else conductors and directors would not put up with it. We have eliminated both the peaks and the troughs of the earlier part of this century and the preference is for singers who are immaculately professional in every way, who can be relied on for excellent musical and vocal performances and who will not step too far out of line. There has been a removal of risk, and I do not believe that the operatic profession in which I have spent the last thirty-five years would have room for a Maria Jeritza. It is just possible that we are all a little the poorer for it.

JOHN
McCORMACK

IRISH TENOR

b. Athlone, 14 June 1884
d. Dublin, 16 September 1945

Although John McCormack came to represent many people's idea of the quintessential Irishman, both his parents hailed in fact from Galashiels in Scotland. They moved to Athlone, on the River Shannon, because there was work to be had in the local woollen mills, and it was there that John was born, one of five children to survive out of a family of eleven. A clever child with an aptitude for languages, he won a scholarship to Summerhill College, Sligo, at the age of twelve and missed another for the Dublin College of Science by one place when he was eighteen. This, however, was not regarded by John himself as a major tragedy because shortly before taking the examination he had participated as a solo vocalist in a charity concert in Sligo Town Hall and was now irredeemably bitten by the singing bug. He eagerly accepted the offer of a place in the Palestrina Choir of the Pro-Cathedral in Dublin whose choir-master, Vincent O'Brien, gave him his first lessons in tonic sol-fa and voice production.

While he was still only nineteen McCormack was entered by O'Brien for the National Music Festival, or Feis Ceoil, and although he was by far the youngest in the tenor section the adjudicator, Luigi Denza of 'Funiculì funiculà' fame, had no hesitation in awarding him the gold medal. This led to McCormack's first transatlantic engagement as one of the vocalists in what was known as The Irish Village at the 1904 Exposition in St Louis, Missouri. It was an alluring prospect, both because of the salary – £10 a week, equivalent to roughly £425 at the time of writing – and because he had lost his heart to a young soprano called Lily Foley, who had already set sail for St Louis, and who subsequently became his wife. He did not, however, remain *in situ* for the full term of his contract. He was a hot-headed, outspoken young man and when the management decided to spice up the musical programme by enrolling the services of an 'Oirish' comedian he offered his resignation, which was accepted with noticeable alacrity. His burning ambition was to study in Italy, a tall order for a twenty-year-old with no money behind him, but he raised part of the necessary funds by giving local concerts back home in Ireland, and the rest in a remarkably enterprising manner. He went to each of the three main gramophone companies which were active in London and all of them offered him money to make recordings. Hard though many aspects of the operatic profession were in those days, the possibility of an unheard-of twenty-year-old walking into any recording company's offices today and coming out with a contract seems remote indeed.

The teacher to whom McCormack entrusted himself was Maestro Vincenzo Sabatini, in Milan. He is reputed to have said to his wife 'I cannot place that boy's voice; God has done so already', and after only three months' work McCormack was considered ripe for a professional début. This took place in the small town of Savona under the assumed name of Giovanni Foli (an Italianised version of his wife's surname) and in the title-role of Mascagni's L'AMICO FRITZ – a fine example of opera's illogicality, as it is one of the few Italian pieces in which the leading tenor plays the part of a middle-aged man. When McCormack reached the climax of his main aria, 'O amore, o bella luce del core', realising that he was going to fluff the high B flat, he had the good sense to strike a tenorial pose with his mouth wide open and stop singing altogether. The audience, deceived by the crashing orchestra into believing that they had heard a faultless top note, applauded vigorously – a perfect instance of what is called 'acquiring stage experience'. After further rigorous studies with his Maestro, a kindly man as well as an expert teacher, Sr Foli progressed to the role of Gounod's Faust in an even smaller town than Savona, called Santa Croce del Arno, near Florence. There he did unfortunately allow himself to crack on a high note and fled from the stage rather than face the cat-calls with which Italian audiences like to greet these little mishaps. He was in fact forgiven – a greater degree of kindness tends to be shown to youthful beginners than to established stars – but it soon became evident to him that if he stayed in Italy he would have a hard path to tread. His wife was expecting their first child and they decided that it would be wise to move back to London.

After a somewhat threadbare period, picking up any singing jobs he could at a pound or two a time, McCormack secured his real breakthrough with an introduction to the music publisher Arthur Boosey, who presented a popular series of so-called Ballad Concerts at the Queen's Hall, events which used to feature singers, instrumentalists and theatrical celebrities. On 1 March 1907 McCormack appeared alongside such well-known names as Harry Plunket Greene, Edith Evans and Mischa Elman, creating enough of a stir to ensure regular employment from Arthur Boosey as well as several invitations to sing at private soirées in aristocratic houses, a useful source of income for performers of all levels in the London of those days.* Most importantly, his success in the Queen's Hall brought him to the attention of Sir John Murray Scott, a man of remarkable wealth and equally remarkable size, a leading patron of the arts and the person responsible for the Wallace Collection being secured for the nation. He decided to take the young Irish tenor under his wing and one of the many services which he performed was to arrange an audition with the general manager of Covent Garden, Mr Harry Higgins. Higgins was impressed by the quality of McCormack's voice but dubious about its carrying power. 'He'll never be heard over the orchestra,' he objected; a remark which elicited from Sir John the immortal reply, one that has been at least mentally echoed by countless singers and audiences ever since, 'Then make your

---

* Caruso's fee for such events was £500, more than £20,000 or $30,000 at the time of writing.

damned orchestra play softer.'

McCormack's (as opposed to Foli's) operatic début* took place at Covent Garden on 15 October 1907 as Turiddu in CAVALLERIA RUSTICANA. At twenty-three he was the youngest tenor ever to have appeared in a principal role in the Royal Opera House, and Turiddu is not a part which any conscientious management nowadays would dream of entrusting to an untried beginner whose voice is remarkable more for its quality than its quantity. The press was lukewarm, with *The Times* indicating that in the first act (CAVALLERIA was played at that time as a two-acter) McCormack was outsung by his Norwegian partner, Borghyld Bryhn, a young lady whom the conductor Percy Pitt had discovered working as a governess in London; though it conceded that in the second act he was 'more at ease and used his voice with admirable effect'. The *Illustrated London News* found that 'it would be flattery to suggest that he had made a successful first appearance', and on the subject of his acting nobody had a good word to say – to quote *The Times* again he 'showed his inexperience by strolling about the stage and allowed himself ineffective actions'. Several of the critics, however, were forced to admit that the production was better attended than on previous occasions that season, and that certain sections of the audience were noticeably more vociferous than usual in expressing their enthusiasm. The reason for this was a simple one – McCormack had already become a hero of the Irish community in London, and some 250 members of the Irish Club in the Charing Cross Road had marched to the Opera House to ensure their compatriot a rousing reception.

It would be misleading, though, to give the impression that McCormack's operatic career was dependent on packing the house with personal supporters. His second role, Don Ottavio in DON GIOVANNI, was more natural territory for his particular talents,

---

* Unless, that is, one counts appearances in CAVALLERIA and FAUST with the Dublin Amateur Operatic Society.

and although he was never destined to be hailed as a blazing stage performer, the fact remains that he quickly established himself as a fine enough singer to be re-engaged by the Royal Opera every season until the outbreak of the First World War in a repertoire of sixteen different roles, as well as being prominently featured in the most exalted of international company when a gala performance was mounted to celebrate the French President's state visit in 1908.

Even more important to McCormack than his steadily growing reputation at Covent Garden was his engagement in 1909 by the American impresario Oscar Hammerstein to appear as the leading lyric tenor of the Manhattan Opera House, New York, a company which Hammerstein had set up as a rival to the Metropolitan Opera. McCormack was indebted for this to the advocacy of that ebullient figure Luisa Tetrazzini* whose Covent Garden début in the same season as McCormack's had been one of the most sensational in the entire history of the Royal Opera, and with whom McCormack had taken the stage in only his third role there, the Duke in RIGOLETTO. In her autobiography Tetrazzini was to write: 'When singing in London I had met John McCormack, the Irish tenor with the God-given voice. I found that his rich voice went so well with mine that I took him back with me to America . . . the Americans took John McCormack to their hearts.'

More importantly for us today, they also took him to their recording studios, those of the Victor Company to be precise, and on two well-chosen CDs, Pearl GEMM *9335* and Nimbus *NI 7820*, we are treated to a rich feast of the young McCormack's operatic recordings. Several of the titles overlap, two arias from LUCIA, for instance, and 'Una furtiva lagrima' from L'ELISIR D'AMORE, all three of which give McCormack a perfect opportunity to display his most prominent virtues. If I were to seek one word to describe the basic quality of the voice I think it would have to be 'beguiling'. It is a voice whose

---

*   See *Legendary Voices*, pp.231–48.

straightforward beauty falls with an instant and uncomplicated effect upon the ear. It is gentle, caressing when it needs to be, and yet capable through the clarity of its focus of an impressive assertiveness in the upper reaches. Maestro Sabatini's comment on the placing of the voice seems to hit the nail on the head – it sounds gloriously natural and uncontrived. In this I have no doubt that McCormack's native accent came in handy, because consonants as well as vowels, when spoken with a brogue, tend to be well forward and easy to project.* The breath control is immaculate, and although this is usually taken as a sign of uncommonly capacious lungs, an equally important element is the sheer efficiency of the singer's emission of tone. To these technical virtues McCormack adds quite unusual elegance of style and phrasing, not necessarily characteristics which one would connect with a man as boisterous and gusty as himself, and in several arias one becomes aware of the same infectious rhythmic buoyancy that was such a feature of Richard Tauber's singing. One example of this is Alfredo's aria from LA TRAVIATA, in which Verdi has characterised the young man's eagerness by frequent breaks in the melodic line, breaks which are fatal if any tenor allows them to cut off the surge of the melody, but which add wings to it when the singer has the knack of suspending the line in mid-air, and singing *through* the rests – a knack of which McCormack was a supreme exponent.

I am aware that an expression such as 'elegance of phrasing' can seem irritatingly non-specific to any reader who is not versed in the subject of performing styles, but it brings to my mind a remark which, I think, neatly sums the matter up. A few years ago another master stylist, Nicolai Gedda, kindly came to London to participate in a concert which I was presenting for a children's charity, and after he had rehearsed some Schubert songs I asked

---

* This question of helpful and unhelpful accents for singers is an interesting one. I have always felt that the various Antipodean accents help to explain the disproportionate number of outstanding singers from Australia and New Zealand; while what used to be called 'Oxford English', with its plummy vowels and swallowed 'l' and 'r', can be a distinct handicap.

the accompanist, Wyn Davies, how he had enjoyed playing for Gedda. Davies replied that he had never before worked with a singer who gave him so strong a sense of knowing on the first note of a phrase exactly where the rest of the phrase would be taking him – and that is precisely what I feel over and over again with McCormack.

In certain of his operatic recordings McCormack produces some surprisingly dramatic outbursts for an essentially light-voiced tenor. One such is the duet 'O grido di quest' anima' from LA GIOCONDA, with his great friend Mario Sammarco, another Manhattan stalwart, as his baritone partner. Inevitably singing of such panache led to comparisons between McCormack and Caruso, but I suspect that this is a case of McCormack's voice being flattered, not in its beauty but in its size, by the acoustic recording process. When McCormack undertook the role of Cavaradossi in TOSCA at Covent Garden the general verdict was that he had overstretched himself. The *Pall Mall Gazette*, while granting that he was now 'far from being the "stick" he was when first seen in opera' concluded 'For all that he is still little more than an everyday Cavaradossi, the part demanding a more forceful artist for a red letter occasion'; while *The Daily Telegraph*, despite praising his work in the lyrical passages, found that 'during the scene in the torture chamber and throughout the second act the voice seemed to lose its fine colour, and the "Vittoria" failed to produce anything of the note of superb triumph to which we have recently become accustomed even from other singers than Caruso'.

Others may have compared McCormack with Caruso but McCormack himself never made that mistake. From the day when he first went to a performance at Covent Garden, back in 1904, and heard Caruso in LA BOHEME, the great Neapolitan became and remained his hero. 'That voice still rings in my ears after thirty-six years,' he was to say to his biographer, L. A. G. Strong. 'It was like no other voice in the world. The memory of its beauty will never die.' In later years, when the two of them had become firm friends, a story used to go the rounds about McCormack greeting Caruso with the words 'And how is the world's greatest tenor today?' to which he received the reply 'And since when, Giovanni, did you become a baritone?' If it was based on fact – it is an attractive idea to think that it might have been – it can best be seen as a typical example of Caruso's celebrated bonhomie, and the easy relationship between them is nicely illustrated by another story which McCormack used to delight in telling. So smitten was he after first hearing his hero in action that he bought a photograph of Caruso and forged his signature on it, adding an inscription to himself. Six years later, in Boston, he told Caruso about this, whereupon the great man, vastly amused, produced another photograph and inscribed it 'To McCormack, very friendly, Enrico Caruso'. It remained one of McCormack's most prized possessions.

To return, though, to the operatic recordings. One other track which is common to both the CDs under discussion is the aria from LA BOHEME, and this tells us a great deal about McCormack as an operatic performer. He once said in an interview, after admitting that he was 'the world's worst actor', 'There are a few operatic roles that I enjoy playing. My favourite is Rodolfo in LA BOHEME. He's a *real fellow*. I can sing him and still feel like a human being. I can pace up and down the stage with my hands in my trouser pockets and seem true to character.' His singing of the aria is indeed flawless. The vocal quality is youthful and fresh, the legato is immaculate, the diction (as always) is exemplary, and the top notes, including a glorious high C, are taken with an enviable ease. Yet, to me at least, there is something missing; the characterisation is low on sensuousness. Rodolfo, after all, is not solely interested in exchanging life stories with his pretty little neighbour, but McCormack gives me the impression that Mimi could afford to blow her candle out on a fairly regular basis without her virtue coming under serious threat. It was doubtless this quality of charming innocence which led one of his soprano partners in CAVALLERIA, a certain Mlle

Mazarin, to try gingering him up with the observation, 'Monsieur McCormack, if Turiddu was like you, I should never have had to complain to his mother about my unfortunate predicament.'

It may perhaps have been this lack of Latin *élan* which left Puccini unimpressed by McCormack's singing. The first time the composer heard him was as Rodolfo at Covent Garden, opposite Melba as Mimi, and he mentioned to McCormack afterwards that there were certain points in the role on which he would do well to consult an authoritative coach. McCormack, nettled by the remark, replied that there could be no greater authority than the Maestro himself; perhaps he would be kind enough to take him through these passages? – to which Puccini somewhat dismissively replied 'Oh! it does not matter. Good-night, and bravo.' The next time they met was when McCormack had just sung the first-act duet from TOSCA with the beautiful Canadian soprano Louise Edvina at one of Lady de Grey's soirées, and Puccini, who was effusive in his thanks to the soprano, wasted not a word on the tenor.*

One other track which appears on both of our CDs has an interesting history. This is Tonio's aria from the first act of Donizetti's LA FIGLIA DEL REGGIMENTO, which McCormack sang with Tetrazzini for the Manhattan Company, and which many people considered his most successful role. The opera had originally been written in French, and the Italian version, which the Manhattan Company used, did not contain the tenor aria. By luck, though, a member of the cast had the French score in his possession and halfway through the rehearsal period he suggested to McCormack that it would be a pity not to sing it; so McCormack made his own Italian translation, and this is it, 'Per viver vicino a Maria'. It is a wonderfully cultivated performance, giving a fine demonstration of McCormack's exquisite piano singing, and one particular high

---

*   One brief passage in a letter which McCormack wrote to his concert manager in 1920 throws an interesting light on his views about the singing of Italian opera – 'Look out for tenor called Gigli, hell of a good voice, but sings like a Wop, nuff sed!'

B flat, cleanly attacked on an open vowel and then reduced through a steady diminuendo to the merest thread of sound, is the sort of thing which only the rarest vocal technicians are able to achieve.

Turning to various of the tracks which only appear on one or other of the two CDs, Pearl offers a typically mellifluous 'Spirto gentil' and a surprisingly mature 'Celeste Aida', recorded for the Odeon company before the days of the Victor contract; also a couple of Rossini's duets from the collection known as 'Les soirées musicales' – 'Li marinari', with Sammarco once again, and 'La serenata' with the great Czech soprano Emmy Destinn. In the first of these, an extremely rare recording, McCormack lets fly with unusual abandon, scoring two memorable high Cs in the process, and in the second he adapts himself to the amplitude of his partner's voice by using a more baritonal quality than I can recall in any of his other recordings.

On the Nimbus issue we have several samples from McCormack's French repertoire (though all are sung in Italian), and here he seems to me to be more comfortably at home than he is with the verismo Italians. The FAUST aria, the MANON Dream, Nadir's trance-like reminiscences from the first act of LES PECHEURS DE PERLES, Gerald's romance from LAKME – they are all treated to vocalism of impeccable elegance; and if Don José's Flower Song leaves me feeling that this particular soldier-boy would have been more likely to settle for Micaëla than risk a tussle with Carmen, it is undeniably a lovely piece of singing. Into this same category – and here I am aware that I am sticking my neck out an unhealthy distance – I would place McCormack's most celebrated operatic recording, his 'Il mio tesoro' from DON GIOVANNI. Ever since 1916, when the recording was made, connoisseurs of Mozart singing have hailed it as the last word on how to sing the aria, and I can see why. The full panoply of McCormack's skill is on parade. The ease of delivery, the majestic phrasing, the flowing coloratura nonchalantly taken on one effortless breath – I fancy that I am not the only tenor who has ever stood on stage and wished that this artistry of McCormack's would magically descend upon him, as he realises that Leporello is about to bolt after his 'Ah pietà!', and that nothing on earth is going to prevent the 'Il mio tesoro' from coming next. Yet once again – and I am talking here about perfection – I personally would like more vehemence behind the delivery. When Ottavio announces that he is off to avenge the wrongs perpetrated against his betrothed, Mozart's orchestra depicts a man who means business. We should sense the iron fist, whereas McCormack is still proffering the velvet glove.

It is a great pity that McCormack never recorded Ottavio's first aria, the gentle, contemplative 'Dalla sua pace'. That, I feel, would have been one hundred per cent up his street, as are the last two items on the Nimbus disc. These are both Handel arias, 'O sleep, why dost thou leave me?' from SEMELE and 'Come my beloved' from ATALANTA, to both of which I would feel inclined to apply the highest praise I know, namely that I cannot imagine any other tenor singing them better. In the opening phrase of 'O sleep' McCormack gives a deft demonstration of how to sing a trill, and as the vocal line soars mercilessly upwards he soars with it, creating an extraordinary impression of weightlessness; while anyone who is not familiar with the melody of 'Come my beloved' is likely to be caught by surprise when it suddenly takes an upward swoop from a low G to a piano high A flat, because on the lower note McCormack does not betray by the minutest sign of effort or audible preparation that he is about to indulge in any such vocal acrobatics.

Although these two Handel arias are indeed operatic in origin it was as part of his concert programmes that McCormack used to sing them; and if on the operatic stage he was something less than supreme, on the concert platform he was in a class of his own. It was only there that he could be what he essentially needed to be as a performer – himself. His own description of the role of Rodolfo clearly indicates this; he enjoyed playing it for the simple reason that it imposed less necessity on him than any of his other stage roles of assuming a personality that was not his own. To many of us in the operatic profession that is exactly what we enjoy doing. On the concert platform you miss the freedom which the operatic stage provides, the freedom not only to express yourself in movement and gestures, but also to leave yourself and your problems in the dressing-room and step into the skin of someone else – someone who is allowed to let fly with all sorts of emotions which in normal circumstances have to be kept under wraps. You cannot go through life screaming *Maledizione* at everyone who incurs your displeasure, and it has a pleasantly cathartic effect to work off your feelings of aggression on the wicked baritone. Concert singers can have no recourse to such external sources of comfort; they are dependent for their effectiveness on their vocal skill, their musicianship, and their ability to make their own personalities attractive to the public – three areas in which McCormack needed to have no inhibitions.

Some of the statistics concerning McCormack's concert career, particularly in the United States, make extraordinary reading. Between November 1912 and May 1913, for instance, he gave twelve concerts in New York alone, every single one sold out, with ticket-buyers numbering 58,000; the last concert took place in the vast spaces of the Hippodrome, when 7000 people were admitted and another 5000 were turned away. During this half-year he also gave fifty-five concerts in other American cities, as well as appearing in twelve operatic performances, and this in the days before air travel was invented. In the season of 1914–15 he stepped up the number of his concerts to ninety-five and in Boston he sold out the city's largest hall four times in the same week. His popularity was one of the phenomena of the day, and the doyen of the New York critics, W. J. Henderson of the *Sun*, probably came closest to explaining it when he wrote: 'If ever there was a brilliant object lesson in any department of art, it has been furnished by John McCormack. The musical style is the vocal revelation of the heart within the man.'

The content of McCormack's programmes was a careful blend

of something for everyone; as he himself put it, 'First I give my audience the songs I love. Second, I give them songs they ought to like and will like when they hear them often enough. Third, I give them the folksongs of my native land. Fourth, I give my audience songs they want to hear, for such songs they have every right to expect. After all, the first duty of any artist to his public is to consider its tastes, and I have always done so.' To glance for a moment at group three, on Pearl GEMM *9338* there are twenty-two Irish songs, and for a perfect example of how this kind of number should be put across you can dip in where you will. To take one track at random, McCormack's 1930 version of 'The garden where the praties grow' really says it all. To attempt a serious analysis of how it is done would be totally against the spirit of the performance. Suffice it to say that with the opening phrase McCormack buttonholes his listeners as if he were joking with them in his favourite pub, and the story he is telling is one that nobody in his right mind would wish to interrupt. If anyone not possessed of McCormack's sheer professionalism tried to pull off the same trick he would find out fast enough that it is not as easy as it sounds. Although I have no doubt that Ernest Newman, that sternest of critics, was right when he said that only someone who had conquered the niceties of singing Schubert and Wolf could bestow so much hidden artistry on these humbler numbers, technique is not the whole story – it has to be backed by an inborn gift. Another track on the Pearl disc, taken from a broadcast late in McCormack's career, includes a shameless bit of blarney in which he talks about the supposed origins of the Londonderry Air – readers may not be surprised to learn that leprechauns had a hand in it – and it rapidly becomes evident how narrow was the gap for this master communicator between chatting in speech and chatting in song.

Another Nimbus disc, *NI 7854*, offers a wide spectrum of McCormack's repertoire of songs and ballads. It includes such stalwarts of the Victorian drawing-room as Sullivan's 'The Lost Chord', as well as Thomas Dunhill's setting of W. B. Yeats's 'The

Cloths of Heaven', one of the finest of McCormack's late record-ings; and it also offers us the song which, more than any other, continues over the years to have his imprint upon it – 'I hear you calling me'. The composer of this song, Charles Marshall, had first encountered McCormack during the tenor's early struggles to win recognition in London. McCormack had secured an engagement to sing in a series of Sunday Night Supper Concerts in the Queen's Hotel, Leicester Square, the fee to be one guinea and a square meal, and Marshall was his accompanist. A couple of years later, when McCormack was already established at Covent Garden, Marshall sought him out and diffidently offered him the song, saying that though he himself liked it very much no publisher would touch it. McCormack immediately submitted it to Arthur Boosey, and in March 1908 he performed it for the first time in one of the Queen's Hall Ballad Concerts. He subsequently recorded it no less than eight times, and the song far outsold any other indi-vidual number in his entire recorded repertoire. The Nimbus track is one of the acoustic versions, dating from 1911, and it is a performance of consummate artistry, truly remarkable for a singer who was only twenty-six at the time. It may seem strange to talk of a mere sentimental ballad in such exalted terms, but 'I hear you calling me', apart from being a fine song of its kind, is not at all easy to sing. When one listens to McCormack it is hard to believe that the song was not actually written for him, so perfectly does it fit his voice and style. The final pianissimo high A seems to hang somewhere in space, until the glittering, gossamer downward glissando brings the melody back to earth. It is the kind of singing which appropriates a song, and I admire the courage of anyone else who has ever tried to sing it.

Another selection of McCormack's popular songs and Irish ballads is to be found on EMI *CDH 7 69788 2* and apart from an even earlier version of 'I hear you calling me' – vintage 1908, with the composer at the piano; a slightly less assured performance than that of 1911 – this disc is devoted to recordings made between 1930 and 1941. By this latter date he had retired from concert work, and his farewell appearance at the Albert Hall, on 27 November 1938, was a tearful occasion for many members of his vast audience as well as for McCormack himself. The question on everyone's lips, and in virtually all the subsequent reviews, was 'Why?' Ernest Newman wrote of the first song in the programme, the German folk-song 'All mein Gedanken die ich hab', die sind bei dir' ('All the thoughts that I have are of you'), 'Instead of McCormack singing it to us, *we* should have risen *en masse* and sung it to him.' He continued: 'John McCormack's like we shall certainly not hear again. In Handel's "Where'er you walk" we were given a lesson in the rounding of Italianate phrases, while in two of the smaller and quieter Wolf songs he once more achieved a miracle in showing them to us exactly as they are even in the circus maximus that is the Albert Hall.' On the subject of retirement, however, the question 'Why?' is an altogether preferable one for a singer to be asked than 'Why not?', and it is undeniable that many recordings made after the date of McCormack's official retirement* indicate that the voice did lose some of its quality and its steadiness. What remained intact, though, were McCormack's personal charm and his exceptional ability to reach the heart of a song and reveal it to his listeners. A number such as 'Off to Philadelphia', despite its swagger and its rough-and-ready humour, has a moving element concealed within it – its protagonist Mr Paddy Leary and thousands like him did not, after all, turn their backs on Ireland because they wanted to; and 'Down by the Sally Gardens' gains in its effect from being sung by someone who audibly has more yesterdays than tomorrows. While his voice still shone with the brilliant gleam of its early years not even McCormack could have weighted the line 'But I was young and foolish, and now am full of tears' with its full burden of regret.

By and large there were not too many regrets in the life of John McCormack. He was a convivial man with a remarkably wide range of friends and interests. When he went to Australia

---

*   He re-emerged during the war for extensive tours on behalf of the Red Cross.

in 1911 as leading tenor of a company put together by Nellie Melba he spent much of his spare time watching cricket as the guest of the great Australian batsman Victor Trumper, whom McCormack admired above all other sportsmen.* He also notched up the highest score of his own cricketing career during that tour, scoring fifty-one for the opera company's own team against a local Australian side, an achievement of which he was justifiably proud. Twenty years later he was photographed on the tennis court of his house in Hollywood with two Wimbledon champions, Maurice McLoughlin and Elsworth Vines, and he was a well-known figure on the horse-racing scene, spending a great deal of money on his unfulfilled ambition to own a Derby winner. Pictures were another of his great passions – the ambition to own a Frans Hals was one which he did fulfil – and in the musical world his circle of friends, unusually for a singer, included many of the leading instrumentalists of the day. One occasion when it would have been nice to be a fly on the wall was an evening which McCormack spent singing straight through two volumes of Wolf songs with Rachmaninov at the piano and Ernest Newman turning the pages,† while the musician who exerted the deepest influence on McCormack was undoubtedly his cherished friend, the great violinist Fritz Kreisler.

As Henry Pleasants has written of McCormack in his book *The Great Singers*, 'He was, in private life, gregarious, garrulous and disputatious, with a penchant for holding forth on any and all subjects' and there is no doubt that for all his boyish charm he trod on many a toe in his time. To quote the memoirs of Gerald Moore: 'He, like any colourful personality, had lots of rough edges. He was not all smooth by any means. Had he not

---

* Trumper did not in fact have one of his best seasons in 1911–12, averaging only 29.88 in five test matches against England despite a century in his first innings of the series at Sydney.

---

† Gerald Moore regarded McCormack as one of the two best sight-readers he ever encountered, the other being Fischer-Dieskau.

been intensely human he would not have been the great artist
he was . . . If he felt he had given offence to someone he loved
his repentance was expressed humbly and frankly. "Forgive me,
I would not hurt your feelings for anything in the world." He
once addressed these very words to me, having followed me out
of the room to say them. It takes a big man to do that.'

A big man was something McCormack certainly became in
the most literal sense of the expression. Photographs of him at
the beginning of his career depict a slender lad with an unruly
mop of hair tumbling over his forehead and a slightly bemused
look in the eyes, as if he were uncertain how to handle the fame
which had descended on him at such an early age. As his material
fortune grew, however, so did his waistline; his favourite method
of coping with the nervous strain of so many public appearances
was to treat himself to the best in food and drink, and to judge
from his girth by the time the above-mentioned tennis photograph
was taken he could not have been offering McLoughlin and Vines
anything very serious in the way of opposition.

McCormack's friendship with Kreisler dated from a tour of five
concerts which they undertook together in 1912 and it lasted until
the end of McCormack's life. McCormack was to say of Kreisler:
'One cannot imagine any field of endeavour in which he would
not be a success. He has the mental equipment to fit him for any
profession. Add to that his innate refinement, his heart of gold and
his musical soul, and you have Fritz Kreisler.' So congenial did the
two of them find each other's company and each other's attitude
to music-making, that between 1914 and 1924 they recorded some
two dozen titles together, almost all of which feature on another
Pearl disc, GEMM *9315*. Like McCormack, Kreisler was a great
snapper-up of unconsidered trifles, and it is fascinating to hear the
two of them lift so arrant a piece of nonsense as a song called 'The
last hour' by a composer named Kramer into spheres of artistry
to which it has absolutely no right to aspire. There are plenty of
familiar old chestnuts on the list – the Berceuse from Godard's
JOCELYN, the Barcarolle from HOFFMANN, Braga's 'Angel's

Serenade', and so on – and two tracks which particularly appeal to me are de Curtis's 'Carmè', with which the Irish tenor and the Viennese violinist effortlessly combine to sweep us off to the sunshine of Sorrento, and a waltz song called 'Flirtation' by Meyer-Helmund, in which the scene is shifted to some Elysian *thé dansant*. There are, however, several more elevated offerings as well, including what I would hail as the jewel of the collection, Rachmaninov's 'O cease thy singing maiden fair'. It is scarcely an exaggeration to say that while Kreisler's fiddle sings McCormack's voice is played on like the finest of stringed instruments; it is a true marriage of musical minds.

The one area in which I am not always able simply to sit back and enjoy McCormack is that of the German Lied. I accept that this is a minority view and that acknowledged connoisseurs such as Richard Capell, Ernest Newman and Walter Legge whole-heartedly disagreed. I find, though, that while McCormack's native brogue slotted neatly into meticulous and idiomatic enunciation of Italian, it sometimes puts up a barrier between him and the German language. He is always totally intelligible – his diction is as crystal clear in German as it is in English or Italian – but the vowel sounds are often distorted to a degree which I find disturbing. Funnily enough a selection of McCormack in Lieder and Art Song on Pearl GEMM *9343* indicates that he was singing much better German when he recorded a group of Brahms songs in 1924 than when he turned to Wolf in the 1930s. In 'Die Mainacht', 'In Waldeseinsamkeit' and 'Feldeinsamkeit' I am happy to trade a veneer of his native tongue against the ease with which he achieves Brahms's mood of rapt enchantment, and the mesmerising poise and beauty of such phrases as 'ferne, ferne, sang eine Nachtigall'. In the Wolf group, however, despite the depth of McCormack's insight and his dedication to the spirit of the music, the linguistic distortions detract excessively from the merging of poetry and melody which is so essential to these songs. I quite accept that to anyone unfamiliar with the German language none of this need be a problem. If

McCormack had recorded Rachmaninov songs in faulty Russian I am sure that I, not being conversant with that language, would be perfectly happy with the result.

Throughout most of his career McCormack was as deeply loved by British audiences as he was by their Irish and American counterparts, but it was a love affair which underwent one nasty hiccup. He was born a British citizen* but in 1917, as *The Times* put it, 'the Irish tenor renounced his allegiance to King George and declared his intention of becoming a citizen of the United States'. To Britons at that particular moment this could only be interpreted as an evasion of his obligations to the war effort, and although McCormack laboured mightily, and at his own expense, to raise huge sums of money for the American Liberty Bond Drive he was not quickly forgiven. Even in Australia he met with such hostility that he abandoned his concert tour of 1920 halfway through, and in a letter to his manager he wrote: 'There is no doubt that they have never forgiven me for becoming an American and in fact one man said in a public place that they would have forgiven me if I had become anything but a "damn Yank".' As far as Britain was concerned he had further undermined his popularity by speaking out from America during the war against what he perceived as England's maltreatment of his native land, and as long as the Troubles persisted in Ireland he felt it wisest to stay away from London.

In 1924 McCormack decided that the time was ripe for a come-back, and a concert was announced in the Queen's Hall. This produced a spate of threatening letters, and though his misgivings were somewhat allayed by the assurances of support which he received from many of his English admirers – no less an embodiment of British patriotism than Clara Butt declared: 'If they talk of making a fuss when you go on the platform, John, I

---

* The present Republic of Ireland was an integral part of Great Britain from 1800 to 1922, when, by virtue of the Anglo–Irish Agreement, the Irish Free State was established as an independent member of the British Commonwealth, before being declared 'a sovereign, independent, democratic state' in 1937.

will take your hand and walk on it with you. Then we will see what they do!' – it was nevertheless a nail-biting occasion both for McCormack himself and for his family and friends. As Compton Mackenzie was later to recall: 'I can see now John's face, chalk white as he came on the platform. There was a moment's silence and then the audience broke into mighty applause and cheering. John's face grew whiter, if possible. A silence fell. Then as if from another world he started the aria "O Sleep" on that high opening note without the ghost of a tremolo in it. The return to London was a triumph, and not one of the gallant band of anonymous letter-writers ventured as loud a hiss as a moulting gander.'

McCormack represents a rare example of a tenor whose stock stood as high with the critics as it did with the man in the street. A number of other Pearl CDs are dedicated to the more populist end of his repertoire, including a selection of American songs, and this leads me inevitably to the question which will doubtless continue to intrigue his admirers for many years to come, namely how on earth could so fastidious a musician have recorded so much rubbish? The McCormack–Kreisler lollipops are one thing, but 'Sonny Boy' is another. Why poach on the preserves of the great Al Jolson when he himself already held sway over so wide a territory? McCormack certainly did not need the money, as Tauber did when he was an impoverished refugee, and Tauber's choice of pot-boilers was discriminating compared with McCormack's. An explanation of sorts lies in his own remarks, quoted above, about the artist's obligation to consider the tastes of his public, but that is at best a somewhat specious principle, and no other great singer has ever stretched it as far as he did. Yet a man of Ernest Newman's stature was still able to write: 'I never knew him in his public or private singing to be guilty of a lapse of taste.' How did McCormack manage this tightrope trick without ever once tumbling off? He himself declared that he had never sung music that he did not want to sing, so perhaps we should leave it at that; and I must admit that as far as I am concerned anyone who performs 'Come my beloved' as matchlessly as John McCormack is welcome to have a crack at 'Sonny Boy' as often as he feels inclined.

LAURITZ MELCHIOR

DANISH TENOR

b. Copenhagen, 20 March 1890
d. Santa Monica, California, 18 March 1973

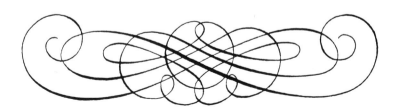

If the gramophone had never been invented, and if Lauritz Melchior's reputation were solely dependent on the opinions expressed in contemporary reviews, we would be left today with a strangely confusing picture. When critics praised him it was their habit to do so grudgingly and when they ridiculed him they did so with conspicuous glee. The image they have left us is predominantly that of a huge man with a huge voice who could sing Wagner for hour after hour without audible or visible fatigue, but who lacked the necessary attributes to qualify as a serious artist. His recordings, on the other hand, show us the greatest Heldentenor of the century, against whose strengths the weaknesses of virtually all his successors have been judged.

Lauritz Melchior was born on 20 March 1890 but his mother survived his birth by less than a month. His father, the owner and joint headmaster of a large private school in Copenhagen, eventually engaged a housekeeper named Kristine Jensen to look after the family – Lauritz had three sisters and a brother – and she turned out to be the first of several people who entered Melchior's life as if they had been hand-picked by some particularly competent guardian angel to smooth his path. She was responsible for introducing a lady boarder into the household who happened to be a singing teacher; the Melchior girls took lessons with her and so from an early age Lauritz regarded singing as a natural part of everyday life. Strangely enough, through the coincidence that one of his sisters was blind, he also gained early experience as a theatre-goer; the Royal Theatre, which presented plays, ballets and operas, had special seats under the stage on either side of the prompt box for blind children, and when his sister was allocated one of these places Lauritz frequently acted as her escort. Sitting there, able to hear but not to watch the action on stage, he acquired a deep respect for what could be achieved solely through the use of the human voice, and by the time he was eighteen he himself had set his heart on singing as a career. He had already been admitted as a bass to Copenhagen's leading choir – his father, an exceptionally talented amateur baritone, was also a member – and for a time he worked in a music shop where one of his duties was to sing new songs to potential purchasers of the sheet music. His father had always hoped that Lauritz might pursue a career in medicine, but as singing was his own greatest passion he made no real effort to discourage his son's ambitions.

There was, however, one serious problem. As a result of improvements in the state educational system people stopped sending their children to the fee-paying Melchior School, which had to close its doors. This had a painful effect on the family's finances, but Kristine Jensen stepped into the breach. Whether she was a lady of independent means or whether the sole source of her prosperity was *Miss Jensen's Cookbook*, which had made her the Mrs Beeton of Copenhagen, I am not able to say; but in any case it was she who paid for Lauritz's lessons with a reputable teacher named Poul Bang – she also made it possible for his elder brother to study painting in Paris – and furthermore she insisted that he should be given private tuition in diction and stagecraft. At the age of twenty-one, after a brief period of national service in the Royal Danish Guard, Lauritz was accepted as a student by the Royal Opera School.

In those days he was thought to be a high baritone, and in 1912 he made a début of sorts as the elder Germont in LA TRAVIATA with a small touring group called the Zwicki and Stagel Company. The standard of this production was doubtless unremarkable, but any experience which a young singer can acquire working with an orchestra and in front of a public is of value; it all helps in cracking that initially daunting problem of how to move around on stage *and* get your music right at the same time. Within a year a more formal début beckoned, as Silvio in PAGLIACCI with the Royal Opera, and this went well enough for the management to put Melchior on a three-year contract. Most of the roles assigned to him were in the supporting category – Morales in CARMEN, Douphol in LA TRAVIATA and so on – but in 1916 he was engaged to sing the taxing role of di Luna in IL TROVATORE on a tour of Sweden, and it was then that the next of the providential helpers stepped into his path. For the role of Azucena the company had engaged an American contralto who sang under the name of Mme Charles Cahier. She had appeared at the Met and in the Vienna Opera and had sung the first performance of Mahler's DAS LIED VON DER ERDE, all of which made her a figure to be reckoned with, and when she heard the ease with which Melchior took a high C one evening in order to help out his indisposed soprano partner in their last-act duet, she became convinced that he was singing the wrong roles. She addressed herself forcefully to the directors of the Royal Opera in Copenhagen, telling them that they had a potential heroic tenor, or Heldentenor, on their hands and that as this is the rarest of all human voices they had a moral obligation to do something about it. To their credit they agreed, withdrew Melchior from his baritone repertoire, and offered him a stipend to see him through his period of re-studying, which was to be entrusted to the recently retired Heldentenor Vilhelm Herold. Herold was anxious that Melchior should make his tenor début as Lohengrin, a more lyrical part than most of the other Wagnerian heroes, but in the end it was the tougher assignment of Tannhäuser which fell to his lot. Melchior only achieved a semi-success and the directors demoted him for the time being to smaller tenor roles.

It was at this point that Melchior's talent for landing on his feet reached its apogee, and if I were writing a work of fiction I would never dream of trying to get away with the following chain of events. In 1919 a family friend paid for Melchior to go to London in order to explore the possibility of professional opportunities in England, and one day Melchior happened to hum a Danish tune while in the men's room at the Savoy Hotel. It so chanced that the only other gentleman present was also a Dane and a very rich one; he was just about to leave London for a while, and as he would not be needing his suite in the hotel, his Rolls-Royce, his chauffeur or his valet he put them all at his young compatriot's disposal free of charge. Taken up by his new friend's friends, Melchior met the conductor Sir Henry Wood who listened to him sing and was impressed. The following year Melchior made his first appearance at an orchestral concert in one of Sir Henry's Proms in the Queen's Hall, and with the notable exception of *The Times* he was warmly welcomed by the British press.

The Danish network in London appears to have been singularly efficacious because it was another chance meeting with a compatriot during Melchior's second London visit which led to one of his most unlikely engagements. This time the Dane in question was employed as an engineer by Guglielmo Marconi, who was conducting experiments to help him establish at what range it was possible to hear a voice transmitted by wireless waves. He had already made one successful test with no less a figure than Dame Nellie Melba as his female vocalist, and now he selected Melchior to be the first male singer heard via the new medium. A disused barrack-room in Chelmsford was converted into a studio and stuffed full of what appeared to be totally makeshift equipment. Melchior sang into a telephone held in an upright position by a rubber police truncheon, accompanied on a grand piano which was swathed in a vast paper cone, but nevertheless his programme of six songs, each sung in a different language, was audible as far afield as Russia and the United States. Thus did Melchior carve a little niche for himself in musical history long before his name meant anything to the public at large.

Now the stage was set for the entrance of the last and most influential of Melchior's providential benefactors. His Queen's Hall concert had been attended by the writer Hugh Walpole, a man whose literary star shone at that time with dazzling brightness, and who appears to have been on intimate terms with numerous people in high places. So taken was he with the singing of the unknown young Dane that he wrote him a congratulatory letter, telling him amongst other things that he had rapped the critic of *The Times* over the knuckles for his opprobrious review. In due course the two of them met, and Walpole, convinced that if only Melchior could afford to cease operating as a workhorse tenor in Copenhagen he could become *the* Heldentenor of his generation, came out with an astonishingly generous offer. If Melchior would move to London Walpole would not only take him into his own home and pay for his further training but he would also undertake the financial security of Melchior's family, which by then consisted of a wife (whom he had met on the TRAVIATA tour) and two small children.

The voice lessons started with a teacher named Victor Beigel, a bon viveur who moved in the smartest artistic circles but who evidently knew his business.* He had at one time been accompanist to that legendary dramatic tenor Jean de Reszke and he was reputed to have picked up from 'le beau Jean' the secret of how to sing Wagner and live to tell the tale. Melchior always attributed his own phenomenal breath control, that *sine qua non* of dramatic singing, to Beigel's tuition, and Beigel certainly had Melchior ready for the next stage of the Walpole training programme well within the allotted time. This was to consist of a year in Munich working with Anna Bahr-Mildenburg, one of the great Wagnerian sopranos of the previous generation, on the roles which were to be Melchior's staple diet for the rest of his operatic career.

The next essential step in Walpole's campaign was for Melchior to gain acceptance into that holy of holies, the Festspielhaus, Bayreuth. It was still presided over in those days by Wagner's widow,

---

* The accompanist Ivor Newton wrote of Beigel: 'At first nights in Covent Garden he was earnestly sought after by socialites eager to ascertain his opinions, which they afterwards passed off as their own.'

the formidable Cosima, in conjunction with her son Siegfried, and when in the spring of 1923 Melchior was summoned to sing an audition it was almost akin to undergoing a rite of initiation into some religious sect. Melchior was not even aware that Cosima was present, but when he had finished his two arias Siegfried climbed a long wooden stairway to a gallery high above, where a wispy figure could be espied sitting there like some motionless wraith. Shortly afterwards Siegfried came down again and informed Melchior that he had won his mother's approval. He was to sing the title-role in PARSIFAL and Siegmund in DIE WALKÜRE in the Festival of 1924.

The rest of the year was principally devoted to the preparation of these two roles, but room was also found in Melchior's programme for a concert of Wagner excerpts in the Berlin State Opera conducted by Leo Blech and with the great soprano Frida Leider (who soon became one of his most treasured friends) as his partner – all of which had been organised and paid for by Walpole. This was Melchior's first contact with collaborators of the highest international calibre and it was a revelation to him. He must have made a good impression because the Polydor record company, presumably anticipating that his Bayreuth appearances the following year would turn him into a star, recorded him in no less than seventeen titles, all conducted by Leo Blech, fourteen of which are now available on *Lebendige Vergangenheit CD 89032*. Predictably there are signs of immaturity in the singing. There are occasional minor slips in the German, and the wonderful trumpeting sound around high G and A, which was to characterise the Melchior of a few years later, has not yet swelled to its full magnificence. Otherwise, to my ears at least, almost all of his outstanding qualities are already on parade, including the characteristic which I personally treasure above all others in his singing; the voice may be a huge dramatic instrument, but he uses it as if he were a lyric tenor. He sings wherever possible with a smooth legato – in Wagner's music this is more often possible than many singers believe – and however red-hot the emotional moment he never commits violence against the vocal line. The price one has to pay for being able to hear a Heldentenor over the orchestra is so often a loss of beauty in the tone but Melchior's voice never becomes harsh or ugly. The typical Melchior timbre is covered and rounded; it always sounds wonderfully safe. Even in Siegfried's Hammer Song the boisterous cries of 'Hoho!', 'Hahei!', 'Heiaho!' and so forth are sung, not barked; and as the penitent Tannhäuser he manages to bestow a genuine touch of poetry on the tenderer phrases of the Rome Narration. All of these recordings were made by the old acoustic process, but the quality of this particular disc is outstandingly good and there are several tracks which strike me as being of special interest. One is the Amneris–Radamès duet 'Gia i sacerdoti' from AIDA (sung in German with the mezzo Margarete Arndt-Ober). Radamès was a role which Melchior sang twenty-five times later in his career, but I assume that he must have learnt the duet specially for this recording, and a fine martial piece of singing he gives it, complete with a high B flat which any of his Italian colleagues would have felt good about. Also of particular significance are several excerpts from DIE WALKÜRE including the Sieglinde–Siegmund duet, starting with 'Du bist der Lenz' and extending to a slightly detruncated end of the act. Not only does this give us a rare opportunity to hear Frida Leider, the leading Brünnhilde of her day, as the more vulnerable figure of Siegmund's incestuous twin, but it also gives us Melchior in the very role with which, just a few months later, after his long and arduous grooming, he was to take his first hair-raising bow before a cosmopolitan public.

In the summer of 1924 the Syndicate which managed Covent Garden mounted the first season of German opera since the end of the First World War. Great excitement was generated by the prospect of a new generation of international stars; Frida Leider would be appearing as Brünnhilde, Maria Olczewska as Fricka, the lovely Swedish soprano Göta Ljungberg as Sieglinde and Friedrich Schorr as Wotan, all artists who had established themselves in Berlin or Vienna as the leading Wagnerians of the day, and the

conductor would be Bruno Walter. Through the good offices of
Hugh Walpole, Melchior was to be pitched into this dazzling
company for two performances of DIE WALKÜRE, and pitched
is the *mot juste*. He arrived in London eight days before his first
performance in order to have plenty of time for rehearsals with
Walter and the stage director, but these did not materialise.
Walter was far too busy with DER ROSENKAVALIER, in
which the classic cast of Lotte Lehmann, Elisabeth Schumann,
Delia Reinhardt and Richard Mayr was to be heard for the first
time in London, and nobody dared tell him that he was about
to be lumbered with a Siegmund who had not only never sung
the role before (or indeed any other Wagner role except for one
unremarkable Tannhäuser in Copenhagen six years earlier) but had
never even seen DIE WALKÜRE. When at last, on the morning of
the performance day, Melchior managed to catch Walter briefly
on the telephone he explained the circumstances and asked for as
much assistance as possible. If Walter had had a chance to replace
him then and there he would have done so, but as Siegmunds do
not grow on trees he had to accept the situation and hope for the
best. In the event there was only one major mishap. Worried that
he was not in the right place on stage Melchior asked Leider
the wrong question first in the 'Todesverkündigung' scene,
and she, being uncharacteristically nervous on behalf of her
new friend, answered the question he had asked instead of the
one he should have asked. It has, however, always been my
experience that as long as one looks as if everything one does
on stage is what one is supposed to be doing very few people
will notice even the most appalling disaster, and this was the case
with Leider and Melchior; the critic of *The Times* was the only
one to mention that the new tenor 'seemed to be not altogether
sure' of this particular scene.

On the whole the critics, who had as little idea of the circumstances of Melchior's début as Walter had had, were reasonably
welcoming; the *Evening Standard* summed up the general tone
with the opinion that 'his faults are those of immaturity, for he

is full of promise and has a fine voice'. When he went back to Bayreuth for his first Parsifal a couple of months later he was much more roughly treated by certain sections of the press. 'A tenor called Lauritz Melchior made his début in the title-role,' one newspaper reported, 'but it is not necessary to mention his name again as nothing more will be heard of him.' I sometimes wonder whether this type of critic ever reconsiders his reviews when time proves him to be so spectacularly wrong; Melchior returned to Bayreuth as one of the mainstays of the festival for the next eight years and would have done so for much longer had Hitler's influence on the place not poisoned the atmosphere. The truth of the matter was that Hugh Walpole's predictions were being fulfilled; by dint of steady application both to his vocal technique and to his repertoire Melchior was gradually leaving his more experienced competitors behind.

Five years after making the recordings discussed above he re-recorded several of the titles by the new electrical process, and as one can hear on *Lebendige Vergangenheit CD 89068* there was by then nothing left in his singing which could be called the remotest bit tentative. As the despairing Siegmund calling on the dimly remembered figure of his father to provide him with a weapon in his hour of need Melchior produces some of the most thrilling sounds ever to have been recorded by a tenor voice. His cries of 'Wälse, Wälse!' on the high G flat and G natural are reminiscent of Caruso in his pomp, the baritonal fullness and the tenorial brilliance perfectly combined, and the tones, still without a hint of forcing, hurled at the listener with a power and a passion that only the rarest of singers can hope to achieve. Melchior's voice in those days was a remarkably versatile instrument, too. On the same disc there is a performance of Carl Leopold Sjöberg's song 'Tonerna', Scandinavia's answer to 'An die Musik', in which Melchior floats some ravishing mezza voce tones, swelling them into an effortless forte without for one moment breaking the poise or focus of the vocal line. It is the singing of a considerable technical master, and although later in his career he lost interest in the more delicate areas of his craft, a song recital which he gave in New York a few months before making this recording had earned him some of the most respectful reviews which ever came his way. W. J. Henderson, a critic of considerable perceptiveness, opened a long panegyric with the words: 'It would be cataloguing most of the essentials of song interpretation to go into details in describing Mr Melchior's art as revealed last night,' and ended by stating: 'Such a Lieder singer should be able to make a brilliant concert career in this country.'

Further evidence of Melchior's versatility is to be found in an intriguingly devised selection on Nimbus *NI 7816*. Besides many outstanding Wagnerian recordings it includes a stupendous 'Vesti la giubba' from PAGLIACCI, a beautifully vocalised 'O paradis' from L'AFRICAINE, and two extracts from OTELLO, the 'Dio mi potevi' monologue and the Death Scene. Although all four pieces are sung in German they display stylistic virtues of which many an Italian tenor should be envious. Melchior was very proud of his Otello, but when he first sang it at Covent Garden in 1933 he had not yet learnt it in Italian, which understandably irritated some of the public. To the critics, curiously enough, a German Otello seemed less disturbing. The *News Chronicle* found that he 'gave one of the greatest performances of his career. He inspired the other singers to do better work than any of them had previously done this season', and even that revered Verdian Francis Toye wrote in the *Morning Post*: 'The opening "Esultate" was splendid and the various nuances of the soliloquy of Act III could hardly have been better.' When in the following year (and again in 1939) he repeated the role in the original language, he must have been expecting everyone to be happy. But no – he was unanimously hauled over the coals for his poor Italian.

When Melchior made his début at the Met, singing the role of Tannhäuser on 17 February 1926, it must have seemed to him almost like a rerun of his first experiences of Covent Garden. Once again the management's apparent determination not to let him rehearse turned the occasion into a baptism of fire. It was to be his first appearance in the Paris version of the opera, which differs extensively from the Dresden version with which he was familiar, so he was naturally anxious to go through the piece as thoroughly as possible with the conductor, Artur Bodanzky. This, however, was not how things were done. He was granted a piano run-through, but it took place in the cramped quarters of the ladies' dressing-room with neither the conductor nor any of the other soloists present, and when he was at last allowed on stage for an orchestral rehearsal, still without Bodanzky, it was limited to one scene for which no sets were provided. As his Elisabeth was to be the temperamental Maria Jeritza, Melchior went on stage for the performance, a matinée, with the feeling that anything might happen – a feeling which was not dispelled by the fact that throughout the first act a team of carpenters was hammering away happily backstage. The event of the day, he was given to understand, was not his début, but that of a young soprano from Kansas City named Marion Talley in the evening performance of RIGOLETTO, and the hammering was caused by the Associated Press setting up a telegraph line in order to transmit an act-by-act commentary to her home town. In any case, like many a Tannhäuser before and since, Melchior was adjudged to have sung poorly in the first two acts and to have redeemed himself with the Rome Narration. At least no serious disaster occurred.

The more one reads about the manner in which Wagner was performed at the time the more extraordinary it seems that anyone should have been prepared to put up with it. Vocally it was without a shadow of doubt a Golden Age. The standard international casts of the Twenties and Thirties, with singers of the calibre of Lehmann, Leider, Melchior, Schorr, the baritone Herbert Janssen, and the bass Alexander Kipnis – not to mention Kirsten Flagstad from the mid-Thirties onwards – have probably not been equalled since, but scenically and dramatically most of what was on display was of a standard which no modern public would tolerate. Bayreuth was virtually the only international house which saw fit to mount rehearsals but even there the style had become fossilised. Although Wagner himself had been all in favour of changing things where necessary, once Cosima was in charge her main concern was to ensure that nothing, not an inflection, not a gesture, should vary from the manner in which it had been done under The Master. As all the Wagner singers on the international circuit were steeped in the Bayreuth style there was no need for the various other opera houses in which they appeared to waste time and money on preparing the performances. Like the top twenty tennis players of today who fly round the world playing against each other, the top twenty Wagner singers of the inter-war years travelled between Berlin, Vienna, Paris, London, New York and Buenos Aires (with a few other stops *en route*) to give the same stylised performances on the same standardised sets, the only preparation being a quick chat with a member of the music staff to settle which cuts would be used. Occasionally they would have to ask somebody whether the next entrance should be taken stage left or stage right – during his first Siegfried at the Met Melchior had to ask a stage-hand how to get to the top of the mountain where Brünnhilde waited to be woken with a kiss – but that was about as far as 'production' went, and it was an actual stipulation at the Met that guest artists should not require rehearsal.

Nothing, I think, describes this state of affairs more vividly than a famous passage written by Walter Legge in *The Gramophone* under his pseudonym of 'Beckmesser'. He was reviewing DIE WALKÜRE on 25 May 1936 at Covent Garden, which happened to be Melchior's hundredth performance as Siegmund; Elisabeth Rethberg was the Sieglinde, Emanuel List the Hunding and Sir Thomas Beecham the conductor. 'Rethberg, Melchior and List', wrote Legge, 'made such nonsense of Wagner's dramatic intentions that an audience composed of people understanding German would have laughed themselves hoarse. The fun began as the door opened. Melchior bounded in so exuberantly that

I believe he thought he had to sing Siegfried that night. Then hearing orchestra sounds that were obviously WALKÜRE, he changed his mind and manner, and took on some of Siegmund's weariness. Rethberg strolled in from an inner room, walked down to the footlights completely ignoring the prostrate Siegmund, had a look at Sir Thomas, and remarked to the audience "Ein fremder Mann? Ihn muss ich fragen" ("A strange man? Him must I question").' Legge's account of the passionate developments later in Act I is equally revealing: 'For the love duet this Siegmund and Sieglinde clambered onto a pile of cushions like a couple of long-married and weary hikers seeking the softest piece of grass on which to rest their weary limbs before they settled down to their sandwiches.'

When reading the confusingly mixed reviews which Melchior habitually received I have the impression that for critics who were quite legitimately fed up with this level of theatrical sloppiness he was simply the most tempting target available. For one thing he was invariably the largest and most cumbersome person on stage. He was just over six feet three inches tall, and although photographs of him in his baritone days reveal him to have been a young man of handsome and imposing presence, by the time he had been enjoying Hugh Walpole's hospitality for a couple of years he had become, not to put too fine a point on it, disgracefully fat. He was an intensely convivial man, whose idea of a good time was eating vast quantities of food washed down by equally generous supplies of beer and aquavit, surrounded by as many like-minded friends as possible. A party to Melchior was something which needed to go on until four o'clock in the morning, and although his second wife, a petite and glamorous German lady known as Kleinchen,* was intimidatingly successful in the management of every other aspect of Melchior's existence she consistently failed in her attempts to restrict his diet. In roles which allowed him to wear flowing robes or a carefully corseted

---

* An approximate translation would be 'Little Tiny'.

suit of armour, and in which he was not required to leap around the stage – Tristan, for instance, or Lohengrin – he could maintain a certain degree of dignity, but when he tackled the more lively and less formally clad of Wagner's heroes his appearance was apt to provoke merriment. I remember one opera-goer some years older than myself – I alas never heard Melchior in person – telling me that in the role of Siegfried 'he looked like a vast pink baby wrapped in a tiger-skin rug', and when Hugh Walpole tried to improve on Covent Garden's Siegmund costume by ordering a new one from a famous London designer the result led to so much laughter from the audience that the singers had difficulty in hearing the orchestra.

The other aspect of Melchior's work which came in for constant criticism was his musical inaccuracy, and certain *bons mots* to which this gave rise were freely circulated amongst the Wagnerites of London and New York. Bruno Walter once said to him: 'Don't forget, Melchior, my left hand is at your exclusive disposal' (the left hand being the one with which errant singers are brought back into the fold, while the right hand continues to provide the beat); both Fritz Busch and Fritz Stiedry were credited with the quip that Melchior was entirely dependable because he made the same mistakes every time; and Beecham, inevitably but I suspect apocryphally, was said to have ended his congratulatory speech after Melchior's hundredth Siegmund with the words: 'Quite soon we shall expect you to know the role by heart.' Melchior's principal weakness appears to have been an uncertain sense of rhythm, and most particularly a tendency to race ahead in moments of musical excitement. Such things are obviously hard to judge from studio recordings, in which mistakes can usually be corrected,* and as this was Melchior's universal reputation one can only assume that it was based on fact.

This whole question of musicianship in singers, however, is

---

* For the story of the famous MEISTERSINGER Quintet recording please see p.245.

an intriguing one. I have worked with colleagues who have an enviable ability to read the most terrifying modern music at sight, but I have also noticed that those with the greatest facility as readers do not necessarily find it easy to memorise their roles. Then again, I know singers who are apparently incapable of making the minutest mistake, but who have no flair for bringing the music to life for the listener. This, to my mind, is an essential talent for any opera singer, and it is one which Melchior possessed in abundance. The first Wagner record which I ever bought was his version of the MEISTERSINGER Prize Song with the London Symphony Orchestra under John Barbirolli, and listening to it now as part of a selection on EMI *CDH 7 697892* I can see exactly why it so grabbed my imagination when I was a schoolboy with no experience of opera. Melchior sings with such relish, with such boundless enthusiasm for the job in hand, the voice aglow with vitality, riding the great melodic phrases with irrepressible energy, secure in the knowledge that nothing will douse his flame. Wagner ventured the whole of DIE MEISTERSINGER on this one song being a truly unchallengeable masterpiece, and the kind of performance which would win you second place with a special commendation from the judges is no use at all. It is a song which needs to be delivered with a conscious sense of triumph, and from the opening note until the final exultant cry of 'Parnass und Paradies!' Melchior *knows* that he is going to win.

Melchior may not have been a convincing actor in the physical sense, but by the time he made the recordings on this EMI disc (1929–31) he had become, in purely vocal terms, a considerable one.* The death of Siegfried from GÖTTERDÄMMERUNG and excerpts from Acts II and III of TRISTAN UND ISOLDE reveal a very different side of his musical persona from the

---

* The management of the Met, recognising after Melchior's first season there that with his lack of routine he would not survive their working methods, encouraged him to take a year's contract in Hamburg. There he rehearsed intensively with the head producer and conductor who helped him to smooth off many of his rough edges.

romantic outpourings of Walther von Stolzing or the dramatic panache of Siegmund. The dignity of Tristan's response to King Mark's reproaches and the depth of feeling in Siegfried's farewell to Brünnhilde are genuinely affecting, and with the possible exception of Jon Vickers I have heard no other tenor who could project the dying Tristan's delirious cry of 'Ach, Isolde, Isolde, wie schön du bist!' so directly into the listener's heart.

So many of Melchior's recordings are now happily available on CD that it would be out of the question to discuss them all, but there are two which I find particularly fascinating because they enable us to hear him in more extended passages than the usual 'bleeding chunks', which were originally tailored to the limitations of the old 78 r.p.m. format. The first of these, one of the great classics of the gramophone, is the full recording of Act I of DIE WALKÜRE, with Lotte Lehmann as Sieglinde and Emanuel List as Hunding, accompanied by the Vienna Philharmonic Orchestra under Bruno Walter, made in Vienna in 1935, and now reissued as EMI *CDH 7 61020 2*. I have already expressed elsewhere my enthusiasm for Lehmann's contribution,* but I cannot understand why it has always been the accepted wisdom in critical circles that she outshines her tenor partner. Melchior, to my ears, is equally magnificent. Some of the qualities that he demonstrates are different from those which make Lehmann's interpretation so memorable, but Siegmund is a different character from Sieglinde and he has a different job to do.

I have often noticed that if a singer is capable of singing exceptionally loudly, however beautiful his loud singing may be, and however often he proves that he can also sing softly, some people will inevitably put the label 'bawler' round his neck; while another singer who is only capable of a modest output of decibels stands a much better chance of being regarded as 'artistic'. Melchior, I think, was a victim of this tendency. Again and again in this recording he emerges not only as an artist of the tireless

---

* See *Legendary Voices*, pp.150–1.

stamina which even his most voluble critics could not deny him, but also of a moving sensitivity both to the text, which he declaims with a riveting incisiveness, and to the music. To give but one brief example from the opening scene, as Siegmund recovers from his exhaustion after drinking the draught handed to him by Sieglinde, he sings 'Erfrischt ist der Mut, das Aug' erfreut sich des Sehens selige Lust' ('My spirit revives, my eye delights once more in the joy of sight') and with the slightest of rubati and a gentle downward portamento on the word 'Sehens', followed by a delicately shaded diminuendo on 'selige Lust', Melchior conjures up in two bars the wonderment of a man returning to his senses and scarcely able to believe his eyes. Though the recording engineers lose their nerve at his cries of 'Wälse, Wälse!', so that they do not have quite the electrifying effect to which I have referred above in my discussion of the earlier version, the rest of the heroic passages come over with a glorious impact, culminating in a spine-tingling high A on the final exultant cry of 'so blühe denn Wälsungen Blut'. Both in these dramatic outbursts and in the passionate flow of the love duet one is reminded again and again of the technical skill with which the original high baritone had been transformed into the burnished and refulgent Heldentenor. The lower register still retains its ample baritonal substance, including resonant low Cs on 'Tief in des Busens Berge glimmt nur noch lichtlose Glut', and it was always Melchior's contention that the only way to build a true Wagnerian tenor voice is to use this baritone quality as its foundation and then work upwards. If, he maintained, a lyric tenor tries to develop the necessary tonal body for the Wagner roles he will inevitably be obliged to force the lower and middle registers in which three-quarters of the vocal line lie. He can become a Lohengrin or a Walther von Stolzing (a role which Melchior carefully avoided), but if he tackles Siegmund, Siegfried, Tannhäuser or Tristan he will not have a long career – a theory which several tenors of my own generation have put to the test and proved to be correct.

It is to Melchior's Tristan that I would like to turn next,

in the form of a 'complete' recording (in fact slightly cut), ingeniously and fortuitously created from performances given at Covent Garden in 1936 and 1937, conducted partly by Beecham and partly by Fritz Reiner, and now available as a set of three CDs on EMI *CHS 7 64037 2*. The quality of the recording is not, of course, up to studio standards; there are the usual noises off and the soloists' voices come and go according to whether or not they were facing the microphones, but it is a fascinating experience to hear Melchior sing his way through a whole evening. At no point in the first two acts does he spare himself in order to husband his resources for the notoriously taxing final scene, and yet his voice sounds as brilliant and as limitless at the end of his last monologue as it does in any of his studio recordings. In the Act II Love Duet his mezza voce is of a ravishing quality, and the tenderness which he achieves with a phrase such as 'vor deinen Augen süss zerronnen', rising as it does from a low F to a piano high G, is something which one hardly dares expect from a singer who can unleash such a tempest of tone whenever the role requires it.

Melchior had prepared himself gradually for the part of Tristan, wisely trying it out for the first time in Barcelona, where the audience was known to be chatty and inattentive, unlikely to spot any little things that might go wrong in a German opera. The following year, however, in 1930, he sang it at Bayreuth under Toscanini, a conductor who demanded accuracy above all things. There was a certain amount of apprehension on the subject of what might happen if Melchior started indulging in his famous rhythmical waywardness, but in the event the diminutive maestro and the gargantuan tenor got along splendidly, and it was Toscanini who bestowed on Melchior the nickname of 'Tristanissimo'. I must also admit that even listening, score in hand, to the live recording of TRISTAN I find it hard to spot any evidence of serious inaccuracy. He occasionally allows himself a certain amount of freedom within a bar, especially in a declamatory scene (something which Wagner himself regarded as entirely legitimate), but that is about all. Beecham and Reiner,

I suppose, may have been working hard to curb his eagerness in rapid passages, but if so their left hands were doing a fine job, and this enthusiasm of Melchior's for keeping on the move and never getting vocally bogged down is one of the things which invests his singing with such an infectious sense of vigour.

Melchior's partner in the TRISTAN recording is the incomparable Norwegian soprano Kirsten Flagstad, who had burst upon the international scene the previous year at the age of nearly forty with her first astonishing season at the Met,* and who made her Covent Garden début as Isolde in 1936. If supreme Wagnerian sopranos and supreme Wagnerian tenors have always been rare phenomena, to find representatives of both species who are in their artistic prime at the same time and in the same place borders on the miraculous. The teaming of Flagstad with Melchior produced extraordinary results at the box-office of the Met, where the public's favourite fare had traditionally been the Italian repertoire.† Assisted no doubt by the influx of German émigrés to New York it was the Wagner operas which enabled the management at the end of the 1936–7 season to declare their first profit for six years, and the real gilt-edged attraction was a Flagstad–Melchior TRISTAN. One recording which gives probably as faithful an impression as any of the sound of these two 'voices of the century' at work together is a studio version of the Act II love duet, made in 1939 and now available as part of a Melchior recital on RCA Victor *GD87914*. Though Melchior disappointingly does not attempt the soft high G on the word 'zerronnen', which he brought off to such memorable effect on the Covent Garden stage, the warmth and amplitude of his tone are captured in the studio in a way that they could not be in the

---

* See *Legendary Voices*, pp.76–8.

---

† It is interesting to note that in 1931, during the Depression, Melchior's contract was for twenty performances at $1000 each, while that of Giovanni Martinelli, the leading dramatic tenor of the Italian wing, was for more than forty performances at twice Melchior's fee.

live recording, and one can only marvel that any two artists should be so ideally matched in the power, the breadth and the beauty of their singing.

Unfortunately in the Bridal Chamber scene from LOHEN-GRIN, which dates from the following year and is also included on the same CD, some equally stupendous singing has the shine taken off it by a strangely fuzzy recording. This was another opera which they sang together at the Met, and Flagstad first undertook it in typical Met-style circumstances. Despite not having sung the role for six years, and having only ever sung it in Norwegian, she was given four days in which to learn it in German and no time for a stage rehearsal, so Melchior behaved in appropriately knightly fashion, steering her round the stage and hissing at her what to do next. By an odd coincidence, within a month he found himself participating in a LOHENGRIN performance in which it was he who needed all the help he could get. Arriving as a member of the audience for the opening night of the season at Covent Garden, attired in full evening dress and his impressive array of decorations, he was pounced on in the foyer by an opera-house employee who begged him to come backstage immediately; Max Hirzel, scheduled to be making his Covent Garden début as the Knight of the Holy Grail, had gone down with a cold. Somehow the massive Melchior was squeezed into a makeshift costume just in time to glide on stage aboard the magic swan, and to keep the pot on the boil during those passages with which Melchior was not familiar because they were always cut at the Met, the voiceless Hirzel chipped in as best he could from the wings while Melchior stood there opening and shutting his mouth. Beecham, whose fifty-sixth birthday it was, made a great show of thanking him during the curtain-calls, but even in these circumstances the critics could not refrain from baying at Melchior's heels. Neville Cardus, who should have known better, wrote in the *Manchester Guardian*: 'His acting and general attitudes were as inanimate, and as childlike, and as bland as ever. From time to time he produced the big resonant tone and vocal flourish of the authentic Heldentenor but never for a moment was he more than a distant and very corporeal relation of Lohengrin.' Blow, blow, thou winter wind.

Sadly the Flagstad–Melchior partnership was not as harmonious off-stage as it appeared to be in performance and disagreements between the two became so severe that for two years Flagstad refused to accept any engagements in which Melchior would be involved.* There appear to have been two reasons for this falling-out, the first of which could be attributed to Melchior's exuberant and frequently puerile sense of fun. He was forever indulging in practical jokes both on- and off-stage, a typical example being the occasion when Frida Leider as Brünnhilde approached the corpse of Siegfried in one of the tensest moments of GÖTTERDÄMMERUNG only to find some total stranger lying on the bier, while Melchior, already changed into his dinner jacket, waved to her from the wings. Leider and Lehmann, being devoted friends of Melchior's, were prepared to go along with this kind of thing, but Flagstad (and she has my fullest sympathy) could not bear anyone fooling around backstage and disturbing her concentration.

The other cause of friction lay in the fact that Melchior had engaged the services of a publicity agent – he and Lehmann were two of the first opera singers to do so – who, in Flagstad's opinion, was blatantly plugging the image of herself and Melchior as a team, whereas she quite rightly felt that the name of Flagstad could stand proudly enough on its own.† Basically, I suppose, the two stars' very different temperaments were simply incompatible, but in due course Flagstad appears to have relented, and both the RCA recordings referred to above, as well as one of the duet from

---

* See *Legendary Voices*, p.82.

---

† It was this agent, Constance Hope, who dreamt up the story that Melchior and Kleinchen had first met when she, a stunt-girl in German films, had landed in his garden on a parachute. Melchior faithfully repeated the story in many a press interview, but in fact they met in a Munich cabaret while Melchior was still married to his first wife.

the GÖTTERDÄMMERUNG Prelude, now part of a Flagstad recital on RCA Victor *GD87915*, were made after the dust had settled.* I scarcely imagine that even Flagstad and Melchior would have dared to set about this duet on stage as they do in the recording – it is an alarming piece of music with which to *start* a vocal marathon – but in the studio they let rip to electrifying effect and this time the engineers do them proud. It was made the day after the TRISTAN duet and both recordings catch these two magnificent singers at their absolute peak. Wagner singing like this has not been heard since, and I cannot help wondering if it ever had been before.

Two months prior to the making of these recordings war had broken out in Europe and thereafter Melchior settled permanently in the States. He had long since ceased to sing in Germany, not merely at Bayreuth, finding it intolerable to work under a Nazi regime, but it was a bitter blow for him to have to abandon the resplendent sporting estate which he had bought at a place called Chossewitz, about an hour and a half's drive from Berlin. Apart from eating, drinking and playing the fool Melchior's great passion in life was shooting, and whether his quarry was duck, deer, wild boar, antelope or mountain bear he was never happier than when he was dressed in his oldest clothes with a rifle or shotgun under his arm.† In 1939 he and Kleinchen were spending their summer holidays at Chossewitz as usual when they were warned by the Danish Embassy in Berlin to leave Germany with all possible speed. Many of their most valuable possessions were hidden in

---

* Even in these sensitive circumstances Melchior still saw nothing wrong in arriving for the TRISTAN session at the very last moment straight from an all night duck-shooting expedition, unshaven, unwarmed-up and smoking a foul-smelling black cigar – which makes the quality of his singing even more amazing, but which may explain the disappointing absence of the piano high G!

---

† American writers naturally refer to his prowess as a 'hunter', and this is also the usual translation of the German word *Jäger*. To a Briton, though, 'hunting' means riding to hounds, usually in pursuit of a fox, and as far as I know the vast form of Lauritz Melchior was never seen, squeezed into a pink coat, galloping around the English countryside.

special compartments under the false floor of one of their barns, though none of them survived the subsequent occupation of the place first by the Nazis and then by the Russians. After the war it emerged that numerous irreplaceable test pressings of unpublished recordings had been used for target practice.

In 1941 Flagstad left New York to return to Nazi-occupied Norway but Melchior was lucky enough to find a new partner at the Met in the American dramatic soprano Helen Traubel. It was by now impossible for anyone to deny his status as the leading Heldentenor of his generation and in his early fifties he was vocally as vigorous as ever. After he had lost his European contracts, however, his performances at the Met were not enough to finance his expansive style of living and he did his reputation no good in the sterner artistic circles by introducing more and more music of an unashamedly popular nature into his concert programmes. Nor was that all. In December 1943 he was guest star on a radio show hosted by the famous comedian Fred Allen, and so successful was he at timing his one-liners that in no time he was invited onto the Bing Crosby Show, the Al Jolson Show, the Dinah Shore Show and many others. His publicity agent swung into action selling him as a national character – Lauritz Melchior the regular guy, who could crack your ribs with his wise-cracks or your chandelier with his high Cs. The next step was to Hollywood, where he featured in a series of big-budget movies starting with *Thrill of a Romance* starring Esther Williams and Van Johnson, and where he and Kleinchen built themselves a palatial hilltop home. His film roles were carefully tailored to his twin abilities for singing and clowning, and they distanced him still further from the more fastidious opera-lovers' image of a Tristan or a Parsifal.

Gradually Melchior was becoming a problem figure at the Met. Secure in the knowledge that he was the last singer to have been personally trained in the Wagner style by Cosima and Siegfried he saw no reason to change any aspect of his performances. He who had originally been so keen on rehearsing had by now long decided that rehearsals were superfluous, as Beecham had already discovered at Covent Garden. On one occasion Melchior sent him a note saying 'I am afraid I shall not be able to come to the rehearsals on Thursday. The terrific heat at the Otello made me so tired, that I think I rather be carefull to be fit for the Ring where I should not like to disappoint you.' (I am not sure how many days elapsed between the Otello and the Thursday in question, but in any case fatigue was not a thing from which Melchior was often known to suffer.) Then, in October 1936, he wrote as follows to Sir Thomas with reference to the next year's season: 'I want you to understand that the rehearsals must be *definitiv planned in the contract for the Ring*, as I by experience know Mr Furtwaengler and his *unending* rehearsals. As I have sung in the Ring over a hundred times I am sure you will agree that five days rehearsing is sufficient.' I should also mention that he sweetened this somewhat peremptory ultimatum with the good news that he had (temporarily) shed twelve and a half kilos.*

In other respects, too, Melchior was growing lazy. Early in his career he had explained in an interview with the paper *Musical America* why Parsifal was his favourite role. 'You must act every minute of the time,' he said, 'even during the long scene where Parsifal has to stand motionless with his back to the audience for three-quarters of an hour. He must be absorbed in contemplation of what he sees, and if the singer relaxes for a moment, then the audience will relax too and lose interest in the scene.' During his later years at the Met, however, it became his practice not only to relax during this scene, but to do so in his dressing-room, having worked his way towards a shadowy spot at the side of the stage and slipped discreetly into the wings. His explanation for this new piece of production was that the spot he was supposed to occupy on stage was dangerously draughty; others felt that it had more to do with his desire for a nice cold beer.

In January 1940, following the death of Artur Bodanzky

---

* Twenty-seven and a half pounds, or just under two stone.

who had been chief conductor of the Met's German wing for twenty-four seasons, Melchior made an absurdly ill-judged statement to the press about the unsuitability of Bodanzky's youthful successor, Erich Leinsdorf. When the press sought the views of the Met's general manager, Edward Johnson, he came out with some trenchant remarks about 'old boats' in the company whose exalted egos led them to believe that because there was no one to compete with them for their roles they could become dictators at the Met. 'The operatic art and this institution', he concluded, 'are greater than these and will be here, along with Mr Leinsdorf, long after they are gone.' At that time there was no question of Johnson being able to dispense with Melchior's services – there *was* no one to compete with him – but when Rudolf Bing became general manager ten years later one of his first and most controversial decisions was not to re-engage Melchior. He gave neither Melchior nor anyone else a word of explanation – for which many people, including Melchior himself, were never able to forgive him. Bing's attitude towards Melchior is made apparent on the opening page of his memoirs, where he describes the most vivid impression of his very first visit to the Met, back in 1939, as having been 'the sight of Lauritz Melchior as Tannhäuser, looking like a moving couch covered in red plush'. He was good enough to add in brackets 'though he sounded fine'.

Despite the strength of the case against Melchior he still commanded a loyal body of support amongst the public, and if Bing had allowed him only a single performance he would have been able to celebrate twenty-five years as a company member, a jubilee on which he had long set his heart. His services to the company, after all, were truly exceptional. Not only had he been one of its principal box-office assets throughout a financially shaky period, but he had been tireless in his contributions to special fund-raising events, and nobody who had seen them would be likely to forget his various appearances at 'Save the Met Surprise Parties', in two of which he teamed up with the minute coloratura soprano Lily Pons. In the first Melchior appeared as a circus strongman in spangled shorts and ballet shoes with a similarly attired Pons clambering all over him, walking along his outstretched arm to stand in the palm of his hand, and ultimately (with illusory effects from the technical staff) holding Melchior aloft by one foot; while in the second they performed an apache dance in which Pons as the vicious male (she reached nowhere near Melchior's shoulder) flung Melchior as the defenceless floozie ruthlessly around the stage in a routine for which Melchior had gone so far as to attend rehearsals three times a week for a month.

Melchior's enforced retirement from the Met did not mean that he became idle. He starred in variety, in a musical extravaganza, on television and in his own highly successful touring production, 'The Lauritz Melchior Show', which used to culminate in the beaming, top-hatted Melchior singing 'I'm going to Maxim's' from THE MERRY WIDOW, with a glamorous young soprano on either arm. He even celebrated his seventieth birthday by singing Act I of DIE WALKÜRE in a radio concert in Copenhagen, and though certain concessions obviously have to be made to the effects of passing time it is perfectly evident from the recording of the event that he was still very much a Siegmund to be reckoned with.

In the spring of 1966 Mrs August Belmont, for many years a member of the board of the Met and founder of the Metropolitan Opera Guild, organised a gala performance for the final night of the old opera house, which was to be demolished, and she wrote twice to Melchior begging him to attend as one of the guests of honour. From his reply to the first of her letters it is clear how hurt Melchior had been at the treatment meted out to him by Rudolf Bing sixteen years before. In an immaculately typed and carefully considered reply he wrote: 'You can understand that it is not easy for me not to be present on the 16th, but as I have told you before, a man who deprived me of continuing my work and art at the Metropolitan Opera in which I am sure I can place myself as a faithful and dependable artist, in twenty-four years only cancelling three appearances out of 515 scheduled Wagner operas, is a person of whom I cannot and will not be in company. As I do not want any unpleasant situations to arise . . . I must say, although with a bleeding heart, that I am not going to be present.' When, in 1972, he received an invitation from Bing's successor, Schuyler Chapin, to attend a performance of SIEGFRIED it was the first communication he had received from the administration of the Met for twenty-two years. Sadly he was not well enough to attend, but Chapin read out his touching reply to the cast after the performance, and it was greeted with a volley of applause from the entire company.

I was recently treated to a delightful picture of Melchior in his old age by a lady whose husband used to organise safari trips in Kenya. As the manager of the business he did not often accompany the clients himself but on one occasion, informed that his next guest was some sort of VIP from the United States, he felt that he should do so, though he was by no means thrilled at the prospect of several days in the company of yet another self-important politician or captain of industry. In the event he came home telling his wife that she had missed the treat of a lifetime. His guest had turned out to be a silver-haired giant of a man whose enthusiasm and ebullient good humour had won the hearts of all concerned, and the high-spot of the trip had come one night when everyone was gathered round the camp fire and their VIP had started to sing. At the age of seventy-seven Melchior had loosed off his high tones into the vast spaces of the African night and his listeners had sat there enthralled.

It may seem odd that an incomparable performer who was also a man of this all-embracing bonhomie should have had such a knack as Melchior did for attracting criticism, but I suspect that his problem all along had lain in his favourite maxim 'I do not let singing interfere with living'. Those of us in the operatic profession who can only lay claim to normal human talents cannot afford to adopt this attitude; we cannot stay up all night and still sing Tristan. Melchior's voice amounted to an abnormal human talent and it allowed him to sing certain roles in a manner which no other tenor could match, and to do so without appearing to bother. If he had watched his weight, practised his octave scales and attended endless production rehearsals, would he have been a better Tristan or a better Siegmund? I doubt it, because he would have ceased to be Lauritz Melchior, with all the pluses and minuses that that implies. As Francis Robinson, assistant manager at the Met, once said of him: 'Melchior was a natural phenomenon, something on the order of Niagara Falls.'

At one stage during Melchior's career at the Met the principal soloists were sent a questionnaire by some biographical organisation in which they were asked an endless list of tiresome questions. One's heart, I think, can only warm to a man who answered two of them as follows:

Q: What has been your most thrilling musical experience?
A: Loosing [sic] my pants in TRISTAN.
Q: What is the funniest thing that ever happened to you?
A: That I made a career.

CLAUDIA MUZIO

ITALIAN SOPRANO

b. Pavia, Italy, 7 February 1889
d. Rome, 24 May 1936

As a general rule opera singers tend to be extrovert individuals – we would hardly choose to make a living by pouring forth red-hot emotions in front of a couple of thousand strangers if we were by nature shy and withdrawn. This is the principal reason, I think, why almost all the singers about whom I have chosen to write in these two volumes have ended up by seeming thoroughly familiar to me as people. After the many hours which I have spent listening to their recordings and researching into their lives I feel that if by the action of some magic power I were to meet them in the street I would know what to expect – indeed I would have difficulty in not greeting several of them as old friends. One, however, eludes me. Around the persona of Claudia Muzio there is a tantalising aura of mystery. Was the haunting note of irreversible suffering in her Traviata and her Mimi really an echo of her own self, as certain writers have clearly believed, or was her involvement with the tragic heroines of her stage repertoire so intense that even her contemporaries were unable to differentiate between the woman and the artist? However closely one attempts to approach La Muzio her tall, imposing and intensely theatrical figure retreats with an enigmatic smile.

She was born in a house on the Piazza del Duomo in the university town of Pavia, some twenty miles south of Milan, on 7 February 1889, and she was registered as Claudina Versati of unknown parentage. In fact her mother, a chorus singer, and her father, an operatic stage manager named Carlo Muzio, married at some later date, so that by the time their daughter's career began she had been officially legitimised. She had a strange childhood, much of it spent backstage in the various opera houses where her father worked – all over Italy, at Covent Garden, where he was often engaged for the summer season, and at the Met, where he spent many of his winters. Most of her formal schooling took place in London, which gave her the ability, unusual in an Italian singer, to speak fluent English, and in her late teens she was sent back to live with relatives in Italy. She studied the piano and the harp in a music college in Turin, and subsequently moved to Milan where she continued her piano lessons with a lady named Annetta Casaloni.

Signora Casaloni was a most unusual piano teacher. She was at that time ninety years old, and in her younger days she had been a well-known operatic mezzo; indeed, back in 1851 she had created the role of Maddalena in RIGOLETTO. It is she who is usually credited with the discovery of Muzio's voice, though Carlo Muzio had long predicted a great career for her in opera. 'Since she began to toddle', one journalist reported him as saying, 'she has been in the wings watching my rehearsals. She knows all the dramatic roles, the lyric roles and the coloratura roles – nothing will come amiss to her.' Certainly the extraordinary range of parts which Muzio did subsequently undertake, from the coloratura of Gilda in RIGOLETTO to the unbridled dramatic outpourings of Turandot, bears witness to his prescience, and few if any of her roles could be said to have 'come amiss'.

Muzio's début took place at Arezzo, near Florence, on 15 January 1910 as Massenet's Manon, and within a couple of months she was singing Gilda and Traviata in Messina partnered by Tito Schipa – both of them had just celebrated their twenty-first birthdays. Muzio had no difficulty in establishing herself on the circuit of Italy's smaller opera houses and it can clearly be taken as proof of her exceptional promise that only eighteen months after her début she was invited by the Gramophone Company in Milan to make her first two recordings. One of these, 'Si, mi chiamano Mimi' from LA BOHEME (the other was a passage from LA TRAVIATA), features on a Nimbus recital, *NI 7814*, and it provides a fascinating glimpse of a great artist in the making. To set against the brilliant freshness of the tone there is a strange and not entirely attractive edge on the vowel sounds. They are very open and unrounded and in the upper register there is more than a hint of shrillness. The wonderful cornucopia of vocal shadings for which Muzio was to become famous is entirely absent, and although she does attempt an emotional gearchange as she glides into the big tune on 'Ma quando vien lo sgelo' – the phrase which to me is the litmus test for whether or not a soprano is worthy of this heaven-sent role – it is almost touchingly unsubtle. The same CD also offers us her recording of this aria made twenty-four years later, within a short time of her death. I shall return to it later; the difference between the two versions encapsulates a lifetime.

My strictures concerning this youthful recording would not be half so severe were it not for the standard which Muzio herself was to set as a mature artist, and the speed of her rise to prominence is a clear indication that even in those early days her virtues greatly outweighed her shortcomings. In the season of 1911–12 she reaped a rich harvest of success in Milan's Teatro Dal Verme and by 1913 she was considered ready for her début in that holy of holies, La Scala. Her Desdemona there made a deep impression, and she was invited to repeat it the following year in Paris, where she was heard in rehearsal by Mr H. V. Higgins of the Covent Garden Syndicate. Mr Higgins surprised her by asking if she would come over to London the following week and sing Puccini's Manon, which she did to the delight of one and all – 'In turn voluptuous, seductive, defiant, passionate and tender, Mlle Muzio promises to be a great acquisition to Italian Opera,' wrote the *Pall Mall Gazette* – and it is an indication of the short-term planning which characterised international opera at that time that she stayed in London to sing no less than six different roles at Covent Garden during the next ten weeks. Three times she stepped in as a last-minute replacement – once in OTELLO for Melba, who had to return to Australia because her father had been taken ill, once in LA BOHEME for Claire Dux, who had eye trouble, and once in TOSCA for Louise Edvina, who was 'indisposed'. For the TOSCA she found herself in formidable company – Antonio Scotti as Baron Scarpia and Enrico Caruso as Cavaradossi – but as one of the critics expressed it: 'Edvina's misfortune was Miss Claudia Muzio's opportunity and right excellently she seized it. It was no light ordeal for a young and comparatively inexperienced artist to essay such a role in such circumstances, but Miss Muzio rose gallantly to the occasion and gave a very good account of herself indeed. Her acting and her singing were both really remarkably fine.'

The 1914 season at Covent Garden was an eventful one in many ways. At a Royal Command performance, in the presence of King George V and Queen Mary, a suffragette attempted to address the monarch, and when prevented from doing so locked her arms to a metal rail. According to *The Daily Telegraph*, when an attendant eventually succeeded in releasing her she struck him for his pains, and when she was bundled out of the building the crowd which had gathered outside 'denounced her action in vigorous terms'. In sharp contrast to these unseemly goings-on the outstanding event of the season in an operatic rather than a political sense passed unnoticed. As Caruso took his curtain-call after the last performance of TOSCA no one could know that this was his final bow before the London public; nor indeed could anyone have guessed that after such a row of successes as Muzio had enjoyed, her first Covent Garden season would also turn out to have been her last. She was invited to return in 1915, but as things turned out it was to be five years before another season was mounted there, and inexplicably the post-war management never asked her back.

During the first two years of the war Muzio continued to distinguish herself in Italy. In September 1915 she was reunited with Caruso for two performances of PAGLIACCI in the Teatro Dal Verme under the baton of Toscanini, and the following year she was heard by Gatti-Casazza, the manager of the Met, in a piece called MADAME SANS-GENE by Giordano. Though Gatti made a tentative suggestion to her about singing in New York, he carefully refrained from formulating an actual offer, until he returned to the States and found that he was running into soprano trouble. Two of his stars had become unavailable, Lucrezia Bori because of a throat operation and Emmy Destinn because she was under house arrest in Bohemia for disseminating extreme Czech nationalist views. Gatti turned to Claudia Muzio and on 4 December 1916 she was introduced to the New York public as Tosca, once again sharing the stage with Caruso and Scotti. With her acting as much as with her singing she achieved the feat of rousing the traditionally icy Monday evening public to an unusual pitch of enthusiasm – 'no finer acting has ever been seen on the Metropolitan stage than that offered by Miss Muzio last night,' wrote the critic of the *Morning Telegraph* – and for six years she remained one of the company's most fêted prime donne.

One amusing aspect of Muzio's appearances both at Covent Garden and at the Met was that although she was unknown to the public she was very well known indeed to many of the people backstage. To them she was Carlo Muzio's little girl whom they had last seen running around amongst the stacks of scenery, and she was warmly welcomed in her new capacity as star performer. Indeed the Met went so far as to negotiate with the Geneva Opera, where Carlo Muzio was currently working, to have him released from his contract so that he and his wife could accompany Claudia to New York, thus turning the whole occasion into something of a family reunion. Carlo, who was a jolly, chatty fellow, unfortunately died the following year, and thereafter Muzio's mother, who seems to have been Carlo's exact opposite, tall, silent and forbidding, became Claudia's constant companion. Several of Muzio's colleagues felt that it was her mother's influence which made her for the next ten years almost a recluse in their midst, the two women habitually taking their meals together in the furthest corner of any hotel dining-room and never even nodding to other members of the company as they came in. Frida Leider,

who shared a dressing-room with Muzio in Chicago, has left us
an intriguing picture of her arriving at the theatre for rehearsals,
going straight to her dressing-room, donning an outfit which she
used as a sort of working uniform (including hat and gloves),
striding on-stage where she marked through the role standing
stock still in front of the prompt box, then changing again and
leaving the theatre without a word to anyone. The great Russian
bass Alexander Kipnis used to recall how rapidly she would vanish
from the theatre after a performance, and she herself was quoted
in an interview as saying 'I love my art and I permit nothing to
interfere to its disadvantage. I can't understand how singers can
go to suppers and dinners and receptions and still keep in good
trim for their work.' Up to a point she has my sympathy – one
hour in a noisy, smoky restaurant after a performance can put
your voice under greater strain than three leading roles on the
trot – but most opera singers, especially the Italians, are convivial
people, and camaraderie is one of the profession's chief attractions.

It was doubtless this determination of Muzio's to keep herself
to herself during periods of work which gave rise to some of the
strange stories which grew up around her. One writer has left a
graphic picture of Muzio spending her spare time in a room 'from
which all light was excluded', brooding tearfully over the machina-
tions of her rivals both in opera and in love; other witnesses, as we
shall see, have presented a far more human and appealing picture.
A contributory factor to this air of mystery and contradiction
surrounding Muzio lies, I think, in the peculiar circumstances
of her recording career. The only records which she made by
what one might call the 'normal' method were the experimental
titles of 1911, when her career had hardly begun, and the group
of 1934–5 when it was almost over; during her glory years she
sang for the Pathé and Edison companies which used a totally
different recording technique known as the 'hill-and-dale' method.
The effect of this was that once the machines needed to play the
'hill-and-dales' had gone out of fashion so too did the recordings
which Muzio had made in her prime, and without them it has been

hard to appreciate the potent spell which she used to cast over her listeners. Now, however, thanks to the advent of CD, they have become easily accessible and the story they have to tell is one of boundless fascination.

Thirty-seven titles are to be found on Pearl's two-disc set GEMM *CDS 9072*, and thirty-five (all but one of them included on the Pearl disc) on an American two-disc set, Cantabile *BIM–705–2*.* These recordings were all made between 1920 and 1925 and I must immediately emphasise that in terms of hiss and crackle they demand more tolerance from the listener than most of the other CDs to which I refer in this book. Even the experts (and in this instance the Pearl company turned to one of the best) cannot make a 'hill-and-dale' sound as innocuous as a 'normal' 78, but I would urge all those interested in the intriguing subtleties of operatic interpretation to let their ears become accustomed to the surface noise – imagine that the singer was recording during a hailstorm and frying an egg the while – and allow this compelling artist to speak to them across the years and through the interference. To take one track at random, it would be hard to listen to Muzio's rendering of the scena 'Dove son? Donde vengo?' from Catalani's LORELEY and fail to recognise the sheer ability which it reveals. The dramatic singing has an arresting impact, the text is projected not merely with clarity but with genuine theatrical flair, the rapid passages are dispatched with sovereign ease and the tone quality is one of total evenness right up from the thrilling chest notes to the brilliant high C. This was the role in which Muzio made her début in the Teatro Colón, Buenos Aires, on 18

---

* Since this chapter was written a new company has come to my notice which has brought out two highly successful two-CD sets of Muzio. Romophone *81010–2* consists of all forty-three of the titles recorded for Pathé in 1917–18, and Romophone *81005–2* of the complete Edison recordings of 1920–5 plus both the Gramophone Company recordings of 1911. The transfers have been made by Ward Marston, who was responsible for Pearl's splendid 'Complete Caruso', and are of a very high standard. They confirm my feeling that the emotional charge inherent in the quality of Muzio's voice during her heyday was something unrivalled by any other soprano.

June 1919 and so overwhelming was her success that the piece was revived there specially for her in six subsequent seasons. To quote one of the reviews: 'Outstanding amongst the cast was the new soprano Claudia Muzio. An elegant figure, beautiful posture, expressive gestures and a winning vocal style, all are hers. Her voice, so flexible and well controlled, though there are limits to its volume, is capable through its great brilliance of giving new life to less robust pieces such as this one of Catalani's.' To this day no other soprano has held sway over the Argentinian public as Muzio did. Known as 'La divina Claudia' or simply 'La única', she appeared at the Colón in the course of ten seasons between 1919 and 1934 in no less than twenty-three different operas, including several whose names would mean nothing to the public of today, but which enjoyed considerable popularity as long as Muzio was there to appear in them.

In the Edison recordings Muzio's versatility is established again and again. The opening of the recitative preceding Nedda's 'Ballatella' from PAGLIACCI is heady with dread as she contemplates what might happen if her husband were to guess her guilty secret, but in the course of one page her voice is transformed into the perfect instrument for the glitter and abandon of her song to the birds, a passage which she used to sing in the theatre lying on her back, soaking up the sunshine.* When we move on to another Leoncavallo track, the seldom heard soprano aria 'Dir che sono al mondo' from ZAZA, it is almost as if we were listening to a different voice. This is a brooding, introspective piece and the richness of Muzio's chest tones make her sound almost like a contralto – until, with no apparent change of register, she inserts into the stream of sound the occasional ravishing piano high note. Another verismo composer who is well represented on

---

*   She was also one of the few sopranos who have undertaken the roles of Nedda and Santuzza in CAVALLERIA RUSTICANA on the same evening. Tenors sometimes tackle both pieces, but both tenor roles are written for more or less the same type of voice, whereas the two leading ladies are quite different kettles of fish.

these discs is Giordano. We have a marvellously vocalised scene from MADAME SANS-GENE, the piece which brought Muzio to Gatti-Casazza's attention, as well as a powerfully conceived 'La mamma morta', Maddalena's aria from ANDREA CHENIER. Muzio was the Met's first Maddalena and I have heard no other soprano achieve such a sense of desolation with the words 'Porto sventura a chi bene mi vuole!' ('I bring ill fortune to everyone who loves me!').

Another role which Muzio introduced to the Met* was Tatiana in EUGENE ONEGIN, with Giuseppe de Luca in the title-role, and her account of the Letter Scene, unfamiliar though it may sound in Italian, is gripping and intense. In music of this sort, with its very direct emotional appeal, she uses no artifice, but sings with her heart on her sleeve – it comes straight from her to you. In more florid pieces – the two TROVATORE arias, for instance, or the Bolero from I VESPRI SICILIANI – it is inevitable that one should admire the technique as well as the content, but even there the virtuosity never becomes an end in itself. In his review of Muzio's first Tosca at the Met the critic Richard Aldrich wrote 'It was to be noticed last night that she was always willing to sacrifice vocal display to the need of colouring a phrase to suit the dramatic intention of the moment', and that does indeed appear to have been part of her artistic creed. It is also the clue to one of her outstanding virtues as an artist, her knack of shedding light on everything she sings, so that the old and trite can sound suddenly new and intriguing.

Another of the New York critics, the representative of the *Evening Sun*, waxed lyrical about Muzio at her Met début, and he, too, made some interesting points. 'She was the first Italian woman of importance that New York has heard in the one all-Italian melodrama of Puccini. The very stage held pictures of German† Ternina's great creation of the Roman singer, pictures

---

* She also created the role of Giorgetta in Puccini's IL TABARRO there in 1919.

---

† She was in fact Croatian.

too of the American beauties, Eames and Farrar. But Muzio really *was* Tosca. Youth, that gem above rubies, shone like a Kohinoor in her modest crown. The drama, for sheer realism of actuality, had not been so visualised in years before.' I do not know who it was who first bestowed on Muzio the soubriquet of 'the Duse of Song',* but it would not have clung to her as it did unless it had hit the nail on the head. Again and again the use of her huge dark Italian eyes, her elegant gestures and the intensity of her stage persona are singled out by the critics for as much praise as her actual singing. She was an impressive figure – at five foot nine inches tall enough, indeed, to be self-conscious about it, especially as so many of her regular partners, Gigli, Schipa, Martinelli and others, were noticeably shorter – and she possessed the ability to create an atmosphere of place and period in her performances. This partly came, no doubt, from the thoroughness with which she researched her roles. For her Tosca costumes she sought out those which Sarah Bernhardt had worn for the original Sardou play and had copies made; and when she was preparing the last of her new roles, Cecilia in Refice's opera of that name, she read everything she could find about the life of Saint Cecilia, visited the church built over the saint's old home and the catacombs where her statue lies, and based her costumes on portraits of her in various stained-glass windows. There was, however, much more to Muzio's impact on stage than these external considerations. She carried with her the aura of the tragedy queen, and I remember a great British connoisseur of opera, Rupert Bruce-Lockhart, once telling me that when the curtain went up on the last act of Muzio's LA TRAVIATA 'you could almost *smell* the sick-room'.

With this theatricality of Muzio's in mind I suspect that one particular track on the two CD selections mentioned above brings us closer than any other to her real self. The heroine of

---

* Eleonora Duse, 1858–1924, the great Italian classical actress, was acclaimed for her ability to create every role afresh and to seem a different person in each of them, whereas her French opposite number, Sarah Bernhardt, always strove to project her own personality from the stage.

Cilea's opera ADRIANA LECOUVREUR was another famous actress.* In the first act of the opera we meet her as she finishes one of her greatest performances and is greeted in the green room by the applause of her colleagues. She responds by assuring them that she is nothing but the humble handmaid of her art – 'Io son' l'umile ancella del Genio creator'. It is a beautiful evocation of that very special tone of self-effacement which great actresses do tend to employ on such occasions; they know they are great, you know it too, and, most important of all, they know that you know it, so they can afford to pretend they are not. The scene is one of Cilea's finest achievements, the sweet sighing of the violins depicting the humility of the artistic soul, and Muzio's response calls vividly to mind the famous phrase written about her by the tenor Giacomo Lauri-Volpi – 'that unique voice of hers made of tears and sighs and restrained inner fire'.

The Edison recordings are not limited to operatic offerings, but include a dozen song titles as well. Some of these are classical in style, Rossini's 'La Separazione', for instance, vocalised with extraordinary delicacy on a poised thread of sound, and there are others in which she lets her musical hair down to intoxicating effect. There is a splendid Edwardian romantic ballad called 'Shepherd's Love' in rumpty-tum waltz time, including such immortal couplets as 'Love cannot always be in vain / Love soon will come to us again', and another piece of more garish frippery, also in 3/4 time, with the challenging title of 'Guardami!' ('Look at me!'). There is a gorgeously swooping, swooning performance of 'Aspiration', based on Chopin's E flat Nocturne, op.9, no.2, and an equally evocative rendering of Mascheroni's 'Eternamente', complete with a rousing re-attack on a high B flat and a tasteful obbligato played by a violinist named Albert Spalding. In Sodero's 'Crisantemi' and Bachelet's 'Chère nuit' the vocal quality is strongly reminiscent of

---

* Adrienne Lecouvreur, 1692–1730, was a star of the Comédie Française. She died in her prime and it is interesting to note that as she had never renounced the theatrical profession she was refused Christian burial.

the young Renata Tebaldi, and as the pick of a wonderful bunch I think I would settle for Muzio's version of 'A kiss in the dark' from Victor Herbert's ORANGE BLOSSOMS, a performance to be treasured alongside Ponselle's unforgettable 'Kiss me again' from the same composer's MADEMOISELLE MODISTE.

During the period represented by these recordings Muzio's professional calendar underwent an important change. When she returned to the Met in January 1922 after one of her sojourns in South America she found that much had altered. For six years she had been Caruso's most regular partner and now he was gone. His place as the company's leading box-office attraction had been taken by the newly imported Maria Jeritza, who was, both as a performer and as a person, the very antithesis of Claudia Muzio. No longer feeling at home at the Met Muzio managed to get on the wrong side of Gatti-Casazza, who complained to his opposite number at La Scala that Muzio's South American and Mexican triumphs had turned her head, and that now, unable to bear playing second fiddle to Jeritza, she, who had always been so obliging, had taken to presenting him with 'tantrums, whims, long faces, rebellious attitudes worthy of a prima donna of forty years ago'. He did not re-engage her, and she transferred her allegiance to Chicago where she shared pride of place with the Scottish lyric soprano Mary Garden, another renowned singing actress, and the Polish dramatic soprano Rosa Raisa, famous for her clarion top notes. Despite the competition of these two established favourites Muzio had no difficulty in winning a secure position in the hearts of her new public, and she remained with the Chicago company until its collapse in 1932.

As the Chicago seasons were shorter than those at the Met she was left with more time available for guest performances in Europe, and in 1926 she returned after a gap of almost a decade to La Scala. This was a testing assignment, because Italian singers who have absconded to America are traditionally subjected to even more searching criticism than usual when they come home trailing their clouds of transatlantic glory. Muzio survived unscathed. As the critic of *Il Sole* expressed it:

> We remembered Claudia Muzio's exceptional beauty of voice and gifts of temperament before she won for herself solid renown and substantial wealth in America. We have looked forward to her return, and now we can affirm that no damage has befallen her beyond the ocean, but that, on the contrary, her original gifts now bear the hallmark of perfection. Traviata sung by Muzio represents exquisite musical enjoyment, and it will long remain in the mind.

Having conquered with LA TRAVIATA Muzio confirmed her victory the following week with IL TROVATORE. To quote *La Sera* this time:

> Muzio triumphed with Leonora as she had with Violetta; her magnificent voice, full and even in timbre, soared with masterly assurance from the highest register to the lowest, always rich and resonant, the mezza voce a thing to treasure, the dramatic feeling deep and sincere. Her regal figure and highly distinguished deportment made this a perfect, a faultless Leonora.

Muzio was a tireless worker, and with regular obligations in Chicago, Europe and South America she maintained a punishing schedule.* If it was a period of unremitting professional success, however, it also brought set-backs in other ways. Over the years Muzio had earned spectacularly, especially with her tours of South America, but through the efforts of a man named Scotto, who doubled for a time as her manager and her lover, she lost vast sums of money. His extravagance was appalling – to show off his (in fact her) wealth he would scatter jewellery and gold cuff-links around the front-of-house staff – and much of what was left after his depredations was lost in the Wall Street crash. Muzio was doubtless dramatising when she confided in a friend

---

* One memorable experience of Muzio's during this period was a modern-dress production of LA TRAVIATA in Rome in 1928 in which Alfredo's off-stage voice in Act I was heard over the wireless.

that if she worked for a hundred years she would never be out of debt, but in the last few years of her life money problems were often on her mind. She added considerably to her worries by being a poor picker of men – Sr Scotto was not her only unfortunate choice of lover – and in 1929, at the age of forty, she married a certain Renato Liberati who was not only several inches shorter than her but seventeen years younger. The union did not prosper.

Soon after her marriage Muzio's health began to give cause for worry. During 1930 she had to cancel a number of performances – her doctor in Rome came up with the somewhat non-specific diagnosis of 'nervous exhaustion' – but whenever she did sing the results were as stunning as ever. In 1932 she opened the new War Memorial Opera House in San Francisco as Tosca and was given the Freedom of the City, at that time the only opera singer apart from Luisa Tetrazzini to have received the honour. Before her return to Buenos Aires in 1933 after an absence of five years certain wagging tongues put about the theory that she had lost her voice, the main effect of which was to raise the public's enthusiasm to a new pitch of frenzy as she reeled off LA TRAVIATA, NORMA, TOSCA, ANDREA CHENIER and LA FORZA DEL DESTINO, all inside seven weeks. In 1934 she returned in triumph to the Met and gave two performances, as Violetta and Santuzza,[*] which have taken their place amongst the legends of the house – the ovation after LA TRAVIATA was said to have lasted for fifteen minutes – before going on to Rome for the première of Refice's CECILIA. It was at this point that she made the first of the Columbia recordings on which her reputation has been largely based ever since, nineteen of which (along with the youthful version of the BOHEME aria) are available on the Nimbus CD, *NI 7814*.

If Muzio had never made any other recordings than the two tracks on this CD which date from 1934 they would be enough

---

[*]   She also sang one Violetta with the company in Philadelphia.

to establish her reputation as an artist of rare emotional range. The first is a searing account of 'Voi lo sapete, o mamma' from CAVALLERIA RUSTICANA, in which Santuzza pours out the tragic story of her love for, and abandonment by, Turiddu. Muzio sings it as if with all her nerve-ends exposed, and anyone wanting to hear a vocal actress at work need only listen to one phrase from Santuzza's description of her rival Lola – 'arse di gelosia' ('she was aflame with jealousy') – to find what they are seeking. It had always been Muzio's achievement in these all-stops-out verismo pieces to give them the impact they need without resorting to crudity of expression; the emotion was shattering, but the artistry never splintered. To move on from this track to the next is to step out of a swirling tempest into a carefree cloudless day. In Buzzi-Peccia's little ditty 'Colombetta' Muzio displays something which we have not had a chance of glimpsing so far, namely an infectious sense of fun, and the neatness, the skittishness with which she puts the number over are as immaculately judged as the pathos of the operatic aria. To bring off a song like this on a recording, with so much charm and without a trace of archness, is no mean achievement, and one can only regret that with the exception of Alice in FALSTAFF she never turned her hand to comedy on stage. What a Rosalinde she would have made in DIE FLEDERMAUS, or rather in IL PIPISTRELLO!

The rest of the Columbia recordings on this Nimbus CD were made fourteen months later, in June 1935, and although the voice is still one of a fascinatingly individual beauty there is no denying that by then a technical decline had set in. The climax of Tosca's 'Vissi d'arte' is laboured and out of tune, and Muzio falls back at one point on just the kind of gulp that one is so happy not to hear in the earlier verismo recordings. 'Tacea la notte' from IL TROVATORE no longer has quite the sweep or security of the earlier version, and two breaths are needed where there used to be only one. What we are offered in compensation, however, is an intense and deeply personal dramatic insight into the plights of these various luckless heroines. There is a memorable conjuring up of inescapable doom in Margherita's 'L'altra notte' from MEFISTOFELE, while the anguish behind her diction in 'Esser madre è un inferno' from Cilea's L'ARLESIANA almost leads her into a kind of *Sprechgesang*. The heroine's 'Poveri fiori' from ADRIANA LECOUVREUR, which spares her too many excursions into the uppermost range, is vibrant with theatrical poignancy, a *tour de force* of which the original Adrienne would surely not have been ashamed; and in the Act III duet from OTELLO, in which Muzio is powerfully partnered by the tenor Francesco Merli, we have a vivid memento of her celebrated Desdemona. Lest anyone should suppose that these 1935 recordings do nothing but shred the listener's emotions there is also a spirited rendering of Delibes's 'Les filles de Cadiz' and another nice touch of humour in the same composer's 'Bonjour, Suzon'. The singer depicts a gentleman who has never had much luck with Mlle Suzon, but who feels that since he last walked past her door she may have changed her mind. Compared with Supervia's blatantly cheeky version Muzio's is restrained and suave, but one feels that her Suzon would be no less likely than Supervia's to accede in the end to the request 'ouvre ta porte'.

To judge from various accounts of her recurrent ill health it is reasonable to suppose that by the time Muzio made these 1935 recordings she knew her days were numbered, or at least her days as a front-rank operatic soprano. Most of the imperfections which they display are those which come from straightforward loss of physical strength; when previously comfortable phrases seem longer than they used to be, and the high notes higher, no singer of Muzio's intelligence could fail to read the signs. One normally reliable authority has stated that she herself financed these recordings, and if that is true it seems likely that she saw them as an artistic legacy to be achieved while there was still time. As I indicated in my discussion of the one early track on this Nimbus CD, the aria 'Si, mi chiamano Mimi' from LA BOHEME charts the course of Muzio's career. The 1911 version is naïve but radiant with promise; the 1921 'hill-and-dale' (to be found in the Cantabile set) finds the voice at its best and the characterisation attractive and assured; while the 1935 version, vocally on the wane, packs an emotional punch far beyond anything contained in the other two. It is like an echo of Mimi's own words in the last act of the opera; when Rodolfo assures her that she is still as beautiful as the dawn she corrects him with the words 'No, as beautiful as the sunset'. When the Muzio of 1935 opens the flood-gates with that make-or-break phrase 'Ma quando vien lo sgelo' she is no longer just a sweet little girl artlessly yearning for the first touch of warm spring sunshine; there is an undertone of desperation, as if she herself knew how little sunshine was still to come. It is beautifully done, but its beauty is that of the sunset, not of the dawn.

Mimi's other principal solo, 'Donde lieta uscì', usually referred to as Mimi's Farewell, was recorded the day before the Act I aria and is one of the most beautiful tracks on the Nimbus disc. The essential word 'addio', taken by Muzio off the singing voice and into a bleak parlato, may smack of a loftier style of tragic heroine than the stricken little seamstress, but only the flinty-hearted could cavil at so lived-in a performance. The brightening of her tone, as Mimi remembers the little pink night-cap under the pillow and suggests that Rodolfo might like to keep it as a memento of their love, suffuses the music like a sudden flash of sunshine through a crack in the clouds, then vanishes as quickly as it came.

And so to the most famous recording which Muzio ever made, the recording which, more than any other, has come to be regarded as the quintessence of her art and even, somewhat misleadingly, of herself – Violetta's 'Addio del passato' from LA TRAVIATA. Violetta is dying and the one hope which keeps her clinging to life lies in the letter she has received from Alfredo's father saying that all misunderstandings have been cleared up and that Alfredo is on his way to her. Over the melody to which Alfredo expressed his first declaration of love in Act I, this time played pianissimo on the violins, she reads out the letter. Listening to Muzio's Violetta one has the feeling that she does not need to read it – every sentence is already engraved on her heart. This is indeed the Duse of Song at work, and as she lays the letter aside all her sufferings are summed up with a terrifying intensity in her last two spoken words, 'È tardi!' ('It is too late!'). They are marked in the score to be spoken *con voce sepolcrale* and Muzio leaves us in no doubt that the grave is indeed yawning wide. The aria itself opens in a tone of utter desolation, the phrases short and painful. It is one of the hardest tasks for a singer to lend credibility to the operatic convention that characters who are at their last gasp should still express themselves through the medium of song, but this is exactly what Muzio achieves in such agonising fashion. Gradually the exhausted tones gather strength and grow into a fever of desperation, but it is too much for her and the final high A is a shriek cut off into sudden silence. Perhaps this was a classic example of making a virtue of necessity – the note is marked in the score to be sung 'on a thread of voice' – but the ability to sing a pianissimo high note surely indicates a greater degree of conscious physical control than is suitable for the spent Violetta.

These recordings were made in the June of 1935 and on 24 May the following year Muzio died in her hotel room in Rome at the age of forty-seven. The cause of her death is another of the many Muzio mysteries. Described simply as 'heart failure' it has been attributed by various writers to the side-effects of all sorts of maladies, Bright's Disease, a kidney condition, being perhaps the most frequently cited. Nor can the rumours be lightly dismissed that, aware of a mortal sickness, she took her own life.* Her body lay in state for three days surrounded by banks of flowers including a floral crown from the Queen of Italy, and the building of her tomb, now officially a national monument, was paid for by

---

* Robert Tuggle, in his splendid book *The Golden Age of Opera*, feels sufficiently confident on this point to have written 'Suffering from heartbreak and failing health, she died in Rome . . . almost certainly by her own hand'.

her colleagues in the form of a subscription headed by Giacomo Lauri-Volpi.

As I have mentioned before, I always feel that a singer can receive no higher praise than that of other singers, and within the ranks of the operatic profession Claudia Muzio was a universally admired, even a revered, artist. The great Italian mezzo Ebe Stignani, who sang with Muzio in the 1920s and with Callas in the 1950s, said 'Muzio was above all comparisons – to me she was on an altar'; and on one occasion Mafalda Favero, herself a prima donna at La Scala, went to Muzio's dressing-room after a performance and instinctively dropped on her knees before her. Ponselle, the one soprano of the day who was incontestably Muzio's superior in purely vocal terms, regarded her Aida and her Maddalena in ANDREA CHENIER as being performances 'which could not be surpassed', and I well remember the heart-warming enthusiasm with which Dame Eva Turner once spoke to me of Muzio when I was preparing a BBC radio programme about her. Muzio had been kind enough to invite her younger colleague to visit her while they were appearing during the same season in Chicago, and to her surprise Dame Eva found herself participating in a thoroughly English tea and being closely questioned about current affairs in Hammersmith and Tottenham, two London boroughs in which Muzio had received her early education. Dame Eva described her as the singer who had made upon her 'the most unforgettable impression of all', and she was particularly enthusiastic about Muzio's qualities as a recitalist. In her own gorgeously rounded tones* she said, 'Every word was pregnant with meaning, and she encompassed the phrases so beautifully with her flowing tone. She held us all entranced, and any chance to hear her was an opportunity not to be missed.' I remember, too, asking my own teacher, Alfred Piccaver, who, in his opinion, was the greatest soprano with whom he had ever worked. I expected that he might pause to think – Lehmann, per-

---

* See *Legendary Voices*, pp.260–1.

haps, or Selma Kurz? I knew it would not be Jeritza – but without a second's hesitation back came the answer 'Claudia Muzio'. He sang Cavaradossi to her Tosca in one of his Chicago seasons and to him she was incomparable.

I was given another personal glimpse of Claudia Muzio, and the touching vulnerability of her character, while I myself was appearing recently in the Teatro Colón, Buenos Aires. The mother of one of my colleagues had been a chorus singer there in Muzio's day, and she recalled an evening when Muzio was seriously concerned about a sore throat. The leading clarinettist in the orchestra, a particular friend of Muzio's, went into her dressing-room before the performance and, gently laying his thumb and forefinger either side of her larynx, he assured her that she had nothing to worry about. *'Hai una gola d'oro'*, he said – 'You have a throat of gold'. She sang that evening like an angel, and for the rest of the season she was unable to go on stage until he had come to her dressing-room and performed exactly the same action to exactly the same words. I also enjoyed another of the old lady's memories concerning Muzio and one of her most regular partners, Beniamino Gigli. Gigli was taking a solo curtain-call at the end of a performance of TOSCA and was shamelessly milking the applause. When he at last came back through the curtain Muzio looked at him disdainfully and said *'Tenore da cantina!'* – an English equivalent might be something like 'tea-shop tenor!' – before sweeping out to take her own call. You either have to be the best of friends or the deadliest of enemies to make remarks like that, and they were the best of friends.

The person who has left us the most convincing picture of Muzio in private life is a lady named May Higgins. She was a member of the Muzio Fan Club in Chicago and became personally acquainted with her idol after summoning up the courage to speak to her in the street. In 1929 Muzio invited her to become her personal secretary and for six years Miss Higgins accompanied her wherever she went. At regular intervals she would send back detailed reports of their doings to the

Fan Club, each one opening with the words 'Hi Gang!', and the picture she paints is very different from that of the depressive in the darkened room. No doubt her views were initially coloured by heroine-worship, but heroine-worship can scarcely survive six years at the closest of quarters, and May Higgins's devotion to Muzio deepened as time went by. She describes a very dedicated, very private person – 'She appreciates the adoration and applause of the people but would rather hide than face them' – but one of infinite kindness and generosity. When a memorial mass was held for Muzio in Chicago the pastor said 'Many is the child she has dressed in this parish', but she had preferred not to let her light shine before men. Her favourite relaxations, according to May Higgins, were playing the piano, which she would do for hours at a time, taking long drives on days when there was no performance, and going to the cinema, especially if there was a Laurel and Hardy film to be found. She was at her happiest whenever they could take a holiday in Italy. Muzio used to rent a large apartment in an old hotel in a place called Riolo Bagni, and on one occasion, in July 1931, she agreed to sing Gounod's 'Ave Maria' and the aria 'La vergine degli angeli' from LA FORZA DEL DESTINO during a service in the local church. In Miss Higgins's words 'the population increased miraculously overnight', the seating had to be taken out of the church to make room for the crowd, and the priest explained to the congregation that as the Signora was not giving an operatic performance, but was singing a prayer to the Virgin, there was to be no applause. With difficulty the people restrained themselves until the service was over, and then mobbed Muzio's hotel, where she had to appear on the balcony to receive their homage. One other vignette provided by May Higgins which particularly appeals to me concerns their occupation of the apartment in the Grand Hotel, Milan, in which Verdi had habitually stayed. In the sitting-room hung a life-sized portrait of the composer, and Muzio addressed it with the words 'I wonder if you know how much work you have brought my way'.

Perhaps the keynote to the Muzio mystery lies in the fact that she brought both to her life and to her work a quality which is comparatively rare in the operatic profession – genuine humility. She was an artist for whom there was no such thing as a routine performance; she herself used to say that whenever she went on stage she was filled with profound emotion and with the feeling 'tonight my career begins'. As the Argentinian writer Enzo Valenti Ferro has expressed it, she embodied the Stanislavskian precept 'Love your art within yourself and not yourself within your art'.

TITTA RUFFO

ITALIAN BARITONE

b. Pisa, 9 June 1877
d. Florence, 6 July 1953

F̶ew Italian conductors of the twentieth century have enjoyed wider respect than Tullio Serafin. During an active career of well over sixty years he was familiar with virtually every singer of note in the Italian repertoire, from Tamagno to di Stefano and from Tetrazzini to Joan Sutherland, and it was a favourite dictum of his that although he had worked with many wonderful artists, there were three whom he regarded as being in a class apart. These were his 'giants', singers so gloriously gifted that no one else could be mentioned in the same breath. They were the tenor Enrico Caruso, the soprano Rosa Ponselle and the baritone Titta Ruffo.

Ruffo was born in Pisa on 9 June 1877, and his name, which he changed around for professional purposes, is an oddity. Titta was in fact the family name, and his father, Oreste Titta, who worked as a blacksmith in a foundry, chose to have his second son baptised Ruffo because it was the name of a recently deceased dog to which he had been deeply attached. To say that during his childhood Ruffo led a dog's life would be an exaggeration, but only a slight one. While he was still small the family moved to Rome; there were six children in all, two boys and four girls, money was desperately scarce, and instead of being sent to school Ruffo was kept at home until the age of eight as a full-time mother's help. When one of his sisters had become old enough to take his place he was sent to work in a factory, and from there into the foundry where his father was employed. Following a savage falling-out between the two of them Ruffo decided to leave home; like some juvenile hero in a Dickens novel, he took to the road. Such was his thirst for independence that despite appalling hardships he managed to keep his head above water for six years, eventually finding a craftsman in ironwork who was prepared to take him on as an apprentice, and he only went back to rejoin his family when his mother, whom he adored, became seriously ill.

When Ruffo was eighteen his elder brother Ettore, a talented musician, took him to a performance of CAVALLERIA RUSTICANA in Rome's Teatro Costanzi; the roles of Santuzza and Turiddu were sung by their original creators, the husband and wife team of Gemma Bellincioni and Roberto Stagno. Afterwards Ruffo asked his brother to play the 'Siciliana' on his flute and casually began to sing along with him. Out came, as he himself was later to describe it in his memoirs, 'a tenor voice of such beauty and spontaneity' that the two brothers could only look at each other with amazement, and at that moment it became evident where Ruffo's future lay.

He was not able to start taking voice lessons immediately; he was still too young and the family too poor. His father by now had a workshop of his own and he needed his son, who had become an expert craftsman, to assist him. Eventually Ruffo was allowed to apply to the Accademia di Santa Cecilia as long as he continued his manual labour as well. He auditioned successfully with the aria 'Sei vendicata assai' from Meyerbeer's DINORAH, but was told that there was no point in his studying the piano, an essential faculty for anyone wanting to graduate, as his hands were too stiff and calloused to be any use at the keyboard. Nor were his voice lessons quite what he had hoped for. He was assigned to the famous Maestro Persichini, teacher of Mattia Battistini amongst several other stars of the day, and in his memoirs Ruffo gives an hilarious account of the great man's arrival for the morning class, handing his top hat to one obsequious pupil, his gloves to another and his cane to a third, before sitting down with many a satisfied glance in the mirror to sip his cup of coffee. As this routine took twenty minutes of the two-hour class, and as there were seven students to receive instruction, it followed that nobody could expect more than a quarter of an hour or so of the Maestro's valuable time; and in fact it was usually a great deal less as he customarily devoted forty-five minutes to his favourite pupil, Giuseppe de Luca.* To add to all this frustration, when Persichini did turn his attention to Ruffo he seemed determined to train him as a bass, whereas Ruffo, despite his initial flirtation with the idea of becoming a tenor, was convinced that he was in fact a baritone. After only seven months he left the place in disgust.

By putting in many extra hours in the workshop Ruffo saved enough money to buy some reasonably presentable clothes and take himself off to Milan, armed with a letter of introduction to a well-known baritone named Lelio Casini. Casini immediately recognised Ruffo's potential and agreed to teach him in between his own engagements, though the arrangement did not last for long. Ruffo's financial plight was so severe that he often went dangerously short of food; it became urgently necessary for him to make his début and start earning a living. This came about on 9 April 1898 when he sang the Herald in LOHENGRIN in the Teatro Costanzi, the very same theatre which had already played such a fateful part in his career, and he made an instant impression. The title-role was taken by a distinguished Spanish tenor named Francisco Viñas who prophesied a great future for the young man, and who, fifteen years later, was to present Ruffo with a splendid photograph of himself as the Knight of the Holy Grail inscribed 'To the most select of artists, the good Titta, I offer this reminder of the day which, for the king's herald in the Teatro Costanzi, marked the first step on his glorious road'.

Glory did not tumble immediately into the young man's lap, but within two years he had appeared in a dozen of Italy's provincial theatres and had acquired a repertoire of no less than sixteen leading roles. There were still set-backs to be encountered, such as the occasion when he invested all his savings in a magnificent pea-green overcoat in order to impress an impresario

---

* See *Legendary Voices*, pp.55–68.

who had engaged him to sing in Ferrara. First, in his eagerness to get off the train in time, he left the coat behind with his wallet in the pocket; then he discovered that the impresario had absconded with the opera company's money and his performances had been cancelled. By the autumn of 1900, however, when he was still only twenty-three years old, he had learnt his business well enough to embark on an international career; on the first of many trips to South America he appeared with success, though without causing a sensation, in the opera houses of Valparaiso and Santiago.

To judge the speed of a singer's ascent in the ranks of the operatic profession there is no better yardstick than the fees which he or she receives. For his Herald in Rome Ruffo was paid a fee of three and a half lire a day. On his return from South America two years later his fee for six performances in the Teatro Massimo, Palermo, was one thousand lire, almost fifty times as much; and by the time he made his Chicago début in 1912 he was commanding a fee of $2000 a night, which is well over three thousand times as much.* The main cause of Ruffo's rocketing market value was the sheer magnificence of his voice – in fact his old class-mate Giuseppe de Luca used to say 'It wasn't a voice, it was a miracle.' The evidence of Ruffo's recordings fully bears this out, and one excellent selection of them is to be found on Nimbus *NI 7810.* They date from 1907 to 1926, and although it would be impossible to give pride of place to any single one of these twenty-one tracks, the Prologue from PAGLIACCI is enough to show what de Luca was talking about. From the first

---

* To give some idea of today's equivalent to these sums one pound around this time equalled $4.80 or 27 lire, and these figures need to be multiplied by roughly 40 to reach their value at the time of writing. In other words today's equivalent to Ruffo's LOHENGRIN fee would be approximately £5.18 per performance, his Palermo fee £247 per performance and his American fee £16,666 per performance. In fact his Chicago fee breached an agreement which Gatti-Casazza, manager of the Metropolitan Opera, had made with other leading theatre directors in the States that no one except Caruso should be paid more than $1000, but as half Ruffo's fee was paid by a wealthy patron of the Chicago Opera named Edward Townsend Stotesbury it was felt to be legitimate.

utterance of 'Sì può?' the sound is one of an arresting quality, rich, beautiful, and yet with a strange almost threatening snarl behind it. As he introduces himself with the phrase 'Io sono il Prologo' the glorious high E may be clothed in velvet but behind the ease and suavity there is the impact of a battle-cry. With an opening such as this many a baritone would have put himself in the tricky position of having nothing with which to cap it when the real climax comes, but in Ruffo's case there are herculean reserves still to be unleashed. After a mocking, dangerous mezza voce as he slides into the big tune on 'E voi, piuttosto . . .' he climbs with a gradual piling-up of pressure first to a high F of glorious potency and then to a shattering high A flat – the absolute ceiling for most baritone voices but for him something to be taken for granted and positively revelled in. Nor is the effect merely one of a man with a gigantic voice putting his top notes on parade. Thanks to Ruffo's imaginative treatment of the text this is also a classic piece of musical characterisation; we are dealing with a Prologo who oozes contempt for his listeners.

There was something titanic, something elemental in Ruffo's singing which clearly reflected the man's personality as well as his voice. He was known as '*Il leone*' ('the lion'), as much for his imperious presence, his mane of hair and his piercing gaze as for his vocal prowess, and he was one of those people who, in defiance of biblical precept, do by giving thought succeed in adding cubits to their stature. He had received no schooling whatsoever and yet he turned himself into a cultural polymath. He became a voracious reader, with Shakespeare as his favourite author, and his memoirs* are widely regarded as a work of genuine literary merit. He was fascinated by the spoken word and though it is to be assumed that he grew up using a rough-and-ready dialect, several people who knew him in his maturity reported that he spoke the purest Italian they had ever heard – not for nothing did he claim that the recitation classes given by a certain Virginia Marini in the

---

* *La mia parabola*, written in 1924 but not published until 1937.

Accademia di Santa Cecilia were the only ones from which he had derived any benefit. He was a passionate lover of modern painting and the first thing he did when visiting any city for the first time was to scour its picture galleries. His stage characterisations were arrived at by thought and observation, never more so than in the case of Tonio in PAGLIACCI. On holiday in the Val di Ledro he had once witnessed a strange and touching scene. A peasant, clearly mentally defective, with a nervous tic and an idiot grin and carrying a bundle of wood, tried to detain a girl who passed him in a country lane. She shook him off and walked on leaving the wretched creature standing there with a strange look in his eyes, half misery and half desire. To Ruffo he was the embodiment of Tonio, and whenever he played the role he based his whole presentation on the man, down to the crudely cut reddish hair covering the low forehead, the blisters on the lips and the toothless leer. It was one of the many roles he sang in Chicago and the city's leading critic, Edward Moore, later wrote of his characterisation: 'No one else has ever done Tonio the same way. Ruffo's Tonio was mournful, tragic, imbecilic, trembling on the verge of epilepsy, a condition portrayed with almost the accuracy of a clinic. But it was a whirlwind of passion, and as far as the audience was concerned it was a riot. They said that ushers gathered up split white gloves by the basketful after the performance was over.'

Ruffo's first role in Chicago had been Rigoletto, of which Moore wrote: 'RIGOLETTO with Ruffo in it was suddenly converted from just another Italian opera into a shuddering masterpiece of tragedy.' It was a role which he had used for several important débuts – La Scala, Milan in 1904; St Petersburg, where he was a tremendous favourite, in 1905; and Vienna, with Selma Kurz as Gilda and Caruso as the Duke, in 1906. The complex figure of the hunchback jester, riven with hatred for most of his fellow human beings but rendered vulnerable by his over-protective love for his daughter, was one of those towering theatrical figures with which Ruffo so happily grappled. The Nimbus disc includes perhaps the most revealing of his Rigoletto recordings, that of the monologue 'Pari siamo', in which he compares his destiny as jester to a master whom he loathes with that of the professional assassin Sparafucile. Where Ruffo's PAGLIACCI Prologue was flung disdainfully at the listener, here the thought processes are kept marvellously contained within himself, the introspective shifts of mood dramatically reflected in subtle variations of vocal colour. The resonance takes on a veiled, slightly nasal quality, and it is interesting to note that when, in the same year that this recording was made, Ruffo submitted to an exhaustive scientific examination by two Roman laryngologists anxious to establish whether his phenomenal voice resulted from abnormal physical attributes, one of their findings was indeed that he possessed 'a vast nasal cavity'.* They established, too, that his vocal cords were 'very muscular and very large', which, backed by the powerful physique developed during his years of exertion in the forge, doubtless helps to explain the extraordinary range and volume which Ruffo had at his command.

Curiously enough, though the role of Rigoletto brought Ruffo so much success elsewhere it was indirectly responsible for wrecking his career at Covent Garden. He made his début there in 1903, before he had established himself as a superstar, in LUCIA DI LAMMERMOOR, followed by his very first Figaro in IL BARBIERE DI SIVIGLIA, of which the Milan paper *Il Trovatore* reported that 'the audience erupted into an ovation such as has seldom been heard in that theatre'. He was then requested to take over the role of Rigoletto from Maurice Renaud, who was not well, and sing it opposite the uncrowned queen of the house, Nellie Melba. Ruffo was only given one rehearsal and to his surprise Melba did not participate, but contented herself with observing the proceedings from a box. After Ruffo had given such a tremendous account of himself in the 'Cortigiani' scene that

* A singing teacher who attended this examination reported that although Ruffo was wired up to an alarming collection of scientific gadgets, he managed to let fly with the high A flat in the PAGLIACCI Prologue, whereupon the two doctors 'ran from the room, screaming from pain in the teeth'.

the chorus and orchestra burst into spontaneous applause the diva informed the director of the house that Ruffo was too young to sing with her and that Renaud must be persuaded to rise from his sickbed. When Ruffo discovered the following day that his name had been removed from the posters he demanded to see the director and expressed himself, as he himself later described it, in such 'imaginative Italian' that the director, once the tirade had been translated to him, threatened Ruffo with legal action – whereupon Ruffo abruptly departed from London and never sang at Covent Garden again.* A heaven-sent opportunity for revenge did, however, come his way. Eight years later Melba stopped off in Naples on her way home to Australia and heard Ruffo, by now the most sought-after baritone in the world, as Nelusko in Meyerbeer's L'AFRICAINE. So impressed was she that she offered to sing a performance as Ophelia in Ambroise Thomas's HAMLET with Ruffo in the title-role. The director of the Teatro San Carlo begged Ruffo to agree, but the lion's old wound had not yet healed and he sent back the message, to be delivered verbatim, 'Signor Ruffo considers that you are too old to sing with him.' The incident could of course be taken as an example of petty-minded vindictiveness, a fact of which Ruffo was well aware, but he had trudged a hard road to achieve his pre-eminence, and I hardly think that anyone could have shaped his own destiny to the extent that Ruffo had without a keen sense of his own value. In fact he and Melba *were* subsequently cast together, and in RIGOLETTO too, in Philadelphia on 18 February 1914. There are no records of any untoward eruptions, but I somehow doubt whether Ruffo took much trouble to hold back in their numerous duets.

---

* Ruffo's subsequent London appearances were restricted to a couple of recitals in private houses, and three concerts during 1922, one in the Queen's Hall and two in the Albert Hall, of which Walter Legge, in his first published article, wrote: 'His infinite subtlety, varied tone-colour, interpretative insight and sincerity, his magnificent control, stupendous breathing powers, and impeccable phrasing stamped him as a genius.'

The opera in which Melba was so keen to appear with Ruffo, Ambroise Thomas's HAMLET, was one which he made very much his own. The operatic version may fall short of Shakespeare's original, but Ruffo was fascinated by the role of the prince and after he had sung it for the first time in Lisbon in 1907 it featured in his repertoire almost wherever he appeared – in all he performed it some 130 times. When the magnificent new Teatro Colón was opened in Buenos Aires in 1908 it was the second opera to be mounted there, and it marked the beginning of the closest association which Ruffo was to form with any individual house. In that first season alone he sang no less than forty-three performances in ten different roles – rather different from today, when a singer of Ruffo's status is more likely to fly in, do one role three or four times and fly out again – and in his final season there, in 1931, Hamlet was still on the menu. Pictures of him in the part by that stage of his career would not match many people's notions of the ascetic young Dane – he looks rather like one of the gangsters in Cole Porter's KISS ME KATE when they have been dressed up to go on stage in *The Taming of the Shrew* – but in his early days it had been one of his most compelling impersonations. The vocal high-spot of the performance was invariably the drinking song which the librettists interpolated into the play scene, and his 1907 version of this vocal *tour de force* is also included in the Nimbus selection, complete with an astonishing pyrotechnical cadenza. This was another of the passages with which Ruffo obliged the two doctors during his scientific examination and they timed his breath on this one phrase at fourteen seconds, a feat 'so fantastic that it left us open-mouthed with astonishment'.

I do not, of course, wish to give the impression that Ruffo should be principally regarded as a kind of vocal equivalent to the circus strong man. It is true that critics did occasionally pounce on him for indulging his public with fortissimo high notes held rather longer than the composer had indicated but the Nimbus disc amply demonstrates that there was no shortage of more refined weapons in Ruffo's armoury too. There is, for instance, no crude ranting about Iago's 'Credo' from OTELLO. It is a devilishly multi-faceted exposition of evil, and he delivers the fictitious narration of Cassio's dream in a slimy, insidious mezza voce, almost a pre-echo of the way Tito Gobbi used to sing this passage. In Figaro's entrance song from IL BARBIERE DI SIVIGLIA, with which he took his long-delayed first bow as a member of the Met in 1922, one might expect him to sound muscle-bound, but despite the vastness of his voice the rapid parlando passages come positively tripping from his tongue; and though I do find his tone too massive for Falstaff's featherweight 'Quand' ero paggio' it is by no means lacking in humour.

Ruffo's ability to switch vocal colour in order to match the character he is playing is nowhere better exemplified than in King Alfonso's 'Vien, Leonora' from Donizetti's LA FAVORITA. The voice here is muted, channelled into an expression of dignified devotion; it is almost as if we were listening to a different instrument from that employed by Tonio or Iago, the only things they have in common being the sovereign ease of the upper register and the endless expansiveness of the breath. When Germont père appeals to his errant son in LA TRAVIATA to desert his ill-chosen love and return to the bosom of the family he does so in accents of pained restraint; when the *passé* music-hall singer Cascart begs Leoncavallo's Zazà to forget her wealthy young lover and return to him the message is the same – 'Come back before it is too late' – but the psychological motivation is entirely different, and so too, to a remarkable degree, is the quality of Ruffo's delivery. As the Cenobite monk Athanaël in Massenet's THAIS, filled with loathing for the foul city of Alexandria, and as Verdi's Nabucco venting his fury against the Temple of Solomon, he lets fly with stentorian outbursts of spine-tingling rhetoric, while as the spy Barnaba in Ponchielli's LA GIOCONDA he indulges in a particular vocal shading of which he always seems to me to have been the ultimate master – unadulterated nastiness served up beneath a veneer of derision. For the singing actor Verdi scarcely wrote a more searching baritone aria than the great 'Eri tu' from

UN BALLO IN MASCHERA and Ruffo turns in a monumental account of it (significantly ducking the low A, which he takes in the higher octave), and as a further demonstration of his remarkable versatility Nimbus also include a skittish little song entitled 'Non penso a lei' which establishes beyond any doubt that the upper reaches of the Ruffo voice were attainable in a playful piano as well as in a cataclysmic forte.

What this all adds up to is that we are dealing with one of those rare voices which transcend normal human limitations of size and scope, and which, when combined with a fertile artistic imagination, are capable of shattering traditional moulds. Ruffo was not a *bel canto* singer of the old school, a direct successor to Battistini or Mario Ancona. The main emphasis of his artistry did not lie in the minutiae of technical refinement, partly, I suspect, because he had not been able to afford a thorough training, and partly because the profusion of his own natural gifts had meant that he could get along without them. Together with Caruso and Chaliapin he was the outstanding exponent of the new wave of verismo, or realism, in operatic performance, and these were the two colleagues whom he admired above all others. When asked in a newspaper interview in 1925 if he enjoyed going to the opera he replied that since the death of Caruso four years previously he never went except to hear Chaliapin. He learnt a great deal from the mighty Russian about the physical aspects of operatic acting and about the art of make-up. One delightful relic of their friendship is a recording which Ruffo made of an imaginary conversation between the two of them, with himself in both roles; he gives an inspired imitation of Chaliapin moaning and groaning in heavily accented Italian about his aches and pains and the general intolerability of life.

It was often said that between Caruso and Ruffo a jealous rivalry existed, but there is no evidence that this was so – indeed, photographs of Caruso and Chaliapin occupied places of honour in Ruffo's study, and at Caruso's funeral Ruffo was one of the pall-bearers. His was the only male voice of the time which could be compared with Caruso's in its combination of power and beauty and they both possessed the ability to take an audience by the scruff of the neck, a flair which rendered them *hors concours* in the works of composers such as Leoncavallo, Mascagni and Giordano. They were both blessed, too, with that fascinating vocal quality of 'chiaroscuro', a dark-hued timbre with a brilliant shine to it – and something else that they had in common was the knowledge of how it felt to have started at the bottom of the pile. They appeared together several times on stage* and the respect which they had for one another is illustrated by one of those anecdotes which seem too neat to be true, but which generally contain at least a grain of fact. One evening Ruffo was attending a performance of Caruso's and a friend asked him what he thought of it. 'He's magnificent,' Ruffo replied; 'he scares me.' A few evenings later the same man met Caruso during a performance of Ruffo's and asked him the same question. 'He's magnificent,' said Caruso; 'he scares me.' In any case, on one immortal occasion the two titans were brought together in the recording studio. It was in New York on 14 January 1914; they recorded the duet 'Enzo Grimaldo' from LA GIOCONDA and the Oath Duet from OTELLO. What became of the former nobody knows – it was never published and it vanished without trace. The latter, however, which is also on the Nimbus disc, remains to this day one of the most thrilling pieces of operatic singing ever committed to disc. Unless you know these two voices well it is sometimes difficult to tell which of them is singing, so richly baritonal is Caruso's tenor, and so brilliantly projected is Ruffo's baritone. Each of them, without doubt, was aware that day that nothing less than one hundred per cent of his best would do, vocally or histrionically, and they both delivered.

The most extensive reissue of Ruffo's recordings on CD is a three-disc set, *Lebendige Vergangenheit 89303*. It includes almost

---

* FEDORA in Paris in 1905; RIGOLETTO in Vienna the following year; RIGO-LETTO and the French première of LA FANCIULLA DEL WEST in Paris in 1912; and finally in 1915 in the first act of PAGLIACCI at the Teatro Colón, followed by the whole of that opera in Montevideo.

all the numbers on the Nimbus disc (though not the PAGLIACCI
Prologue) plus nearly fifty more, and though it would be superfluous to go into too much detail, certain of the additional titles
cannot be left unmentioned. There are numerous songs, including
such familiar favourites as 'Santa Lucia' and Tosti's 'Marecchiare',
as well as a couple composed by Ruffo's brother Ettore and one by
the tenor Tito Schipa, but to me at least it is the operatic excerpts
in which he seems most at home. They include the DINORAH
aria with which he originally gained access to the Accademia di
Santa Cecilia, and even if in those days it had only been the palest
foreshadowing of this stupendous 1914 version it would scarcely
have been possible for the panel to refuse him, calloused hands
and all. Amongst several more Verdi titles there are spacious and
eloquent versions of Ernani's 'Oh! de' verd' anni miei' and 'Lo
vedremo' (this was a role which he sang at the Met with Ponselle,
Martinelli, and Mardones – rather a tempting quartet), as well as
a spritely version of Falstaff's 'L'onore! Ladri!' and a dangerous,
brooding 'Urna fatale' from LA FORZA DEL DESTINO – this
was never issued as a 78, presumably because of one minuscule
frog which has the temerity to hop momentarily into the lion's
throat. We are also treated to three remarkable examples of what
used to happen to poor Mozart back in the Good Old Days. In
two different versions of Don Giovanni's Serenade and one of his
so-called 'Champagne Aria' Ruffo deploys his voice with riveting
skill, but in a manner which would have modern audiences asking
who on earth had written the music. Fastidious opera-goers clearly reckoned that even by the standards of the time the Don was
not natural Ruffo territory; when he sang it in Chicago in 1913
Edward Moore, who, as we have seen, had praised his Rigoletto
and Tonio to the skies and beyond, simply wrote 'it is a role
which he should gently but firmly have been argued out of ever
singing at all'.

One other aria which I would like to mention is Gérard's
'Nemico della patria' from Giordano's ANDREA CHENIER,
one of the most rewarding baritone solos in the literature of

verismo opera. Gérard was a role with which Ruffo scored many successes, including several at the Met during the last years of his career, usually in the company of Gigli and Ponselle. He recorded it twice, acoustically in 1920 and electrically in 1929, and in these two recordings (both on the *LV* set) it is possible to chart the course of what I think one has to regard as his premature decline. In both versions the declamation is intensely gripping but by 1929, when Ruffo was still only fifty-one, the voice is no longer able to look after itself – he has to help it by forcing and pushing it off the breath. The clarion thrill of the upper register has begun to show signs of rust, while at the bottom of the voice a kind of huskiness is beginning to reduce him almost to *Sprechgesang*.* It was shortly before he recorded this second version that he said goodbye to the Met and made a brief but lucrative excursion into the world of motion pictures. Thereafter he only made twelve more appearances on the operatic stage. 1931 saw his final performances in the Teatro Colón, as Hamlet and Scarpia – in the latter role one of the critics praised him for a personification 'now sullen and ironical, now lascivious and cruel, expressed in accents of the grandest eloquence', while another confined himself to hauling Ruffo over the coals for sitting too long on a certain high note in Act I and thus 'provoking such confusion that only the skill of Maestro Calusio and of the chorus could save the situation'. During the next few years he appeared occasionally on the concert platform, and in 1935 he took his final bow in the Casino Municipal in Cannes.

To return, though, for a moment to Ruffo's early years. A CD has been brought out in the United States (*OASI 7004*) which includes all fifteen of the so-called 'hill-and-dale' recordings

---

* He had always had a tendency to neglect the bottom of his voice. This is already noticeable in one of his most famous recordings, the unaccompanied 'All'erta, marinar!' from L'AFRICAINE, made in 1915 when he was at the peak of his powers, and which features in both the Nimbus and *LV* selections. The quality of the middle and upper ranges is astounding, but the lower notes are sketchy in the extreme.

which he made for the Pathé company in Paris in 1904. These are collector's pieces, and presuppose the collector's tolerance of hiss and crackle, but for those who have ears to hear they contain some truly phenomenal singing. This is the voice as it sounded just at the moment when Ruffo was making the breakthrough from being a success to being a sensation. Whether the relentless fortissimo of a passage such as the death of Posa in DON CARLO is a sign of immature artistry or of the need to pump everything he could into the primitive recording apparatus I am not able to say, but if there were nothing more on this disc than the aria 'Tu sola a me rimani' from Leoncavallo's CHATTERTON it would still be worth acquiring. The role of the suicidal young English poet was written for a tenor, and Ruffo sings the aria transposed, but it enables him to produce some of the most exciting sounds I have ever heard from a human throat. Another intriguing track is the trio 'Di geloso amor sprezzato' from IL TROVATORE, in which Ruffo is joined by his sister Fosca, a reasonably successful professional soprano, and her husband Emanuele Izquierdo, who emerges from this recording (not a Pathé, but an HMV dating from 1907) as an imposing dramatic tenor.

With a composer, an operatic soprano and the highest paid baritone in the world amongst their six children there must have been more to the Titta parents than met the eye, and it is an attractive idea, I find, that the star of the family should have ensured his brother's and sister's immortality on gramophone records. This, though, was typical of Ruffo. He was a man with pronounced ideas about his responsibilities and on several occasions during his life he unhesitatingly put what he saw as his duty before his own personal interests. During the years immediately preceding the First World War he sang principally in North and South America with very few performances in Italy, and yet in 1916, at the age of thirty-nine, he decided to go back home and join the armed forces. He was at the peak of his career, a man of wealth and fame, and yet he chose to serve in the ranks, eventually rising to corporal. Between September 1916 and December 1918, when he could have been making a fortune on the other side of the Atlantic, he appeared precisely three times in public, once as Tonio in Nice, once in the same role in the Opéra-Comique in Paris, both times for the benefit of soldiers suffering from tuberculosis, and once in a concert in a French military hospital. Even when the war was over he did not feel vocally ready to return to the States until 1920, and thus during what would probably have been the last five years of his genuine prime he did not make one single gramophone recording.

In the politically turbulent years between the two world wars most opera singers managed to keep their heads down, but Ruffo was not a man who stepped out of trouble's path. In June 1924, while he was singing a performance as Rigoletto in Bogotà, Colombia, he received a telegram informing him that the Italian socialist leader Giacomo Matteotti, who was married to his sister Velia, was missing; he had apparently been kidnapped by henchmen of Mussolini's and was assumed to be dead. Ruffo promptly cancelled all his contracts for the next few months and travelled to Italy to be near his sister. For a time it appeared that the general outcry over what became known as 'the affair Matteotti' might sway public opinion against the fascist party, but Mussolini was ultimately left in a stronger position than ever. When Matteotti's body was discovered two months later Ruffo played a prominent part in the funeral and from then onwards he became a marked man. In October of the following year he returned to his native Pisa to give two benefit performances in the role of Hamlet and his grateful admirers in that city decided to commemorate his appearances with a plaque in the Teatro Verdi. Soon afterwards the Italian ambassador in Buenos Aires started supplying the government in Rome with fictitious reports of Ruffo stirring up anti-fascist sentiment in South America, whereupon the plaque was smashed to pieces by a gang of blackshirts. Ruffo never sang in Italy again; he decided to leave the luxurious villa which he had had built in Rome (complete with wrought-iron decorations designed by himself) and move to France, though even there he was not immune. In February 1931 he was set on by hired thugs as he approached the stage door of the Casino Municipal in Marseilles, where he was due to sing Rossini's Figaro; bruised and shaken though he was he went through with the performance. Worse was to come. In October 1937, when he went on a family visit to Rome, he was arrested and imprisoned on the personal instructions of Mussolini. International protests led to his release only three days later, but the authorities impounded his passport and he was unable to leave the country again until the war was over.

On 14 May 1945, only six days after VE-Day, Ruffo had the pleasure of being present when his fellow citizens in Pisa organised a ceremony for the reinstatement of the plaque in the Teatro Verdi. In his old age he lived on a modest scale – he had lost a fortune during the Wall Street crash of 1929, just as his earning capacity was on the wane – but at least his reputation had been restored. His son, Dr Ruffo Titta, has left a touching description of his father as an essentially extrovert man, a brilliant conversationalist, mimic and anecdotalist, but subject to periods of deep depression, during which he would 'isolate himself in profound silence'. Significantly, when asked why he did not give singing lessons Ruffo used to reply that it would be immoral to take money off people for instructing them in something which he himself had never understood.

For one vivid glimpse of him in his declining years I would like to turn again to the memoirs of Tito Gobbi. Gobbi was engaged to sing Rigoletto in Pisa soon after the war and shortly before the performance someone rushed into his dressing-room in great excitement saying 'The Maestro has arrived!' In Italian the conductor is always referred to as '*il maestro*', so Gobbi felt that it would be odd if he had not arrived. When the next person came bursting in with the words 'The Maestro is in the house!' Gobbi asked 'Whereabouts in the house?' and was perplexed to receive the answer 'In his box of course!' It was then explained

to him that in Pisa 'the Maestro' only meant one man – Titta
Ruffo. After the performance Gobbi had hardly begun to remove
his make-up when he heard the dramatic announcement: 'The
Maestro is coming!' He rose to his feet and, to quote Gobbi's
own words, in came 'about the most imposing figure I had ever
seen. He stood just inside the doorway, dwarfing everything and
everyone, and in deep, resonant tones he announced to the people
accompanying him: "There are only two singers worthy to play
Rigoletto in this house. One is Titta Ruffo and the other is Tito
Gobbi." ' Gobbi, the greatest Italian baritone of his generation,
felt that he had arrived.

ELISABETH SCHUMANN

GERMAN SOPRANO

b. Merseburg, Saxony, 13 June 1888
d. New York, 23 April 1952

Without my realising it at the time Elisabeth Schumann was the first great singer I ever heard; not in the flesh, but on my parents' wind-up gramophone. Their somewhat haphazard collection of records stretched from the various musical comedy stars who had brightened my father's life while he was home on leave from the First World War – Basil Hallam, George Grossmith, Gertie Millar, Melville Gideon and other such grand old names – to Noël Coward, Maurice Chevalier and Fred Astaire; but somehow or other, as an unexpected interloper, there also was this lady called Elisabeth Schumann on a ten-inch record with the special HMV black label singing two songs from what I later learnt to be Viennese operettas. They were 'Sei nicht bös' from Zeller's DER OBERSTEIGER and 'Wie mein Ahn'l' from the same composer's DER VOGELHÄNDLER, the latter sung in delightfully accented English and embellished with a marvellously whistled imitation of a nightingale, complete with trills and all. I used to play this record with particular avidity and though I cannot pretend that at that age I appreciated the finer points of Mme Schumann's vocalisation, looking back on it now I realise that I had succumbed to the most conspicuous of her many virtues; more than any other soprano I can think of she possessed that elusive quality – charm.

Elisabeth Schumann was born on 13 June 1888 in the provincial Saxon town of Merseburg, into a highly musical family. Her father was a schoolteacher and his modest salary was earned teaching several subjects which were more or less of a chore to him; it was in his ancillary activities as piano teacher, assistant cathedral organist and conductor of the local choral society that his enthusiasm lay. His wife was a good enough soprano to undertake important solos in the cathedral and when Elisabeth showed early signs of musicality both parents seized upon them eagerly and did everything possible to foster her talents. There can certainly be no doubt about her innate ability as a mimic because by the age of four she had picked up enough from listening to her mother's singing to cause quite a stir in family circles as a sort of Wunderkind vocalist, and it was by imitating the family canary that she perfected her extraordinary technique as a whistler. In any case her parents were quite set on their daughter becoming a singer – a refreshing change from all the stories one reads of parents who were equally determined that their daughters should not – and they saw to it that she received all the necessary grounding such as piano playing and musical theory. She also caught the opera bug while still unusually young. She was taken at the age of seven to see TANNHÄUSER in the neighbouring town of Halle – such were, and still are, the cultural opportunities in provincial Germany – and a couple of years later when a visiting company came to Merseburg's own Tivoli Theatre she used to climb out of bed, get herself dressed and smuggle herself out of the house and into the theatre while her parents assumed that she was all tucked up and fast asleep.

Schumann was still only sixteen when she set off to Dresden to start serious vocal training. The teacher whom she was originally intending to go to turned out to be a gorgon and Schumann felt that one encounter had been enough, but through the good offices of one of the most illustrious cultural figures in Dresden, Professor Felix Draeseke, she soon fell into kindlier hands, those of a lady named Natalie Hänisch. After only three months of instruction Frau Hänisch selected her to perform in one of the regular house concerts at which the pick of her pupils sang to an invited audience of Dresden's musical *cognoscenti*, and with her performance of Zerlina's 'Batti, batti' from DON GIOVANNI Schumann even managed to secure her first pat on the back in the international press. The audience included the musical correspondent of a German–American paper who described the débutante as 'a young girl yet in her teens, but a future Sembrich,* the owner of a deliciously warbling soprano voice'.

Schumann naturally attended performances in the Dresden opera house as often as she could, and there the great event of 1905 was the unveiling of Richard Strauss's explosive new opera SALOME. Schumann was one of those who were swept off their feet by the flood of exotic tonal effects unleashed in Strauss's revolutionary score, but in the more conservative musical circles to which she had been admitted through the good graces of Frau Hänisch and Professor Draeseke Strauss was regarded as something of an abomination. Schumann began to feel out of sympathy with her surroundings, and believing also that she had learnt all she could from Frau Hänisch she departed for the more progressive ambience of Berlin. There she lodged in an intriguingly bohemian household; had her parents known that the couple who headed it were not even married – or not, at least, to one another – they would never have countenanced their daughter staying there for a single night.

Schumann continued her studies with a well-known contralto named Valerie Zitelmann, only to change again after a year or so to one of the sopranos of the Berlin Hofoper, Marie Dietrich, and it is a noticeable thread running through her early life that however often she hopped from one situation to the next her path was always eased by recommendations from influential sources – something which resulted, I have no doubt, from the powerful combination of a captivating personality and a talent that brooked no denial. At one point, for instance, she needed an eminent musician to support her application for one of the keenly sought-after scholarships offered to young musicians of outstanding promise who wanted to attend the Wagner festival in Bayreuth. She turned to her old benefactor Professor Draeseke, and despite her defection

---

* The Polish soprano Marcella Sembrich (1858–1935) was widely regarded as the outstanding coloratura soprano of her generation.

from Dresden he did not hesitate to write what was required of him. It was a personal recommendation, too, which brought about her first operatic engagement. This was in 1908 as Aennchen in DER FREISCHÜTZ, with a Berlin company called the Lortzing Sommeroper, which, as its name implies, limited its activities to productions during the summer months. It seems to have been a somewhat ramshackle outfit, because when Schumann went to her dressing-room on the evening of her supposed début she found it already occupied by another young lady who told her in no uncertain terms that she and not Schumann was the Aennchen of the evening, and so would Schumann kindly close the door on her way out?

When Schumann did finally get her hands on the role she acquitted herself nobly, and for someone who had had no theatrical training she felt remarkably at home on stage. She was also beginning to pick up occasional engagements for concerts and oratorios, and by the spring of the following year her career was well and truly launched, when she went to Hamburg to visit her boyfriend and on the spur of the moment breezed into the opera house and asked for an audition. Nowadays that would not be at all the way to set about things, but back in 1909 there were no opera schools in which the companies could do their talent-spotting and nothing much in the way of agents to promote promising new artists. In any case, nobody seemed surprised that a young girl should come in off the street asking if someone would like to hear her sing, and the initial briskness of the gentleman deputed to deal with Schumann vanished when she was halfway through her first song. Without more ado she was whisked from the chorus master's room onto the empty stage, one of those dreaded voices from the darkness asked if she happened to know any of Aennchen's music from DER FREISCHÜTZ, and within minutes she was in the director's office clutching a three-year contract.

It is impossible to exaggerate the value of a contract such as Schumann's in a young singer's development. Beginners' salaries in the German houses may never have been princely, but to have three years in which you do not have to wonder where your next engagement will be coming from, in which you can build up a repertoire and find out which roles suit you and which do not, and in which you can be steadily learning your trade from the resident musical and production staffs and from working alongside the established members of the ensemble is invaluable. Sadly this sort of experience is unavailable in countries whose opera houses do not maintain a company as such but merely engage their singers according to the requirements of each successive production. Schumann opened her account in Hamburg with the Shepherd Boy in TANNHÄUSER, followed by other small but important roles such as the First Boy in DIE ZAUBERFLÖTE and Pepa in TIEFLAND. Gradually she climbed the ladder to her familiar FREISCHÜTZ Aennchen and the title-role in Ambroise Thomas's MIGNON, in which she captivated one of the critics with 'the childlike quality, the charm of innocence with which her Mignon was imbued'; and then, still in only her second year, she was considered ready for the role which more than any other will, I fancy, remain identified with the name of Elisabeth Schumann.

On 26 January 1911 the world première of Richard Strauss's latest novelty DER ROSENKAVALIER took place in the Dresden Court Opera, and the highlight of the season in Hamburg was to be their first production of the piece in the following month. The chief conductor in Hamburg, Gustav Brecher, had promised the role of Sophie to the up-and-coming young soprano Lotte Lehmann, who had joined the company a year later than Schumann and who had no idea that Schumann had also been given the part to study. When it came to the final decision it was Schumann who was chosen for the première; although Lehmann had the richer, more powerful voice, Schumann with her extra stage experience had the edge on her as an actress. For a time this brought a sharp halt to the burgeoning friendship between the two young sopranos, because Lehmann could not imagine that she had been robbed of the role by any means other than subterfuge and intrigue. She soon came to recognise, however, that if there was one colleague in the business who would never stoop to such methods it was Elisabeth Schumann, and their happy relationship, once restored, lasted until the end of Schumann's life. Lehmann did subsequently enjoy great success as Sophie, but the selection of Schumann for the Hamburg première was amply justified by the results. Both vocally and visually it would indeed be hard to imagine a more perfect vehicle for the twenty-two-year-old Schumann than Sophie, the ingenue fresh from the convent, but who, by pouring out her charmingly naïve emotions in a stream of high-lying, swooning Straussian melody, needs only a couple of pages of the score to drive all thoughts of Octavian's passion for the Marschallin clean out of his head; and who, despite her girlish innocence, ends up getting exactly what she wants. Schumann was small and provocatively pretty, and her voice was characterised by a purity of tone and ease of emission ideal for the expression of childlike heedlessness. It is, moreover, quite remarkable that although it was to be twenty-two years before she made the immortal Viennese recording of ROSENKAVALIER excerpts with Lotte Lehmann as the Marschallin, Maria Olczewska as Octavian and Richard Mayr as Ochs, her voice still emerges from it as the ideal instrument for the role.*

This famous old recording has now been reissued as a two-CD set by two different companies – Pearl have it on GEMM *CDS 9365* and EMI on *CHS 7 64487 2*. My personal preference is probably for the EMI issue, not only for its sound quality but also for the fact that the second disc is completed by a superb selection of Strauss Lieder sung by Schumann and Lehmann, of which more anon. In any case, whichever the label, Elisabeth Schumann emerges

---

* Physically she had filled out a bit by then, and it was typical of her that she was highly amused when Richard Mayr suggested an alteration to the text. It would be appropriate, he felt, if the expression '*hundsmager*', roughly equivalent to 'thin as a rake', with which Ochs comments on Sophie's figure, were to be changed to '*schön mollert*' ('nice and chubby').

not only as a vocalist of rare technical perfection but also as
a musical and theatrical personality of disarming vivacity. The
schoolgirl whose 'Die Mutter ist tot und ich bin ganz allein'
('My mother is dead and I am quite alone') touches the heart with
its wistfulness, becomes in a flash a very different creature, wide
awake to life's possibilities, as the Cavalier of the Rose appears
before the house in his magnificent carriage; she cannot suppress
the exclamation that though she knows Pride to be a Grievous Sin
she really cannot be expected to conduct herself with humility in
the middle of quite such resplendent goings-on. It is, however,
the ravishing phrase with which she accepts the silver rose which
will, not only for those of an older generation who saw her in
the role but also for many of us who first became acquainted
with DER ROSENKAVALIER via this recording, remain for
ever Schumann's personal property. In this respect (though not,
I hasten to add, in any other) it is somewhat akin to Edith Evans's
'A handbag?' in *The Importance of Being Earnest* – you hear it
excellently done by other performers, but somehow it is the one
version, the ultimate rendering, that you have indelibly in your
ear. The silvery, shimmering quality of Schumann's voice might
have been created to fit not only the music but even the décor
of this particular scene, and she manages to bring to the words
'Wie himmlische, nicht irdische, wie Rosen vom hochheiligen
Paradies' ('Like heavenly roses, not earthly ones, roses from the
holiest paradise') the freshness and the breathless wonder of a
young girl smitten for the very first time – breathless, I must
emphasise, only in the expression with which she clothes the text,
because as an example of breath control her floating of these taxing
phrases could serve as an object lesson to anyone.* Another aspect
of Schumann's expertise revealed by these dauntingly exposed
phrases is her mastery of the difficult art of keeping every vowel
identically placed in the flow of sound, so that, for instance, the

---

*   Breath control had given Schumann some problems during her first season, and
it was after Lehmann had recommended her own teacher, Alma Schadow, to her
that she really mastered its complexities.

shift from an 'Ah' to an 'Ee' does not dislodge the even emission
of tone. At the same time, of course, the vowel sounds must be
differentiated in order to remain intelligible, and never more so
than in this very scene, which contains a trap for the unwary.
Sophie's next phrase, 'Ist wie ein Gruss vom Himmel' ('It is like a
greeting from Heaven'), takes her by means of an octave leap onto
a high B flat on the awkward first syllable of the word 'Himmel';
but singers who round the 'Him–' sound into a more ingratiating
'Ham–' produce a somewhat unfortunate effect, '*Hammel*' being
the German word for a wether, or neutered male sheep.

It is not only in the Presentation of the Silver Rose that
Schumann's Sophie excels, but also through the seraphic ease
with which she glides along the top line in the final trio and duet.
Not even the best Sophie should be able to dominate a well-cast
ROSENKAVALIER but if you play your cards right you can
steal a scene or two, as Schumann certainly proved when she used
the role as her visiting card for three important débuts – the Metropolitan Opera in 1914, the Vienna State Opera five years later
and Covent Garden in 1924. When Schumann travelled to New
York for the first time the First World War had already begun
and transatlantic travel was beginning to involve a certain degree
of risk, but the Metropolitan Opera was nevertheless prepared to
put a remarkable number of its most valuable eggs in one basket
– Schumann's travelling companions on the liner *Canopic* included Caruso, Destinn, Farrar, Hempel, Bori, Scotti and Toscanini!
During a five-month season at the Met Schumann gave forty-five
performances in ten different roles, including Musetta in LA
BOHEME, Marzelline in FIDELIO and Gretel in HÄNSEL UND
GRETEL, and as she enjoyed invariable success it seems strange
that she was never invited back. She did in fact perform there
once again, though not in opera; it was her very last appearance
in New York and it was part of a benefit concert in 1951. As she
waited in the wings the master of ceremonies announced her as 'a
beloved artist who, when she last stood on this stage, was in the
company of Caruso and Farrar'; before making her entrance she

turned to her accompanist and whispered 'Golden Age, here we come!'

Schumann's Vienna début was one of vital importance to her because she had been engaged in somewhat controversial circumstances at the express request of Richard Strauss, who had just been appointed co-director of the State Opera. Vienna is a city in which the Opera stands at the hub not only of artistic but also of political life, and for people who might have felt inclined to attack Strauss's appointment but did not quite dare to, attacking his favourite singers was an attractive alternative. In fact Schumann survived her initial baptism of fire with flying colours, harvesting enthusiastic reviews not only for her Sophie, but also for her Micaëla in CARMEN and her Blonde in DIE ENTFÜHRUNG, which followed within the same week. The backlash was to come a couple of months later, when word got around that Strauss was aiming to bring Schumann's then husband, one of the Hamburg house conductors named Carl Alwin,* to the State Opera when in the opinion of certain of the Viennese critics he was not of the required standard. One in particular, the influential Max Graf, let rip on the subject. Under the title *Freunderlwirtschaft*, which one could loosely translate as 'How to look after your little friends', he claimed that Strauss, instead of employing one of the many talented young Austrian conductors who were unable to find a job, was engaging an old crony so that the two of them could play cards together while Frau Strauss and Elisabeth Schumann settled down to a good gossip. This brought the formidable Pauline Strauss leaping into print to point out that not only had her husband and Herr Alwin never played cards together but they hardly knew one another, and that she had spoken to Frau Schumann precisely once in her whole life. For a time the storm abated but the anti-Alwin sniping went on, with the critic Julius Korngold, father of the composer Erich Korngold, taking up the cudgels. At least he

---

* Although record companies persist in spelling his name Karl, Carl is actually correct.

delivered himself of one entertaining witticism when Alwin conducted a piece by a composer of modest reputation named Julius
Bittner and was written up by Korngold as 'the eminent Bittner
conductor'; but it was all grist to the mill of those who were
aiming at Strauss's removal, and who by 1924 had achieved their
object.*

Schumann's first meeting with Strauss had taken place in May
1917 when she sang Zerlina under his baton during a Mozart festival in Zurich. He had long heard glowing reports of her Sophie
and when he encountered her in person he was not disappointed
– he even volunteered to act as her accompanist when she sang
some of his songs at a concert in a Swiss internment camp. 'He
is a wonderful accompanist,' she later wrote. 'I have never before
heard the sound of a whole orchestra come from a piano.' To
anyone who has heard Schumann's Mozart recordings it will not
come as a surprise that Strauss was equally enthusiastic about
the sounds that came from her. One of the necessities for good
Mozart singing is to aim at vocal and musical flawlessness without
becoming dull in the process, and while it would be hard to fault
the purity of Schumann's style she never loses her sense of fun.
Eight Mozart titles form part of an excellently varied portrait of
her on *Lebendige Vergangenheit CD 89031*, most of them recorded
while she was in London in 1926 for her third Grand Opera Season
at Covent Garden, appearing as Zerlina, Susanna in LE NOZZE DI
FIGARO and Eva in DIE MEISTERSINGER. Her Sophie in each
of the previous two seasons had established her as a favourite with
the London public† and her Mozart roles were eagerly awaited.
As Zerlina she was in starry company – Frida Leider as Donna

---

* Removing famous conductors from the directorship of the State Opera is a
favourite Viennese sport. During my own time there as a student in the
Musikakademie I watched Böhm and Karajan come and go, and there have been
others since.

† Two appearances as the Composer in ARIADNE AUF NAXOS had failed to set
the Thames on fire, but it was the opera itself which disappointed rather than the
singers, and the low-lying role of the Composer was in any case scarcely natural
Schumann territory.

Anna, Lotte Lehmann as Donna Elvira and Mariano Stabile as the Don, with Bruno Walter in the pit – but even so she came close to running away with the notices. The *Evening Standard* considered that she gave 'by far the best performance of the three ladies' and a now defunct journal with the challenging name of *Truth* found that she 'sang and acted to perfection' and that 'her singing of "Batti, batti" and her cajoling of Masetto were perfect examples of the grace and vivacity of this charming Viennese singer'. When one listens to her recordings of the two DON GIOVANNI arias it is difficult not to feel that though this forthright representative of *Truth* may have been a few hundred miles off target with his allusion to her place of origin, with his assessment of her Zerlina he had scored a bull's-eye. Schumann manages to be coquettish without being arch, which is always such a relief, and she allows the seductiveness of text and music to speak for themselves. If her Susanna created less of a stir in the British press than her Zerlina it was largely because at that moment the papers had little space for anything other than the General Strike. To judge by her recording of 'Deh vieni, non tardar', my personal favourite of all Mozart's soprano arias, she could not have failed to bring the house down; the tone is so exquisitely poised, the effort employed *appears* to be precisely nil, and the whole thing breathes, exactly as it should, the enchantment of a moonlit summer night.

As an example of both Mozart and Schumann in an entirely different mood the same disc offers us her gloriously ebullient version of the 'Alleluia' from the Motet 'Exsultate jubilate', the bursts of coloratura spurting forth with joyous abandon; while in a lesser known piece, the aria 'L'amerò, sarò costante' from IL RE PASTORE, whose formidable technical demands Schumann takes in her stride, it is interesting to note how the natural brilliance of her vocal quality could be shaded into a more tragic timbre should the nature of the music require it. Two Bach tracks, 'Aus Liebe will mein Heiland sterben' and 'Es ist vollbracht', also emphasise that Schumann's voice, light though it was, was less limited than one might suppose in its range of expression. With the bubbling femininity of the more 'soubrettish' operatic numbers held in total check it takes on an almost instrumental quality – Strauss, indeed, was fond of telling her 'You sing like a violin' – and when His Master's Voice decided in 1929 to undertake the first full recording of the B MINOR MASS it was to Schumann that they turned as their soprano soloist, planning their recording dates to fit in with her limited availability during that year's Grand Season at Covent Garden.*

To revert, though, from the sacred to the profane this same disc includes two more Mozart arias, from FIGARO again, but this time presenting Schumann in the role which she habitually sang in her early Hamburg days, that of the girl-crazy page-boy Cherubino. Here her voice positively pulsates with a sub-text of potential naughtiness, and this very role did indeed set off a chain of events which led to Schumann becoming the pivotal figure in the twentieth century's most seismic operatic scandal. Schumann had a weakness for men of passionate artistic convictions, and she found herself strongly drawn to a gangling, intense young man who joined the Hamburg company as a staff conductor at the beginning of her second year there – one Otto Klemperer. He too was greatly taken by Schumann and was so enthralled by her in the 'breeches part' of Cherubino that he urged her to abandon the role of Sophie in DER ROSENKAVALIER and switch to the young nobleman Octavian. Artistically it was a disastrous idea, because the role simply did not lie right for Schumann's voice, but that was the least of the problems involved. Klemperer invited Schumann to his flat to rehearse, one thing led to another and in no time they were in love – a situation which would not have bothered anybody if it were not for the fact that only eighteen

---

* This classic recording, featuring the contralto Margaret Balfour, the tenor Walter Widdop and the great Wagnerian baritone Friedrich Schorr, with the Philharmonic Choir and the London Symphony Orchestra under Albert Coates, is now available, along with every one of Schumann's individual Bach recordings, as a Pearl two-CD set on GEMM *CDS 9900*, and is strongly recommended to anyone interested in the history of Bach singing.

months earlier Schumann had at last married her fiancé of several
years' standing, a young architect named Walther Puritz. When
she fled the marital nest to be with Klemperer, Puritz called in
the police and for a short time even had her incarcerated in a
psychiatric clinic. He challenged Klemperer to a duel with pistols
– he was a keen member of his old student corps, very proud of
his duelling scars – and although Klemperer attempted to laugh
it off by announcing that if Herr Puritz wanted to go shooting
he should find some wild duck, he was sufficiently alarmed to
travel round Hamburg in a closed carriage with the blinds drawn
down.

Eventually, on 26 December 1912, things came to a head.
Schumann was in a box in the opera house watching Klemperer
conduct LOHENGRIN. She noticed that several seats immediately behind the conductor's podium were empty, and when she
saw her husband heading for them at the end of the second
interval with a group of his friends she scribbled a note to
Klemperer, warning him to watch out for trouble. He conducted
the last act apparently unperturbed until, during the orchestra's
final bars, Puritz leapt up and shouted 'Klemperer, turn round!'
As Klemperer did so Puritz drew a riding crop from his sleeve,
slashed the conductor twice across the face and sent him tumbling into the pit. Lotte Lehmann, the evening's Elsa, was later
to describe to Klemperer's biographer Peter Heyworth how he
clambered back 'like a huge black spider', and attempted to join
battle, but Puritz's friends were already leading him from the scene
and Klemperer contented himself with making an announcement
to the public, who had of course been following these stirring
events with no little curiosity. 'Herr Puritz has attacked me', he
cried, 'because I love his wife. Good evening.' The following day
both parties in the affray made statements to the press, Klemperer
solemnly declaring (and Schumann, to the end of her life, avowed
the truth of his words) that 'no damage had occurred to Herr
Puritz's marital rights'. This aspect of the situation, however,
underwent a change when the two of them disappeared together

from Hamburg, leading to the suspension of both their contracts.

It was a story with a woefully banal conclusion. Schumann and Klemperer were unable to find work together in any other theatre – Puritz had written to several managements threatening legal action – and Klemperer, who was a manic-depressive, found as his euphoric stage evaporated that his feelings for Schumann were no longer as intense as he had supposed; his psychiatrist was given the painful task of explaining to Schumann that her *grand amour* was at an end. She was lucky enough to be taken back both by the Hamburg Opera and by her husband, to whom in July 1914 she bore a son. The marriage, though, was not destined to survive, and indeed, though Schumann was a lovely person to have as a friend, she appears to have been emotionally too restless for the state of wedlock. When two young people happen to feel lonely in the same place at the same time music can be a quick builder of bridges – one artistically harmonious rehearsal can stir sympathetic feelings a great deal faster than any number of dinner-party conversations – and by 1917 Schumann had fallen for her new accompanist, Carl Gotthardt. This led to the final split with her husband and even for a time to a break with her parents, who not only accused her of behaving like a whore but also tried to claim one-sixth of her income as recompense for their own financial sacrifices during the period of her training. Next came her marriage to the mercurial Carl Alwin, but after a dozen years of that she was ready for another change and varied the pattern by falling for a pedantic Viennese dermatologist named Dr Hans Krüger. By the time she married Krüger she was already aware that she no longer loved him, but it was Hitler time, they were both facing emigration to America and it seemed the sensible thing to do. That union was duly brought to an end by her third divorce in twenty-six years; a depressing record for someone of such a boundlessly affectionate nature.

To return, though, to the *Lebendige Vergangenheit* CD. Apart from a winningly crisp and chirpy version of Handel's 'O hätte ich Jubal's Harf' ' the rest of the disc is devoted to Lieder, with

Strauss, Marx, Mozart, Mahler and Schumann all represented. If I had to select a personal favourite from amongst the baker's dozen under offer it might well be Robert Schumann's 'Aufträge', a perfect example of the enchanting neatness of Schumann's vocalisation. It is a rapid song, marked by the composer *'Leicht, zart'* ('Light, delicate'), and although her voice scampers effortlessly along the vocal line it does not miss a single one of the subtle little points which are lurking in the text. In the poem a rippling wave, a flitting dove and a shimmering moonbeam are each given the task of delivering a message to her boyfriend. Each one is addressed in a minutely different tone of voice – she cannot, we are told, deliver the message herself owing to pressure of time – and at the end of the song, which has so far lain comfortably in the middle of the voice, Schumann serves up her million-dollar trick by launching into the final phrase with a surprise high A attack taken with the ease of a swallow in full flight.

Schumann never retired from the operatic stage, she simply ceased to appear on it. On 1 November 1937 she sang the unremarkable role of the First Flower Maiden in PARSIFAL in the Vienna State Opera and then set off for various concerts and recordings in England and America. She was briefly back in Vienna in March 1938; on the very day that the German troops marched in she left on a tour of France and North Africa, and from then on her professional life was restricted to recital work and teaching. In fact even if the advent of Hitler had not forced this sudden change upon her it is doubtful whether she would have carried on for much longer in opera. Hers was a voice ideally suited to ingenue roles, and though the instrument itself had lost so little of its vernal appeal a soprano of over fifty is unlikely to go on feeling at home in that particular repertoire. For someone whose voice-type hovered between the light lyric and the soubrette Schumann had actually managed to tackle a surprisingly wide range. You do not, for instance, normally expect the same singer to appear in the same week as the social-climbing chambermaid Adele in DIE

FLEDERMAUS, full of pert witticisms and cheeky coloratura, and as Eva in DIE MEISTERSINGER, but Schumann did so at Covent Garden in May 1930 and with resounding success.

The FLEDERMAUS production, the first ever mounted at Covent Garden, was conducted by Bruno Walter and enjoyed such a triumph that an extra performance had to be inserted into the season to enable King George V and Queen Mary to attend. Schumann's Adele was one of its prime attractions and though it is true to say that if you cannot steal the show as Adele you are in the wrong business, it must have been harder to do so than usual with such formidable competitors as Lotte Lehmann, Maria Olczewska and Gerhard Hüsch in the cast. The critic of the *Manchester Guardian* used an apt expression when he described the 'feline grace' of Schumann's voice as being exactly suited to the part. He also found that she acted it 'with inimitable drollery', while his colleague on the *Yorkshire Post* went so far as to say that if she had had no singing voice she would assuredly have found fame as a straight actress. In one way I imagine it must have been a particular pleasure for Schumann to play the role in London, because Adele's dialogue is largely written to exploit the Viennese dialect and the public in Vienna can be understandably sniffy about German singers trying to imitate the way they speak – a few years earlier her old sparring partner Julius Korngold had had some fun referring to her Adele as 'a chambermaid from a good North German family'.*

To judge from the rest of her repertoire Adele would certainly seem to have been more natural Schumann territory than DIE MEISTERSINGER, but when one listens to the famous 1931 recording of the Act III Quintet, with Friedrich Schorr as Sachs and Melchior as Walther, it becomes less surprising that she should have been in demand as Eva, not only in London but in several other major houses too. This has now become available on a four-

---

* Another chambermaid who made a brief appearance in Schumann's repertoire was the jazz-crazy Yvonne in Krenek's JONNY SPIELT AUF. She made her first entrance pushing a vacuum-cleaner and dancing a Charleston.

CD set entitled 'Wagner Singing on Record' (EMI *CMS 7 64008 2*) and the long, sustained opening solo of this matchless piece of music provides a perfect example of the formidable strength of Schumann's 'support' – the voice itself may glide along with weightless ease, but the projection is exemplary and the muscles that do the work are under iron control. In the making of this particular recording it was in fact not the only form of iron control which Schumann needed to exercise, because Lauritz Melchior, who had never sung the role of Walther on stage, came in wrong, not once but four times running. The mood of Eva's solo passage is one of cloudless bliss, but as Schumann found herself launching into it for the fifth time in succession she must have been harbouring a few rather less than blissful thoughts about the Great Dane. This time, however, the conductor, John Barbirolli, coaxed him through it without mishap, and as the final result proves, Schumann's customary spontaneity had somehow survived intact, suffusing her opening line, 'Selig, wie die Sonne meines Glückes lacht', with all the golden promise of a sunlit midsummer morning – such is the power of professionalism. When, in 1951, Schumann was invited to be the castaway in the popular BBC radio programme 'Desert Island Discs' this was one of the eight records which she chose to keep her company. I am not surprised – it is a superb piece of singing.

It was early on in Schumann's career that she turned her attention to the singing of Lieder, and in 1921 came one of her most formative experiences, when she was engaged for a North American tour of sixteen concerts with Richard Strauss as her accompanist. It was a habit of Strauss's to start the day grumpy and unapproachable, then gradually to polish up his mood until by the time a concert began he would be relaxed and charming, with his total confidence in Schumann's ability lending her extra encouragement. He could be remarkably mean – he was delighted with himself when he saved 50 cents by getting his son to clean his shoes instead of having the hotel bootboy do it – and Schumann regarded it as a major triumph when she beat Strauss father and son at poker during one of their train journeys. 'Took $2.60 off them,' she wrote. 'Ha, ha!' Musically Strauss was a source of endless stimulation, and in his own songs he would regularly suggest variants of phrase and nuance, little improvements on the original. In the thirteen Strauss songs which complete the EMI ROSENKAVALIER set to which I have already referred (*CHS 7 64487 2*) they crop up again and again, and I think one can safely assume that whenever Schumann departs from the letter of the song as printed it is an alteration which had had the composer's blessing. It is one of those odd things about the musical profession that once a composer is dead every semiquaver rest becomes sacrosanct, whereas living composers tend to adopt a much more relaxed attitude towards their own music. Strauss often encouraged Schumann to be less concerned about accuracy and to indulge herself more, particularly on some of the high notes – nowadays the ultimate sin, leading to many a critical rap over singers' knuckles. On one occasion when she asked him if she had lingered adequately on a certain climactic tone he replied with a smile *'Ja, aber mit einer inneren Verlegenheit'* ('Yes, but with an inner embarrassment'). Despite this musical fastidiousness, however, Schumann was absolutely not one of those Lieder singers who end up giving a dry-as-dust performance. Every one of the thirteen songs on this particular disc is illumined by the vividness of her own personality, whether it be the rapt serenity of 'Morgen' and 'Freundliche Vision', songs which seem to hang in the air in a state of musically suspended animation, or the chatty exuberance of 'Schlechtes Wetter', a brand-new song on that American trip, and one that brought every house down. The only one of the sixteen audiences which might conceivably have been disappointed was that in St Louis, as the press had prepared them for an even more exceptional event than a Schumann–Richard Strauss concert. Accompanied by a photograph of the famous statue of Johann Strauss II (d. 1899) in the Vienna Stadtpark one paper announced 'The Waltz King is in Town'!

The composer who stood at the centre of Elisabeth Schumann's

Lieder repertoire was predictably Franz Schubert, and on an invaluable EMI two-CD set (*CHS 7 63040 2*) we are treated to no less than forty-nine Schubert recordings, dating from November 1927 right up to her final session in the EMI studios in October 1949, when she was sixty-one years old. By the time Schumann gave her first Lieder recital in London, on 25 January 1926, she was already a favourite with the opera-going public, but nevertheless, for the purposes of a recital largely devoted to Lieder she was still obliged to hire the Wigmore Hall at her own financial risk. It turned out to be a sound investment; the dividends were a useful financial profit (£40, round about £1000 by today's reckoning) and a huge artistic triumph. The critic of *The Daily Telegraph* wrote that 'Many people must have asked themselves whether they had ever heard finer Lieder-singing', and readers of *The Times* were informed that 'her hearers revelled in every subtle nuance of phrase and diction, every hint of personal feeling which she knows so well how to give without destroying the classical purity of her voice and style'. He added that although on this occasion the hall was not quite full, next time it would certainly be crowded, and it was indeed the beginning of a long love affair between Elisabeth Schumann and the British concert public.*

The success of the recital also helped His Master's Voice to decide that there would be a market for her Lieder records and all these years later the artistry of Elisabeth Schumann still lends an unfading glow to every one of the performances on the EMI CDs. I will content myself with mentioning only a few of the many titles involved, and I would suggest that anyone wanting to dip into the set to catch the special flavour of a Schumann–Schubert rendering should start with 'Das Lied im Grünen'. Musically the song is an outburst of high spirits; it sets off at a spanking pace

---

* Those who believe that the day before yesterday was always a golden age may be interested to know that the *Times* review ended with the words: 'Her whole performance reasserted artistic standards which have been lamentably lost sight of in the recent dearth of first-rate singers.'

and it contains masses and masses of text. Now, at this speed, and with so many words to think about, it is easy to let detail go to the four winds, but the manner in which Schumann pronounces 'Da lockt uns der Frühling' ('There the Spring calls to us'), in the very first line lets us know that even in this cascade of poetry not a syllable is going to be taken for granted. There is a sort of chuckle to it, with a momentary lingering on the 'l' of the word 'lockt', but it is obviously not something that she sat at home pondering over; it is something that she did, it is over in a flash and it is marvellous, and again and again throughout these songs it is this delighted reaction of her own to the subtlety and beauty of Schubert's settings that produces these minute but unforgettable responses. At that first Wigmore Hall recital 'Das Lied im Grünen' had to be repeated – as the *Times* critic put it, 'its buoyant rhythm had specially delighted her audience.'

With a voice of her lightness Schumann was naturally more limited in her choice of songs than, say, a Lotte Lehmann, a Janet Baker or a Felicity Lott, but she was extremely perceptive about what did and did not suit her. It would be a mistake, too, to suppose that hers was an instrument which could only laugh its way through 'Seligkeit' or tell the simple tale of 'Heidenröslein' or 'Die Forelle'. These are indeed miniature masterpieces – and her version of 'Der Hirt auf dem Felsen'* with the clarinettist Reginald Kell and the pianist George Reeves qualifies, I think, as a major masterpiece – but there is plenty of heart-break to be found in Schumann's 'Gretchen am Spinnrade' and plenty of grief for the woes of life in her 'Der Jüngling und der Tod'. She herself, after all, though she may have been all smiles to the outside world, had had plenty to cry over in her time.

I myself only heard Schumann once in the flesh, in 1948. I

---

* A year after making this recording she sang the song with Frederick Thurston as her clarinettist at a Promenade Concert in the Queen's Hall, rather curiously sharing the programme with the first performance of Benjamin Britten's piano concerto. Britten was the soloist in his own work, but neither in the concert programme nor in the *Times* review did Schumann's piano accompanist rate a mention!

was in the army, stationed in Windsor, and managed to get hold of a ticket for a recital which she gave in the School Hall at Eton College. She must have been sixty, give or take a week or two, and she was a sweet-looking, dumpy little lady with an angelic smile – every schoolboy in the audience must have wanted her as his granny. As the Schubert recordings of this time indicate, the tone had become a trifle drier than of yore and the delivery was no longer characterised by quite the old miraculous springiness of step, but what I was listening to was still to an extraordinary degree the same voice that I knew so well from the black-label 78, and the personal magnetism was almost tangible. This was not a case of an elderly singer living on the goodwill she had built up during her prime; her recitals were still rewarding artistic experiences, and indeed she was still finding new realms to conquer. In 1951 she toured South Africa for the first time in her life and here again one of the newspapers excelled itself – a photograph of her in the role of Sophie was captioned 'Elisabeth Schumann as Rosie in DER ROSENKAVALIER'.

It was as well for Schumann that her voice did hold up so remarkably because the sad truth is that after all those years of hard work and virtually unremitting success, in her declining years she needed every penny she could earn. As for so many of her friends and colleagues wartime exile was a punishing experience. She and her dermatologist husband (who was Jewish) set up home in New York, but he was unable to work until he had resat his medical exams in a language which was totally strange to him, and various of his penniless relations turned up too, leaving Schumann no alternative but to support them as well. It was also far from easy for her to find lucrative engagements in the States. She gave an annual Town Hall recital in New York but other offers did not come flooding in, and she was fortunate indeed to have landed a steady teaching job at the Curtis Institute in Philadelphia.

Besides all this she had one other truly appalling worry – her only child, a son by Walther Puritz, was a pilot in the

Luftwaffe; once the United States entered the war he was one of the enemy. The emotional dilemma in which this placed her did not end with the war itself. She had discovered that her son had lost a leg when he was shot down during the Sicilian campaign, and back in London in 1945 she turned to one of her most dependable friends for help in getting a well-made artificial limb sent out to Germany. She made the request during the course of lunch at the Dorchester and when her friend replied that in his opinion anyone who fought for Hitler had to put up with the consequences she was so shocked that she walked out and never spoke to the man again. This incident is described in detail in her son's recently published biography* and the reader's sympathies, I feel, are expected to lie entirely with Schumann. I must, however, say that in my opinion in the London of 1945 many people would have given her the same reply. It was only towards the end of the war that we in Britain began to find out the full horrors that had been inflicted on virtually every country in Europe, and at that moment to ask an Englishman to differentiate between a 'good' German and a 'bad' one was to ask a lot – a fact which I do not mention in order to rake over old coals, but to emphasise in what an agonising position Schumann found herself. In any case she was not one to let the grass grow under her feet. Despite the many stringent regulations in force at the time she was determined somehow to get to Germany to see her son, her daughter-in-law and the two grandchildren she had never met. Largely through the good offices of that potent impresario of the gramophone world, Walter Legge, she succeeded in being taken on by ENSA (the Entertainments National Service Association) to entertain the troops – with the bizarre result that at the age of fifty-seven this particular German-born American citizen donned a British army uniform, climbed aboard an old Dakota and flew off to sing to the British Army on the Rhine.

One of Schumann's most moving experiences during this time

---

* *Elisabeth Schumann* by Gerd Puritz, André Deutsch, London 1993.

was her first post-war appearance in London, on 18 September 1945, when she participated in a Promenade Concert in the Albert Hall – the Queen's Hall had been destroyed by bombs – singing two Mozart arias accompanied by the BBC Symphony Orchestra under Sir Adrian Boult, followed by two Schubert songs with Myra Hess at the piano. Schumann's arrival on the platform was the signal for an astonishing display of affection, and Sir Adrian had to raise and lower his baton again and again until the welcoming applause had at last subsided. It was perhaps an even more emotional occasion when she returned the following year to Vienna to give a concert in the Grosser Musikvereinsaal. It was to be several years still before life in that depressed and divided city could return to a semblance of what it once had been, but Schumann ended her programme with Richard Strauss's 'Morgen', and of its opening line – 'Und morgen wird die Sonne wieder scheinen' ('And tomorrow the sun will shine once more') – the Viennese critic Heinrich Kralik wrote: 'It will be a message of promise to us, a greeting of comfort from the other shore.'

Back in 1937 Schumann had been honoured with the titles of *Ehrenmitglied* (Member of Honour) both of the Vienna State Opera and of the Vienna Philharmonic Society, and it is with Schumann as an *ex officio* Viennese that I would like to close this chapter. On a Pearl CD, GEMM *9379*, coupled with the same Richard Strauss songs which I have discussed on the EMI release, we are treated to a feast of Viennese 'light' music, consisting of Josef Strauss's 'Sphärenklänge', Sieczynski's 'Wien, Wien, nur du allein', Benatzky's 'Ich muss wieder einmal in Grinzing sein' and six songs from actual Viennese operettas. With one exception these tracks were recorded in London with English orchestras under the British conductor Lawrance Collingwood or the Berliner Walter Goehr, so they can hardly be called *echt*-Viennese; and yet for anyone wanting to know how this sort of music should be performed here is the answer. To the skills of the fully-fledged opera singer – the smooth legato, the two-octave range, the flawless breath control, the effortless top notes and so on – a special ingredient has to be added; the singer must sound as if he or she is loving every minute of it. This must not come across as artifice, it must come across as real, and in the case of Elisabeth Schumann it would be hard to imagine a happier sounding singer. When she asks us in a number from the Schubert–Berté operetta DAS DREIMÄDERLHAUS 'Was schön'res könnt' sein als ein Wienerlied?' ('What could be more lovely than a Viennese song?') she gives us her own answer – nothing. 'Was jauchzt so im Herzen?', she asks, 'what makes your heart so whoop with joy?', and if ever I have heard a tone which merits the description of a whoop of joy it is Schumann's on the word 'jauchzt'.

Two of the operetta arias, both by Carl Michael Ziehrer, are typical of so much delightful music from this genre which is in undeserved danger of ending on the scrap-heap simply because the pieces from which it is taken would no longer stand revival in the theatre; while in the 'Chambre séparée' number from Heuberger's DER OPERNBALL we once again meet Schumann as a chambermaid, this time in dangerously seductive mode.* Readers may not be surprised, however, when I say that to me the most welcome items are those self-same songs from Zeller's DER OBERSTEIGER and DER VOGELHÄNDLER which I mentioned at the beginning of this chapter. Neither time nor familiarity has laid a withering hand on these two performances, indeed I enjoy them after all these years even more than I did as a child because I am now in a position to recognise how rare is the ability to sing like this – every note is alive with Schumann's own joy in the act of singing. When, in DIE MEISTERSINGER, Hans Sachs says of Walther von Stolzing 'Nun sang er, wie er musst'! Und wie er musst', so konnt' er's' – 'He sang the way he had to; and as he had to, he could' – he is talking about the same sort of thing; this is someone's whole persona bursting

---

*   In its original form this number is an exquisite duet for soubrette and 'breeches-role' – Adele meets Cherubino, so to speak. What a treat it would have been if Schumann and Lehmann could have recorded it together.

forth in song. When he continues 'Dem Vogel, der heut' sang, dem war der Schnabel hold gewachsen' – 'The bird who sang today, his was a well-grown beak' – the parallel with Schumann becomes irresistible; as she launches into her whistling in the VOGELHÄNDLER song (she uses it on several other recordings as well, but never more fittingly than here, as the number is all about a nightingale) a beak is precisely what she appears to have acquired. It is somehow typical of her that she should never have ceased to delight in this trick which she had mastered in her childhood, and it brings to mind a story which I was told by the English critic and broadcaster John Amis. In the summer of 1950 he was on the staff of a summer music school at Bryanston where Schumann was to give some classes. At one point he was intrigued to hear that someone had evidently brought a budgerigar into the house, which was singing away lustily in another room. He went in to take a look at the bird, and was surprised to find that apart from Elisabeth Schumann, who was standing by the window with her back to the door, the room was empty. She *was* the budgerigar.

Shortly before her death in New York Schumann was rung up by Otto Klemperer, who had heard that she was mortally ill. As she put down the telephone she turned to a friend who was visiting her and used a strange phrase – '*Es war der rote Faden in meinem Leben*' ('it was the red thread in my life'). Despite everything she had been through in her early days she was able to say in an interview with the *Daily Herald*, back in 1930, 'A singer must be happy. I am – otherwise how could I feel the wonderful joy of music? True, I have been lucky. I have had no struggles.' Did she herself really believe that, I wonder, or was it something she needed to believe in order to keep that puckish smile on her face? Or perhaps it was simply the product of another typical characteristic of hers, an aspect of her personality which the British critic Alec Robertson summed up after her death in one telling phrase – 'Never was so brilliant a woman so completely without malice.'

CONCHITA SUPERVIA

SPANISH MEZZO-SOPRANO

b. Barcelona, 9 December 1895
d. London, 30 March 1936

One of the most popular misconceptions about the operatic profession, I have found, is that young singers nowadays do not train
for as long as they did in the Good Old Days. To me it seems that
the exact opposite is nearer the truth. Today very few people enter
the profession without first attending some form of music college
and we are quite unused to the idea of singers making a début until
they are comfortably into their twenties. It was not always thus;
especially amongst the ranks of coloratura sopranos débuts used to
be made at a far earlier age. Way back in the 1820s Maria Malibran
was singing Rosina in IL BARBIERE DI SIVIGLIA at seventeen
and at eighteen the great Giulia Grisi was hard at work. Adelina
Patti tackled Lucia di Lammermoor at sixteen, Marcella Sembrich
and Luisa Tetrazzini leapt into the fray at nineteen, and so the list
continues. As far as I am aware, however, despite such doughty
competitors the victor's palm for vocal precociousness has to be
awarded to the Spanish mezzo-soprano Conchita Supervia. She
made her début at the Teatro Colón, Buenos Aires, on 1 October
1910, two months before her fifteenth birthday.

It is in the best traditions of opera's splendid illogicality that
the first role undertaken by this waif of a débutante should have
been that of an old crone named La Mère Marçeau. This was
in a piece entitled BLANCA DE BEAULIEU by an Argentinian
composer called Stiattesi, and it was one of no less than thirteen
productions presented at the Colón by the Goula Company, a
visiting troupe from Spain. Supervia sang in four of them. In the
second, LOS AMANTES DE TERUEL by the Spanish composer
Tomás Bretón, she played a lady named Zulima who was a little

closer to her real age – the production was chiefly distinguished by the presence in the cast of the famous tenor Francisco Viñas – and in the third she had a tailor-made role, appearing as one of the three sirens in CIRCE, by Ruperto Chapí. I imagine, though, that it would have been in the fourth of these operas that she had the best chance of making the audience sit up and take notice. For one performance only the company presented CAVALLERIA RUSTICANA and Supervia was cast as Lola. Lola's principal task is to make trouble for the tenor, Turiddu, first by interrupting one of his big scenes with a saucy song from the wings, and then by crossing the stage in the most provocative manner possible while on her way to church. I have a feeling that even at the tender age of fourteen Supervia would have been fully capable of handling this assignment.

Supervia was born in Barcelona on 9 December 1895 – later in life she herself confused the issue of her date of birth by knocking off four years and having 1899 written in her passport – and she was educated at the Colegio de las Damas Negras in that city, as well as studying voice with a teacher named Alfredo Martini. At an early age she was already a capable pianist, and it is reasonable to assume that by the time she appeared at the Colón she must have been an even more capable singer, because only a short while after her return to Europe she was engaged to undertake no less a role than Carmen in the city of Bari, just above the heel of Italy. This would normally be considered an outrageously risky step for one so young, but Supervia evidently acquitted herself well because in the autumn of that same year, 1911, she received a signal honour when she was selected for the title-role in the Italian première of DER ROSENKAVALIER at the Teatro Costanzi in Rome. This was a truly astonishing state of affairs. Because Octavian, the cavalier in question, is only seventeen years old the part was conceived as a 'Hosenrolle', a trouser-role, the idea being that no singer could meet so demanding a vocal and musical challenge until reaching artistic maturity, and that a mezzo of thirty or forty summers would make a more attractive teenage youth than a tenor or baritone of the same age. I scarcely think that either Strauss or Hofmannsthal would ever have envisaged the part being undertaken by a singer who was actually younger than Octavian is supposed to be, but when Supervia first sang it she was still a couple of months short of her sixteenth birthday.

Seventeen years later Supervia appeared again as 'Il Cavaliere della Rosa', this time at La Scala, Milan, under the baton of Strauss himself. Her Sophie was the soprano Ines Maria Ferraris and the recordings which they made together of the Presentation of the Silver Rose and of the Final Duet are included in an excellent selection of operatic numbers, all sung in Italian, on *Lebendige Vergangenheit CD89023*. From the first note of Octavian's formal peroration Supervia's voice is revealed as one of those rare instruments which is entirely individual, not for one moment to be compared with or mistaken for any other. It is a true mezzo in timbre but with great brilliance of quality and notable for a rapid flutter in the tone. I hesitate to use the word vibrato, which is actually the correct technical term for this particular characteristic, because to many people that conjures up an impression of the dreaded wobble, which Supervia's flutter most distinctly was not. A wobble is caused by lack of control over various of the muscles employed in the singing process, and it is sadly something which assaults many of us after a certain age (as well as some who are young enough to know better); whereas Supervia's vibrato was under total control and is more comparable to that of a string player, a means of giving life to the tone and continuity to the legato. If in the first instant it seems strange to hear Octavian introducing himself in Italian, the confidence, the authority and the vitality of Supervia's delivery soon sweep all preconceived ideas aside, and as both these scenes consist largely of the two voices weaving their ecstatic way through an unbroken flow of melody, in no time at all Italian begins to sound the right language for them anyway.

Another classic German opera in which these same two singers were cast together at La Scala enabled them to show very different sides to their personalities. This was Humperdinck's HÄNSEL UND GRETEL, and on another track of this same CD they abandon their aristocratic formality to give a gleefully uninhibited account of the urchin siblings larking and squabbling their way through the opening scene. Supervia, of course, is the Hänsel and though any shapely mezzo accepts that she will spend a certain amount of her time in trousers, the management of La Scala seems to have had an outright objection to letting her loose on their stage in a skirt, as the third of her roles there was the girl-crazy page-boy Cherubino in LE NOZZE DI FIGARO. His two principal solos also feature on the *Lebendige Vergangenheit* disc and these are gloriously full-blooded performances, so vivid, so strongly projected and so utterly spontaneous that you can almost shut your eyes and *see* Supervia striding around the stage. Her 'Non so più' is hectic and desperate – it must have been a sacrifice for this Cherubino to waste two minutes forty seconds singing the song when in that time he could have caught up with at least another three or four girls. In the 'Voi che sapete', more restrained in tempo, Supervia deploys an intriguing range of vocal subtleties. This is the song which Cherubino has written himself, and which he sings to Susanna and the Countess, begging them to tell him whether the odd sensation which so regularly besets him could possibly be love. In Supervia's hands he is no gauche young fellow singing his party piece; every word is directed straight at his two lovely listeners and his aim is to tug as hard as he can manage at the heartstrings of both of them. There is a nice little touch of chest voice on the lower tones of the opening phrase, to make it evident out of what wells of emotion his rendering is dredged up. In the simple sentence 'Donne, vedete s'io l'ho nel cor', cogency is added by observing the comma between the first two words, while the most discreet of portamenti on the last two syllables of 'vedete', assisted by a perfectly controlled diminuendo, lends the whole phrase a whiff of supplication.

This is Mozart singing which certain conductors nowadays would doubtless want to water down – a singer's own personality must not intrude between Mozart and the audience – but dilution was not part of Supervia's artistic make-up. The very essence of her musical personality was her Spanishness, with all that that comprises in terms of fire and vigour and rhythmic zip, and it inevitably leads to an intriguing clash of interpretative priorities when faced with the role of Cherubino. Although FIGARO is set in Spain, Mozart did not choose to hispanicise his music, but when Supervia is set the task of portraying a lively young Spaniard there is no way that she is going to set about him as if he were a Viennese. It is fascinating to compare her versions of these two arias with the classic Mozartian approach of Elisabeth Schumann. Both artists are to be counted amongst the most charming, the most humorous and the most feminine singers one could possibly imagine, but the means by which they achieve their ends are diametrically opposed. Where Schumann enchants with the limpid purity of her tone Supervia rivets the attention with her vibrant Iberian temperament; where Schumann effortlessly moulds her poised Mozartian phrases Supervia's little spurts of passion momentarily distort the line, but transport Cherubino several hundred miles further south. I would hate to have to state a preference for the one approach or the other; I am happy to settle for both.

Cherubino is not the only Spaniard on this particular CD; we also meet the heroine of Rossini's IL BARBIERE DI SIVIGLIA, of whom more anon, and Bizet's Carmen. Unlike Mozart and Rossini, Bizet did set out to incorporate local colour in his score, and as far as many operatic managements were concerned Supervia was the obvious person to sing it. Within two years of her performances in Bari, and while still aged only seventeen, she was engaged for the role by one of Italy's most prestigious houses, the Fenice in Venice, and thereafter she sang Carmen more often than anything else in her repertoire. Her Italian recordings of 1927 consist of the Habañera, the Seguidilla and the Quintet, and although I have been assured by experts on Spanish music that Bizet's pastiche is frequently off target it is sufficiently genuine to have made Supervia sound very much at home. The vibrato and the chest voice both come gloriously into their own, and it is when she indulges these two essentially Spanish attributes to the full that one really appreciates how totally she had them under technical control. There is no gearchange in the octave leaps on the word 'l'amor', the come-hither gutsiness of the first syllable leading with disarming ease to an innocent purr on the second, while the flutter to which I alluded earlier has become a shamelessly seductive throb. Even when the tone is at its darkest, however, Supervia never loses her lightness of touch. Hers was not a voice comparable in weight to the kind of mezzo who has an Amneris or an Eboli up her sleeve – Grace Bumbry, for instance, or Giulietta Simionato – and I can well understand why critics occasionally found her Carmen too lightweight for the bigger houses. Referring to her season with the Chicago Opera in 1916 the critic Edward Moore wrote: 'There was Conchita Supervia from Spain who did a nice, girlish little Carmen,* a rather pleasant Charlotte in WERTHER, and as good a Mignon as was ever heard on the Auditorium stage'; and when she brought her Carmen to Covent Garden in 1935 at the peak of her artistic maturity Neville Cardus wrote in the *Manchester Guardian*: 'the fact was plain that Conchita Supervia's treatment of the part was vocally small and Sir Thomas Beecham had no alternative but to tone down the score.' I suspect that Richard Capel! of *The Daily Telegraph* put his finger on it when he described Supervia's Carmen as being entirely her own, not a tragic figure or a *femme fatale* but 'merry, saucy and beguiling'. It would be fair to add that several other gentlemen of the press were happy to surrender unconditionally to this somewhat kittenish rendering of the role. 'She is Carmen down to the ground,' wrote the critic of the *Star*; 'there was even something fascinating when she spat the orange pips at poor José; it was so natural and so naughtily done.'

As reviews like these will have made evident, Supervia's voice

---

* She *was* still only twenty!

was by no means the only string to her bow. The description of her in the memoirs of her regular accompanist Ivor Newton* is perhaps the most affectionate pen portrait that I ever remember reading of any singer, and its opening paragraph includes the following passage:

> Unusually beautiful, with large expressive eyes, a small nose and the most beautifully shaped mouth I have ever seen, she had a mass of carefully disorganised auburn hair, and the sort of figure, all curves and charm, that Latin taste adjudges to be perfect. She was always intensely alert and possessed of apparently inexhaustible vitality. Her gaiety, good temper, sympathy and charm cloaked a keen intelligence and adamantine will-power. To be with her was to inhabit a land of cloudless happiness; waiters and railway porters leapt devotedly to her service and everywhere men stopped to admire her as she passed.

Supervia's 'adamantine will-power' was amply demonstrated during the tangled tale of her first season at Covent Garden. She was engaged to appear there in 1934 in three performances of Rossini's LA CENERENTOLA (CINDERELLA) and three of CARMEN, and from the outset she made it perfectly plain to Geoffrey Toye, the managing director of the company, that it would be out of the question for her even to start rehearsing CARMEN until CENERENTOLA, an opera written in a totally different vocal style, was over and done with. When the plans for the season were announced, however, CARMEN had been scheduled as the opening attraction and Toye found himself engaged in correspondence with a formidable opponent. One of Supervia's letters, written in excellent English and in a forthright, highly characteristic hand – it would, I feel sure, bring joy to the heart of any graphologist – contained the sentence: 'I think I need the advice of some experienced authority who would understand the risks and the technical difficulties which this sequence of programs present and I believe the only authority I can appeal to is

---

* See bibliography, p.316.

Sir Thomas Beecham.' Beecham was the artistic director of the company, but as Toye was himself a conductor of some repute I do not suppose that he can have relished the implication that he was not an 'experienced authority'. In any case things went from bad to worse. First Covent Garden fixed CENERENTOLA for two of the dates which they had allotted to CARMEN, then withdrew the latter opera altogether, thus reducing the season by five days and Supervia's contract from six performances to two. If that was how she was to be treated, she declared, she would prefer not to appear at all – which would have left Covent Garden with an expensive production of CENERENTOLA on its hands and nobody to sing the central role. Within three weeks her solicitor had entered the fray and the final scene of the drama consisted of Toye literally beseeching her to sing two evenings of CENERENTOLA at the end of the season. She agreed, and even at the end of all this fracas her letters were still documents of impeccable courtesy starting 'My dear Geoffrey . . .'.

The original reason why Toye and Beecham had wanted to open the season with CARMEN was quite simply because they had no faith in CENERENTOLA as a box-office attraction. It had not been performed at Covent Garden since the early 1890s, and even in Italy it had become a widely held view that apart from IL BARBIERE DI SIVIGLIA Rossini's comic operas were not worth staying awake for. One factor which militated against them was that the leading lady needed to be a mezzo possessed of a dazzling coloratura technique, and such people are amongst the rarest birds in the operatic aviary. IL BARBIERE was kept on its feet by transposing the role of Rosina to make it accessible to a high soprano, but when Supervia first undertook the part, in Barcelona in 1914, she reverted to the original keys and revealed an exceptional aptitude for the singing of florid music. During the next few years her Rosina was seen in several Italian houses and in 1921 she added LA CENERENTOLA to her repertoire. Four years later she undertook a third Rossini heroine in circumstances which attracted widespread attention; under the baton of Vittorio

Gui, later to become familiar to British audiences as principal conductor at Glyndebourne, she opened the new Teatro di Torino in
Turin as the eponymous heroine of L'ITALIANA IN ALGERI.
By now she was being hailed as the saviour of long neglected
masterpieces and she repeated them all over the place, usually
bringing along an entire cast of her favourite colleagues as part
of her retinue. In particular, Rossini and Supervia became the
twin toasts of Parisian opera-lovers, and in 1933 her Cenerentola
was one of the outstanding attractions of the inaugural Maggio
Musicale in Florence.

Clearly any singer who can raise operas from the dead must
have something special to offer, and as the three Rossini tracks on
the *Lebendige Vergangenheit* disc amply demonstrate, Supervia
had. For one thing an aria such as 'Una voce poco fa' from IL
BARBIERE, so familiar as a showcase for the charming twitterings
of many a light soprano, becomes a different piece of music, and of
theatre, when put back into its proper mezzo framework. Young
Rosina, the heiress kept under lock and key by her scheming old
guardian, informs us that as long as things go her way she is
happy to be as sweet as sugar, but if anyone chooses to tangle
with her he had better watch his step. Not only does Supervia's
immersion in the spirit of the piece make us feel that she might
well have written the text herself – Geoffrey Toye could have
been forgiven for suspecting that she had – but the sheer degree
of meatiness in the tone gives an extra substance to the character.
It would be impossible to imagine this particular Rosina growing
up to be the withdrawn and dignified Countess of Mozart's LE
NOZZE DI FIGARO, but it would be equally impossible to
imagine the wiliest guardian standing half a chance against her.
One of Supervia's secrets is that she does not regard the florid
passages as mere vehicles for vocal display, but as a natural means
of expressing effervescent emotion. She is a champagne singer and
when her Rosina wants to get something off her chest she fizzes
and bubbles. From a sumptuous low G sharp to a rock solid high
B natural Supervia can encompass anything Rossini asks of her,

but she never steps back from the character in order to show off the voice.

There are two other Rossini numbers on the *Lebendige Vergangenheit* disc, 'Contro un cor', the music lesson aria from IL BARBIERE, and 'Nacqui all'affanno', the rondo sung by the transformed Cinderella (in the opera she is in fact called Angelina) in the closing scene of LA CENERENTOLA. Here we encounter a slightly different side to Supervia's skill as a vocal actress. At this point Rossini invests his heroine with a touch of regality – the opening of the aria in particular could come from one of his most serious operas – and the teasing quality which characterises Supervia's style in comedy gives way to a timbre of impressive gravity. In this number, too, the individuality of her coloratura technique becomes evident. The agility is dazzling but it is the agility of a child of nature, not the produce of rigorous schooling. This is not the recognised Italian *bel canto* style of immaculate evenness throughout the scale, for which Melba would be the obvious model to quote; this seems rather to have its roots in the wilder regions of Spanish music, so much of it looking back to a Moorish ancestry. Supervia could never be cited as representing the ultimate in classic technique, but as an example of how to make florid music serve a theatrical purpose she would be hard to beat.

I cannot possibly leave the *Lebendige Vergangenheit* disc without mentioning one more track which I think I would have to rate as the most blatantly sexy piece of singing ever recorded by an operatic diva. Back in 1912, at the age of sixteen, Supervia had treated her native Barcelona to a double dose of feminine wiles, appearing not only as Carmen but also as that other arch-temptress of Gallic opera, Saint-Saëns's Dalila (Delilah). Supervia may have been a lightweight, both vocally and physically, compared with others who have assayed the role over the years, but in terms of languorous sensuality the performance which she recorded fifteen years later of the Act I aria 'Printemps qui commence' (or 'O Aprile foriero di sogni') seems to me to be in a class of its own.

I mean it as no disrespect either to Supervia or to Saint-Saëns – indeed I mean it as the highest praise – when I say that to me the opening phrase is like a mezzo recreation of Yvonne Printemps sliding into one of those intoxicating melodies from Oscar Straus's LES TROIS VALSES. It would be beyond the power of most performers to create this almost tangible sultriness even on-stage with set designer, costumier, make-up department and lighting experts doing everything possible to help. To bring it off stone-cold in a cheerless studio is truly an achievement. The music does of course help, but drenched in such overt eroticism 'Little Bo-Peep' would become a dangerous piece to sing in a public place.

When Supervia at last made her Covent Garden début in LA CENERENTOLA both she and the opera triumphed – she was promptly re-engaged for the following year in CENERENTOLA, L'ITALIANA and CARMEN – and it was typical of her that despite all that had gone before she spent the rehearsal period radiating high spirits and goodwill. One morning Beecham, who was conducting, wanted to know how long it would take for the crystal coach drawn by four white ponies to make its way round the stage, and as the coach was not yet available for a trial run Supervia hit on the ideal solution. 'Sir Thomas, Geoffrey,' she called out, 'come and be my snow white ponies'; and with a gravely professional demeanour the two directors of the Royal Opera House trotted round the stage side by side, lifting their knees in approved dressage style, followed by Supervia, whip in hand, while the rehearsal pianist timed them on a stop-watch. After all the problems these two gentlemen had caused her Supervia must have been itching to put the whip to its proper use, but at least as far as the outside world was concerned she showed herself to be of a forgiving nature. In one newspaper interview she was asked what were the necessary ingredients for a successful operatic production and she replied, 'One only needs one or two *esprits animateurs*. At Covent Garden we have two such spirits – the adorable Sir Thomas Beecham and myself.'

At exactly that time the *esprit* of the adorable Sir Thomas was in ebullient evidence. The 1934 season had opened with FIDELIO and although the performance was being broadcast live he turned round during the overture and told some noisy late-comers to keep quiet. Later in the evening he turned on the gallery, where people were still applauding the preceding scene although he had already started to conduct the Leonora Overture No.3. 'Shut up, you!' he yelled, and in an interview the next day he described applause at that moment as 'an incredible piece of barbarism'. He went on to say, 'If it occurs again I shall stop and address the house. I shall ask if they are savages.' He then decreed that late-comers should not be allowed into the auditorium until the first interval, an unheard-of regulation at that time and one which led to a question in the House of Commons by a Member who saw 'danger' in the idea. Finally Sir Thomas declared war on the press, one result of which was that Supervia received very few notices for her début, though peace had been restored by the time she repeated the role the following year, when the critics turned out in force. It is rare to encounter such unanimous enthusiasm as they expressed. 'The whole evening centres on Conchita Supervia,' wrote the representative of the *News Chronicle* in a review typical of the general tone. 'She *is* Cinderella – and what a Cinderella! Other people sing, others indulge in long conversations, but as long as she is on the stage nothing else matters.'

Sir Thomas's next campaign was to encourage the audience to enjoy themselves more by explaining that in Mr Rossini's comic pieces it is not only permissible to applaud after individual numbers but also to laugh at the jokes. Lauritz Melchior, who had attended one of Supervia's early performances, described the audience as behaving like a PARSIFAL public on Good Friday, but people soon caught on, and by the time Supervia appeared in her second Rossini role, that of Isabella, the Italian Girl in Algiers, everyone was having a high old time. On an EMI CD, *CDH 7 63499 2*, we are offered four scenes from L'ITALIANA which Supervia had recorded eight years previously in Barcelona with her regular gang of supporting singers, all of whom she brought with her to Covent Garden. In a typed four-page letter to her agent, Harold Holt, written in December 1934, she had set out her 'suggestions' about the casting of all three of the operas in which she was due to be appearing, explaining in detail why it would be essential to secure the services of every single singer on her list. 'It cannot be said that it is impossible to arrange these matters', she concluded, 'as there are many months to deal with the question, nor can it be a matter of expense, as I can prove to you in a more detailed letter that the fees for all these people are extremely reasonable.' Beecham and Toye must indeed have begun to wonder who was running the company.

In any case Supervia's Italian Girl was received with boundless delight by both press and public, and these recordings give a vivid impression of the style of evening that was on offer. The piece is a total romp, a kind of cross between DIE ENTFÜHRUNG AUS DEM SERAIL and a Feydeau farce, and Supervia's performance froths with conspiratorial glee. At Covent Garden she took it into her head to make her first entrance carrying a small dog under her arm* and, as one of the critics put it, 'many of the more orthodox in the audience were shocked to see it on the boards of Covent Garden'. Luckily, however, there appear to have been plenty of the less orthodox in attendance as well, because even though the dog at one point became entangled in its lead, obliging Supervia to take one high note on her knees while trying to disentangle it, the same critic assures us that 'her singing swept the audience off its feet and the protests of the shocked Wagnerians were drowned in a torrent of applause'.

The third of Supervia's roles at Covent Garden was the long-postponed Carmen, to which I referred earlier on, and the same EMI CD includes seven extensive excerpts which she had recorded

---

* The dog belonged to total strangers and Supervia had spotted it in a restaurant. Its owners were not sufficiently interested in music to accept her offer of free seats to witness their pet's début with the Royal Opera, and sent it to the theatre each evening in a chauffeur-driven car.

in Paris five years earlier. Between them these titles represent something over half of the entire role, and as they are sung this time in the original French and with the assistance of a passable Don José (Gaston Micheletti) they obviously present a more essential memento of her Carmen than the three Italian titles discussed above. There are passages, though, in the Habañera and the Seguidilla in which I find her Italian versions even more intriguing, more magnetic, with the interplay of head and chest tones more tantalisingly deployed. I suspect that in the more extended French version she may have wanted to play down the teasing aspect of the character in anticipation of the tragic undertow of the later scenes and thus to present a more unified characterisation overall. There is certainly nothing superficial about her contempt for Don José's slavish obedience to the bugle's call – her taunts of 'O mon dieu' may be feline, but kittenish they are not – and as the last traces of humour are drained from the role her voice takes on a joltingly tragic timbre. I can still believe that this Carmen would have lacked the sheer weight required for a large house, but as a recorded performance it is full of haunting insights.

Supervia made some 200 recordings in all, and another outstanding selection is to be found on Nimbus *NI 7836/7*. This is a two-for-the-price-of-one set, with the French CARMEN collection on Disc 2, this time in its entirety; it includes Micheletti's Flower Song, which means that the whole of the Carmen–José scene from Act II runs through without a break, adding greatly to its cumulative impact. Disc 1 includes four Rossini titles and Delilah's 'Printemps qui commence', all of which we have met before, but it also offers two positively virginal renderings in Mignon's 'Connais-tu le pays' – with those 1916 performances in Chicago she must have stirred protective feelings in many a male breast – and Marguerite's Ballad of the King of Thule from FAUST. In sharp contradistinction to Delilah these two young ladies were not well versed in the facts of life, and it is fascinating to hear how Supervia cuts back on that sensuous vibrato when innocence is the quality she is wishing to express.

The rest of the Nimbus issue is devoted to song rather than opera, and here, untrammelled by the limitations which any stage role inevitably imposes, even more facets of Supervia's own coruscating personality are released. Two songs by Delibes are so lovingly, so beguilingly conjured up – 'performed' would be altogether too bland a word to use – that had they not been written before she was born one would have to assume that they had been created solely with her in mind. One would also have to assume that her heart belonged in Paris – until she moves on to the group of Manuel de Falla arrangements known as 'Canciones Populares Españolas', in which she is accompanied by the distinguished pianist Frank Marshall.* As a singer of Spanish songs Supervia is mesmeric. Compared with that exquisite soprano of the following generation, Victoria de los Angeles, Supervia's quality has something earthier, more animalistic about it. This may leave de los Angeles the victor in certain songs which require that silkiness of tone which has always been inimitably hers to command, but when passions need to be laid bare Supervia seems to me to stand out on her own. Her performance of the last of the Falla songs, 'Polo', an outburst of resentment at the misery of unrequited love, is as violent a release of pent-up emotion as it is possible to imagine coming from any singer's throat, the energy of the diction given extra momentum by the rocketing impulse of the rhythm.† It seems hardly credible that the touching little Mignon of a few tracks ago could have undergone such a seismic metamorphosis.

The Nimbus set is completed by several Spanish songs with orchestral accompaniment, including one of Supervia's concert

---

* Marshall was for many years assistant to the composer Granados and he was the teacher of Alicia de Larrocha.

---

† The British critic Desmond Shawe-Taylor once used an evocative phrase with reference to this aspect of Supervia's singing – 'the kind of rhythm which makes the non-Spanish world seem only half alive and awake'.

favourites 'Clavelitos' ('Carnations'), and perhaps the most familiar of all Spanish songs to British audiences, 'La Paloma'. Like both Tauber and McCormack, Supervia has the knack of singing such popular numbers as this in a manner which raises them way above their actual status. The tension of the legato at the opening of the second verse, the depth of feeling invested in the text and the sheer wealth of tone devoted to it scatter any memories one may have of jaded bar pianists clattering their way through the tired old melody. Without any inappropriate over-intellectualisation the song has suddenly become something eloquent and compelling.

The group of Falla arrangements also features on an excellent Pearl CD, GEMM *9975*, consisting largely of Spanish songs but also including the heroine's three main solos from Lehár's operetta FRASQUITA, in which Supervia appeared when it first opened in Paris. As the lady in question is a Spanish gipsy who makes her living singing and dancing in a night-club called The Alhambra it is easy enough to see why the producer should have been determined to secure Supervia's services. Before setting about this particular score Lehár had steeped himself in the music of Albeniz, Granados, Chapí and others, and both in her entrance song and in his gipsy number 'Ce que c'est que l'amour' ('Fragst mich, was Liebe ist?') Supervia is given plenty of scope to air her various national trademarks. They are not, however, Lehár's strongest vehicles for a leading lady, whereas in the Act II cabaret number 'Il y avait une fois' ('War in einem Städtchen einst') Lehár is right back on form, and Supervia's response is memorable. If I compared her just now to Yvonne Printemps this time I have to invoke the name of Edith Piaf. Frasquita is telling the story of a girl in a cigarette factory who wonders with each cigarette that she rolls whose lips will eventually be curling round it, a line of thought which leads her into more personal musings, and into the strains of one of Lehár's craftiest waltz motifs. It is a number which sounds effective enough in German ('Wüsst' ich, wer morgen mein Liebster ist'), but Supervia has the knack of making translations seem better than the original, and Piaf is the only other singer I can think of who could have invested this insidious little tune with anything approaching her gravelly, four o'clock in the morning salaciousness.

For the ultimate proof of this extraordinary woman's ability to scale the heights or plumb the depths of any imaginable mood one only needs to turn from the smoke-laden atmosphere of that FRASQUITA track to two songs entitled 'La Fonte' and 'Piogerella, Piogerellina' which are featured on a fascinating disc entitled 'The Unknown Supervia' (Pearl GEMM 9969). During the First World War Supervia had been in love with an Italian lawyer (later to become Mayor of Naples) called Francesco Santamaria and in 1918 she bore a son, Giorgio. She declined to marry Santamaria but Giorgio, or Giorgino as he was known when small, was the apple of her eye. An Italian composer named Gennai wrote a cycle of children's songs specially for Supervia and Giorgino and these are two of them, each one preceded by a chatty introduction delightfully delivered by Supervia in her immaculate Italian. The titles of the songs – the first one means 'The Spring' (in its watery sense) and the second is more or less 'Pitter-Patter Raindrops' – will give an idea of their contents, and the introductions run on the lines of 'How many happy things the chattering spring tells us, glu-glu, as it gurgles merrily down there'. The closest equivalent in English might perhaps be the A. A. Milne Christopher Robin songs set by H. Fraser-Simson, and though the Supervia dubbings have been taken from scratchy old 78s they present yet another disarming side to her chameleon-like versatility.

This disc also includes a group of popular Catalan and Spanish songs which were recorded in Spain but never issued on 78s, though it is hard to imagine why not as every one is a glistening gem. It gives us several zarzuela numbers too; this is a genre which she puts across with predictable relish, and in one duet, as a lady named Señora Rita giving her ex-boyfriend the bird in Bretón's LA VERBENA DE LA PALOMA, she makes Carmen seem like a shrinking violet. There is a group of excerpts from French opera, all unpublished as 78s, which is understandable in the case of the 'Légères Hirondelles' duet from MIGNON in which she is partnered with desperate lack of subtlety by her bass friend Bettoni (who sounded much more at home as one of her merry men in L'ITALIANA), but less so with her moving account of Charlotte's 'Va! laisse couler mes larmes' from WERTHER; and a further curiosity is provided by a pair of excerpts from the sound-track of a British film called *Evensong*.

This film had an amusing history. It was made in 1934, directed by Victor Saville, a leading figure in British cinema at that time, and based on a novel of the same name by Beverley Nichols. The story concerned the eclipse of an ageing Queen of Song and her replacement by an unstoppable young talent, and as Nichols had previously been private secretary to Dame Nellie Melba nobody had much doubt as to the model for his fading star. This role was taken by Evelyn Laye (the cast also included such well-known names as Alice Delysia and Emlyn Williams), and when Saville read about Supervia's withdrawal from her Covent Garden contract he promptly offered her the part of the brilliant newcomer (generally held to be inspired by Toti dal Monte). This suited Supervia admirably, as it kept her on hand in London in case the Covent Garden management should ultimately relent, and it made up for all the fees she had lost. The items reproduced on the Pearl disc consist of Musetta's Waltz Song from LA BOHEME (preceded by some slightly chopped-up dialogue between Evelyn Laye and Fritz Kortner, who played Supervia's manager) and a Spanish song called 'Los ojos negros', which Supervia also used to interpolate into Frasquita's cabaret scene. As recordings these do not rate very highly, but as mementoes of an unlikely chapter in Supervia's career they are well worth their place in the Pearl selection.

So, too, is the one track which she sings in English. It is a song called 'When I bring to you coloured toys', another number whose text is directly addressed to a small child, and it was one of several songs which she learnt in English (a language which at that time she did not yet speak) so that on her British concert tours she could include a group in the audience's own tongue. As a recitalist she was indefatigable and irresistible. In 1931, long before she had been heard at Covent Garden, she had won herself a host of admirers and a sheaf of ecstatic reviews with recitals all round Britain. The following year she undertook a nation-wide tour of no less than twenty concerts in five weeks, including two in the Albert Hall, before departing for an eight-week tour of the United States and a return visit, after a gap of sixteen years, to the Chicago Opera. Her impact on the New York public can be judged by the opening paragraph of one of the reviews: 'The New York début of Conchita Supervia, Spanish coloratura-mezzo, given in the Town Hall on Sunday afternoon, Feb. 7, before an audience of unusual brilliance, heralded the appearance on the New York horizon of a unique interpreter and one of the most alluring figures now before the public.'

A desire to sing to anglophone audiences in their own tongue was not, however, Supervia's sole reason for wishing to learn English. In 1931 she married an Englishman named Ben Rubinstein and, unlikely as it may seem for this archetype of a Latin lady, she became a dedicatedly enthusiastic British resident. Her husband was a wealthy timber broker and they divided their time between their London base, a resplendent flat in Lowndes Square which Supervia had had entirely redecorated in art-deco style, with lavish use of glass and chromium,* and his country property, which included tree nurseries and a fruit farm, at a place called Rustington in Sussex. I have read before now that this was not a happy marriage, but after reading a dozen or more of Supervia's letters written to her husband during her various absences abroad†

---

* A copiously illustrated description of the flat in the *Sketch* refers to a bedroom with tomato-red velvet hangings, white velvet carpet and white walls, and a sitting-room with 'turquoise blue curtains and chairs which make a superb background for her auburn hair'.

---

† These letters, which have never been published, are in the Norman White Collection.

I am unable to believe that this is true. They are deeply affectionate documents, spontaneous, funny and, particularly in view of what was so soon to come, often very moving. Most of them were written from her New York hotel, such as this one, dated 23 January 1933:

> My beloved darling – only a few words to tell you that I have been for two nites to hear Lily Pons and I do not like her at all!!! I think the public is really stupid there and if she is such a great success I must not be proud of mine!!!! . . . I read that in England there is a lot of 'flu' and that people even die!!! Oh! my darling please be more than careful and don't go near anybody that has a cold and gargle with Listerine and keep yourself in good strong condition to fite microbs!

A few days later she evidently received a letter from her husband grumbling that when she was not with him people were no longer so pleased to see him, because on 4 February she had this to say:

> My beloved naughty darling!!
> Why do you put ideas in your head that people does not love you and does not want to talk to you in the parties!! Well!!! first of all which parties – in those which you know so well each other that you are bored with yourselves? It is really an idea of yours quite wrong!! Everybody loves you everybody that is somebody and counts something and *tant pis pour lui qui ne t'aime pas*, they loose more than you do in that game . . . and yet there is not in a certain heart so much love for you to full your ambitions of beeing loved!!!?

When asked in a newspaper interview in 1931 if she missed the sunshine in London she amazed the journalist by replying 'Sunshine? Ah, *amigo mio*, sunshine is very nice – but give me an English fireside, with tea on the table, and friends who know how to joke and laugh, and yet can be quiet, like English people; and let there be outside one of those cosy fogs we have in London!' She must, I think, have been in a similar mood when she wrote to her husband from New York:

> The weather is lovely today and make me remember of one
> of those days blue and sunshiny at Rustington when the nature
> seems so clean and fresh!!! May be it is so today that you are there
> with Giorgio round the nurseries and the garden thinking of me!!!
> May be it is one of those days the sky is dark and cold and windy
> and then it is so nice and restful to be near the fire in the lounge!!!
> I would like to be there and see all the progresses of the flowers
> . . . Oh! my darling I love you every day more and more just
> when I think every day that would be impossible to love you
> more than I do!!! *Je t'aime infiniment*!!!!

It is impossible to read these letters of Supervia's without forming
the impression that in the first half of the 1930s she was on the crest
of a double wave of private happiness and professional success, and
when she discovered that in the spring of 1936 she would be having
another baby there was much excitement in the family. One of the
last people to visit her before the birth was Ivor Newton, who
recalls the occasion in his memoirs:

> She and her husband invited me to their home in Lowndes
> Square to show me the nursery they had equipped for the
> baby she was expecting. The perfection of their elaborate
> arrangements reminded me of the preparations made for the
> arrival of Napoleon's son, the King of Rome. Supervia was
> lively, confident and very happy. 'Do come soon', she said
> 'and see my little Easter Egg.'

Within twenty-four hours her baby daughter had been delivered stillborn, and she herself was dead. She had adopted her
husband's religion and she was buried, the baby in her arms, in
the Liberal Jewish Cemetery in north-west London. The eminent
architect Sir Edwin Lutyens designed her tomb and in view of her
fondness for tortoises – she had adopted the tortoise as a sort of
personal trademark – Sir William Reid Dick, the most famous
British sculptor of the day, engraved it with a tortoise motif as
well as with her favourite motto *'Tuta ad ictus'* ('Strong against

the blows'). The inscription gave 1899 as her year of birth. Her husband clearly knew that even she could not have made her professional début at the age of ten, but it had been Conchita Supervia's wish to disown four years – and to the end her wish remained every man's command.

RICHARD TAUBER

AUSTRIAN TENOR

b. Linz, 16 May 1891
d. London, 18 January 1948

Richard Tauber is one of those artists who confuse people. The most highly regarded Mozart tenor of his day; the matinée idol for whom Franz Lehár wrote his last five sentimental operettas; the conductor who took over from Sir Thomas Beecham for a tour with the London Philharmonic Orchestra; the composer who appeared countless times in the leading roles of his own stage works; the popular entertainer whose renderings of 'We'll Gather Lilacs' or 'Sleepy Lagoon' made the purists' flesh creep; the Lieder singer whose classic recording of twelve songs from Schubert's DIE WINTERREISE was completed in a morning with one coffee break – how do you find a neat pigeon-hole for a person like that? The clue, I believe, lies in something which the Viennese conductor Josef Krips wrote after Tauber's death – 'He was first a great musician, and second a great singer.' Everything Tauber sang was infused with his own instinctive response to the nature of the music in question; and he did not just sing it – he first made it part of himself and then served it up as an extension of his own exuberant personality.

If any of the twentieth century's great opera singers could be said to have had show business in the bloodstream then it is surely Richard Tauber. He was born on 16 May 1891 in the Hotel Zum schwarzen Bären in the Austrian city of Linz, the illegitimate son of a forty-three-year-old soprano, his father being an itinerant straight actor who had disappeared on an extended tour of the United States, and who did not even learn of the baby's existence until he was a year old. This may not sound like a promising start, but in fact each of Tauber's parents, though they never made a home together, played entirely creditable roles in his life and he was devoted to them both. His mother, Elisabeth Denemy, came of dyed-in-the-wool theatrical stock – her father was a Viennese actor and theatre director named Gottfried Denemy and her mother, Caroline Denemy-Ney, was an established opera star and one of the earliest interpreters of the role of Venus in Wagner's TANNHÄUSER – and she herself had been on stage since she was a child. During her prime she enjoyed considerable success in Vienna as a soubrette, reputedly possessing all the most desirable attributes for that particular repertoire, such as a small but expressive voice, large blue eyes and generous quantities of charm; but not even the most talented soubrette enjoys an extended heyday and when the demand for her services had fallen off in the capital she accepted a provincial contract in the Landestheater, Linz. She was a widow, struggling to bring up two teenage daughters, and the realisation that she was expecting another child must have come as a most unwelcome shock. When the baby was born his name was registered as Richard Denemy,* and as his mother needed to get back to work as quickly as possible he was fostered out to a childless woodcutter and his wife. Thus he spent the first year of his life in a remote rustic cottage surrounded by ducks and hens.

When the baby's father, one Richard Anton Tauber, came back to Europe he readily assumed his paternal responsibilities. It was agreed that Richard Jr should initially stay in his mother's care, with the result that much of his early childhood was spent playing on the floor of her dressing-room while she rehearsed, until he became old enough and well enough behaved to hang about in the wings. He started his schooling in the Volksschule, Linz, but when he was nine his father took control of his education, and from then onwards young Richard went wherever his

---

* During his childhood he was also occasionally given the surname Seyffert, his mother's married name, and he did not officially assume the name Tauber until the beginning of his career.

father's career happened to take him. By the age of twelve he had attended schools in Prague, Salzburg and Berlin, until eventually his father, by now a classical actor of some renown, accepted a long-term engagement in the Court Theatre, Wiesbaden.

From early childhood Richard Tauber had shown signs of an exceptional musical talent. He found it easy to pick out any music which appealed to him, whether popular or classical, on the piano, though when his father arranged for him to have formal lessons his teachers never lasted long because the boy had no patience with their methodical approach. Thereafter he taught himself, and very successfully too, but even in those early days it was his almost obsessive ambition to become a singer. He idolised a friend of his father's named Heinrich Hensel, the resident Heldentenor of the Wiesbaden Opera, and at the age of thirteen Tauber was to be seen striding down the street in his father's huge fur coat, with a broad-brimmed hat on his head and the role of Pedro in the latest operatic sensation, Eugen d'Albert's TIEFLAND, tucked prominently under his arm. When his voice had broken and settled into the tenor register his father sent him to Vienna to seek advice of a celebrated singer named Leopold Demuth, but Tauber insisted on bawling his way through several pages of Wagner and was given a succinct thumbs down. Back in Wiesbaden he sang for Professor Schlaar, chief conductor in the opera house, but once again he tried to out-Hensel Hensel, and once again his father received a negative report. It was then decided that as a singing career was clearly out of the question Tauber should apply for a place as a student of conducting in the Frankfurt Conservatory, where he sailed through the entrance examination. He rapidly established himself as the star pupil in the conducting class and no one had any doubt that a brilliant future awaited him; but to quote his own words, 'Only within myself was there a persistent feeling of unrest, because I did not want to sit in the pit conducting, I wanted to stand in the footlights up on stage. The thought of not becoming a singer was discordant to me, and I was totally dissatisfied with my fate.'

At this point, however, fate had a surprise up its sleeve. Tauber fell madly in love with one of the ballet dancers in the Wiesbaden theatre. As a means of insinuating himself into the young lady's household he persuaded her parents that it would be helpful for her to take piano lessons and that he was the ideal teacher – shades of one of his future roles, Count Almaviva in THE BARBER OF SEVILLE! Tauber's desire to shower his beloved with presents necessitated his earning some pocket money, which he did by extemporising on the piano in one of the Wiesbaden cinemas while the silent films were shown, and it was this that brought his love story to an end. Someone told his father about the cinema engagement, Tauber had to admit that he had been creating time for his ballet girl by cutting classes in Frankfurt, and to add to his discomfiture it turned out that she was in any case mistress to Graf von Hülsen, director-general of all the Court Theatres in Prussia, a fact apparently known to everyone in Wiesbaden except Tauber. His father decided that he should be removed from the Frankfurt Conservatory and banished to a family friend, Frau Professor Sarrazin, who ran a *pension* in Freiburg; there he was to attend lectures at the University as well as continuing his training as a conductor in the nearby city of Basle.

If it was one young lady who had got him into this mess it was another who helped to get him out of it. Frau Sarrazin's daughter Lilly was a gifted piano student, and after hearing Tauber sing she did everything she could to encourage him in his vocal ambitions. There were regular musical evenings in the Sarrazin home, guests were invariably astonished by the lodger's talent, and eventually a meeting was arranged with Freiburg's leading voice teacher, Carl Beines. Later on Tauber was to write a detailed account of that first audition, of how Beines immediately told him not to bellow but to sing without strain, of how he took him through endless simple little exercises, and of how he ended up by saying 'So you sang Lohengrin to Herr Demuth and Siegmund to Professor Schlaar – no wonder they told you you were no Wagner singer!' He went on to say, though, that if Tauber felt like studying with him and doing exactly what he was told, he could make him into what he was really destined to be, namely a lyric tenor.

In view of Tauber Sr's insistence on Richard's treading the conductor's path his lessons with Professor Beines had to be kept secret. Beines made no charge, and only the faithful Lilly, who acted as Tauber's accompanist, knew what was going on.* When the year was up Tauber moved on to the tackling of operatic roles, and eventually Beines told him that he had arranged an audition for the theatre in Mannheim. He insisted, however, that Tauber should travel via Wiesbaden and break the news to his father; it was as he waved goodbye to his pupil on Freiburg station that he called out, 'Don't worry, Richard, your father knows the whole story!' Indeed, his father had even arranged another audition for him in Wiesbaden, and this time, after singing Tamino's aria from DIE ZAUBERFLÖTE and 'Champs paternels' from Méhul's JOSEPH, Richard was promptly offered a contract.

It is probably difficult for anyone not involved in the operatic profession to realise what the securing of that first contract means to a young singer – there are so many times during the long period of study when you wonder whether you will ever make the grade. Tauber was naturally jubilant, but in the event the contract was never signed. On the very same day the news arrived that his father had been appointed stage manager of the newly built opera house in Chemnitz (the following year he was promoted to Intendant), so it was decided that Tauber should spend another year working on repertoire with Professor Beines, before making his official début in his father's own theatre. On 2 March 1913, a couple of months before his twenty-second birthday, he appeared there as Tamino, followed a few days later by Max in DER FREISCHÜTZ, but in fact before his début had even taken place his immediate future was assured. A leading agent, Herr Frankfurter, had heard Tauber sing a few

* It was a source of endless sorrow to Tauber that Lilly's devotion to the cause was never rewarded by seeing his rise to fame. Within two years of his leaving Freiburg she died of a heart complaint.

arias after a rehearsal and recommended him to the Court Opera in Dresden. He was summoned to an audition, this time he sang Tamino's aria and the Flower Song from CARMEN, and without further ado he was offered a five-year contract as principal lyric tenor, carrying with it the resplendent label of '*Kgl. Sächsischer Hofopernsänger*', or 'Royal Saxon Court Opera Singer'.

Clearly Tauber's work with Professor Beines had turned him into the kind of singer who only needs to sing a couple of songs to open all doors. It was to be six years before he made his first recordings, and they were years in which he doubtless added many layers of polish to his artistry, but the actual vocal quality which we hear in them will have been much the same as that which launched him on his career. There are several CDs available which offer us selections from Tauber's operatic repertoire, and one which concentrates on his first ten years as a recording artist is Nimbus *NI 7830*. It includes the earliest version of his favourite visiting card, Tamino's 'Bildnisarie' from DIE ZAUBERFLÖTE, and this one track is enough to reveal what it was that made Tauber so special. The voice, of course, is a beautiful one, with a highly individual timbre, and the delivery is natural and authoritative, but what sets the performance apart is the musical imagination behind it. This is such a familiar aria, both to audiences and to singers themselves, who are likely to have studied it *ad infinitum* with their voice teachers and in the opera school, that it is difficult to approach it with any degree of spontaneity. Yet it depicts the mental process of a young man who is waking up to an entirely new set of emotions and describing them as they occur to him, almost in the style of a radio commentator, which means that spontaneity is one of its most essential ingredients. The poor fellow is in a bit of a daze anyway; it is not every day that you come round from a dead faint after escaping death from the jaws of a monstrous serpent to find three rather forceful ladies handing you a portrait of the most beautiful girl in the world, and Tamino's senses have undergone a series of remarkable shocks. Would he have collected himself enough to deliver the opening lines of his monologue, 'Dies Bildnis ist bezaubernd schön, wie noch kein Auge je geseh'n' ('This picture is magically beautiful, such as no eye has ever seen before'), as one poised and confident announcement? Of course it has to flow – it is Mozart at his most melodious – but ideally its flow should include some inner hesitation, and it is exactly this apparent contradiction which Tauber achieves. The phrasing is immaculate, yet each individual word is given just enough weight to make us feel that he is picking his way through his own reactions. As he reaches the phrase 'Dies etwas kann ich zwar nicht nennen' ('I cannot put a name to this indefinable something'), he increases the fluency, but reduces the volume to a marvellously introspective piano, which broadens out to an assertive mezzoforte on the words 'doch fühl' ich's hier wie Feuer brennen' ('yet I feel it burning within me like fire'). So the whole aria proceeds, every minute touch bringing more and more conviction to the portrayal, but – and this is so essentially Tauber's secret – all of it pours out with utter naturalness, apparently a product of the moment.

The second Mozart track on the Nimbus disc, Don Ottavio's 'Dalla sua pace', sung in German and probably recorded in the same session as the 'Bildnisarie', gives Tauber, through the very nature of the aria, less opportunity for imaginative variations of colour and expression, but it must nevertheless stand as one of the most immaculate pieces of Mozart singing available on records. It is a difficult aria to sing, requiring as it does an exceptional degree of breath control, not only to cope with the length of the phrases, but also to match the delicacy with which the vocal line is poised. None of this, however, presents any problem to Tauber, who once again achieves all the necessary technical efficiency without ever lapsing into mere correctness. Many people considered this his finest role, and the comment was often made that he turned what can be a secondary figure into a worthy opponent for the charismatic Don.

The Nimbus selection also includes the second operatic recording which Tauber ever made, the aria 'Selig sind, die Verfolgung leiden' ('Blessed are those who are persecuted'), from a role in which he enjoyed particular success both in Dresden and later in Vienna, that of the preacher Mathias in Kienzl's DER EVANGELIMANN. In the light of what was to come it is ironic to hear the fervour of Tauber's pronouncements, delivered long before there was any reason to believe that he himself might become a victim of persecution.

Several more of Tauber's early successes are represented on this disc – from EUGENE ONEGIN we have a poetical rendering of Lenski's tragic monologue (heavily cut in order to fit onto one side of a 78), and from THE BARTERED BRIDE a defiant perform-ance of Jenik's aria 'Es muss gelingen'. One of the other tracks, though, marks an amusing departure from his stage repertoire. In the spring of 1920, in only his second batch of operatic recordings, he sang Siegmund's 'Winterstürme' from DIE WALKÜRE. Was it, I wonder, to prove a point to all those experts who had told him to keep his hands off Wagner? If so I can only say that I am on the side of the experts. As a performance of an isolated romantic passage it is irresistible, and phrases descriptive of the potency of spring, such as 'seinem warmen Blut entblühen wonnige Blumen', emerge with all the lyrical charm of a Schumann song; the idea, though, that this particular Siegmund should be called on scarcely twenty pages later to tear a magic sword from the trunk of an ashtree while massed trumpets and trombones rend the air is a fanciful one.

In the same session as this gesture of independence Tauber recorded another of the Nimbus tracks, a gloriously full-throated attack on the Italian tenor's aria from DER ROSENKAVALIER, though he did not sing it in the sadistically punishing key in which Richard Strauss had written it. It was a source of regret to Tauber that although so many of Strauss's most popular works started their lives in the Dresden Opera it never fell to him to create a single Strauss role, whereas again and again his time and effort went into new works which were, in his own words, 'sadly never more than a local success, and sometimes not even that'. As the

Viennese opera and operetta composer Richard Heuberger once put it, 'How sad that world premières are so rapidly followed by world dernières.'

Tauber's personal relationship with Richard Strauss got off to a peculiar start. During his Dresden days Tauber built up a reputation as the 'SOS' singer, able to master new roles with astonishing speed should a tenor in any of the neighbouring opera houses fall ill. One such achievement was his first Faust, undertaken at two days' notice to help out the theatre in Breslau. He had worked on the role with Professor Beines, but had never actually prepared it for performance, and was only given one piano rehearsal before going on stage. In March 1915, possibly encouraged by this experience, he accepted an even more daunting challenge. The Court Opera was asked if it had a Bacchus in Strauss's ARIADNE who could undertake the role in two days' time in the Royal Opera, Berlin with Strauss himself conducting. This time it was a role which Tauber had only glanced at, and which is generally thought of as Heldentenor territory anyway, but he unhesitatingly took it on. To quote Tauber himself once again: 'In those days an appearance in the Berlin Opera was the summit of my dreams', and he was not even frightened off by a message from Strauss to the effect that he would only be able to give the guest tenor a brief run-through at the piano of the trickiest passages in the role. Now, no one who has ever sung a Strauss role needs to be told that his trickiest passages are tricky in the extreme, but Tauber survived with flying colours. It was not until after the curtain had fallen that Strauss became aware of the circumstances, whereupon he expressed deep displeasure and declared that had he been informed he would never have agreed to conduct.

Other samples of Tauber's German repertoire to be found on the Nimbus disc include two numbers from Korngold's DIE TOTE STADT. I have already written about 'Marietta's Lute Song' in the chapter on Maria Jeritza, and here we have it in its original form, as a duet for tenor and soprano. As the soprano this time is Jeritza's arch-rival in the role, Lotte Lehmann, interesting comparisons can be made, and as far as Tauber's contribution is concerned that quality of nostalgic resignation with which he could so readily colour his tone makes it one which lingers in the memory. The second excerpt from this intriguing score is the closing scene of the opera, in which the hero, Paul, turns his back for ever on the house which holds such powerful memories of the two women who have haunted his destiny. Even at the age of twenty Korngold had known a thing or two about how to bring down a curtain. In the Lute Song he had written the kind of melody which audiences itch to hear repeated, and when Paul, as a final gesture of farewell, places a cover over the portrait of his dead wife, Korngold gives them their chance. This time Tauber intensifies the passion of his delivery, largely through his extraordinary identification with the text that he is singing, to such a degree that listeners in the theatre must indeed have been drained of their last drop of emotion. It is worth mentioning that the conductor of these excerpts was the twenty-six-year-old Georg Szell, under whose baton Lehmann and Tauber performed the work in Berlin, and even on these old acoustic recordings the combined input of the three of them runs at a high voltage.

The two remaining German tracks on the Nimbus disc consist of Walther von Stolzing's introductory number from DIE MEISTERSINGER, 'Am stillen Herd', and the 'Vater, Mutter' song from Lortzing's UNDINE. The Wagner aria, conducted once again by Szell, is not the piece of cheek which the WALKÜRE excerpt had been, because it was recorded seven years later, when Tauber's voice had become a robuster instrument, and in any case Walther is a role which, in the right circumstances, can be essayed by a tenor of the non-Helden variety. The Lortzing number is something of a curiosity, as it is not sung in the opera by the hero of the piece, one Ritter Hugo von Ringstetten, who was in Tauber's stage repertoire, but by his squire Veit, the buffo, who was not. It is a typical example of the so-called 'Couplets' which regularly crop up in the more folksy German operas and in the works of the early Viennese operetta composers such as Millöcker and Suppé. They always consist of several verses set to a simple homespun tune, with the point lying in the words; and the point in this instance, it must be said, is not exactly a profound one. It is, however, a song in which German audiences take great delight, and I can quite see why Tauber should have wished to record it. Having myself sung the taxing but somewhat unrewarding role of Ritter Hugo I know how it can stretch one's charitable feelings to hear the second tenor cheered to the roof for singing this totally undemanding little number; but if I had ever heard it sung with the uncanny skill of Richard Tauber I think I would have had to admit the justice of the situation. Here we meet Tauber the story-teller, the singer who chats man to man with his audience, a gift which makes something great out of something small, and one which made him such a compelling artist on the concert platform.

The Nimbus selection continues with several examples of Tauber's French and Italian repertoires, with everything sung in German translation, as was the habit in those days in even the most exalted of the German and Austrian theatres. We have another of his audition pieces, the Flower Song from CARMEN, recorded ten years after it had helped to secure his contract in Dresden, and it is to my mind one of his most masterly performances. The vexed question with this particular aria is – do you sing the climactic phrase rising to the high B flat fortissimo, which will always bring the house down, or do you sing it pianissimo, as the composer requested, which is harder to do and involves you in the risk of having half the audience think that you have run out of steam? The ideal answer is to sing it as Tauber does with such an exquisitely graded diminuendo as he climbs to the B flat and such a magical piano tone when he gets there that no one could possibly mistake it for anything other than superlative singing. The ravishing quality of Tauber's mezza voce, and his ability to switch into it from full voice with no apparent gearchange, was very much one of his stylistic trademarks, and is never better exemplified than in the CONTES D'HOFFMANN track 'O Dieu, de quelle ivresse'. He transposes it down a semitone, as he occasionally did with high-lying music in the French and Italian operas, and although some authorities claim that in his prime Tauber could sing a sustained high C, I find it hard to believe. One weapon not included in Tauber's armoury was the gloriously free top register of a Gigli, a Björling or a Pavarotti, and although some of his high B flats are perfectly respectable tones, they are never what is known in the profession as 'bankers', the sort of top notes which add another nought to a tenor's fee.

I imagine that those listeners who are not from the German-speaking countries may initially be put off by a 'Recondita armonia' from TOSCA which emerges as 'Wie sich die Bilder gleichen', but as one who spent much of his own early career singing Verdi and Puccini in German I can only take my hat off to Tauber for the manner in which he maintains an italianate legato while perfectly articulating the German text. I well remember my own struggles in the opera school of the Vienna Academy to retain the flow of Cavaradossi's 'Amaro sol per te m'era il morire' when the words had been converted into 'Nur deinetwegen wollt' ich noch nicht sterben', but Tauber had thoroughly mastered the trick of singing through all those daunting consonants. His recording of the BOHEME aria is another which neatly demonstrates his technical adroitness. This he sings in the original key, though many an Italian tenor has been known to transpose it, and he unfolds the surging melodic line in gorgeously expansive vein. When he reaches the fateful make-or-break high C (which is actually an optional note) he does take it, but with such craftiness that you have to listen carefully to spot whether he has or not. All he does is to sing it exactly as it is printed in the score, the last of twelve triplets in the bar, without lingering on it for a moment, and using the B flat just after it to crown the phrase. Added to that he uses a translation which is otherwise unfamiliar to me, and which enables him merely to flick the C on a weak syllable, and on one of his favourite vowel sounds preceded by one of his most comfortable consonants – 'in meine ar*me* Seele'. He was decidedly not one of those tenors of whom it is said that they have resonances where their brains ought to be.

Before leaving the Nimbus disc I would like to mention one more Puccini track, 'Non piangere, Liù' from TURANDOT, because it is a reminder of perhaps the most astonishing of all Tauber's 'take-over' feats. The outstanding event in the German operatic calendar for 1926 was to be the German-language première of Puccini's posthumous opera, due to take place in Dresden a few weeks after the world première at La Scala, Milan. Tauber was no longer a member of the Dresden company – his main contracts by then were in Berlin and Vienna – but he happened to have been back there for some guest performances as Eisenstein in DIE FLEDERMAUS. On the day of his intended departure he called in at the theatre to say goodbye to the music director, Fritz Busch, and was told that Curt Taucher, the tenor who was due to sing the role of Calaf in the première four days later, was ill and had cancelled. It had been a major feather in Dresden's cap to secure the performing rights, everyone who was anyone in German operatic life was to be there, and now the only hope of saving the event lay with Richard Tauber. He himself was later to describe what happened:

> My car was standing at the stage door ready to go, but I never left! In the prevailing circumstances I could not disregard the cries for help that were coming my way, begging that I should take over the role. My enthusiasm for Puccini and my love of the Dresden Opera prompted me to accept the hazard although it was clear to me that if I failed, which in view of the limited time for the take-over was well within the bounds of possibility, it would be extremely damaging for my reputation.

He signed up on a Wednesday, he sang on the Saturday, and to quote the Berlin *Allgemeine Musikzeitung* of 23 July 1926: 'It was an unprecedented piece of musical heroism, as much of a fairy tale as the production itself. And to add to that he sang the role with such individuality, with such authority of tone and presentation, as if he had been able to immerse himself in it for weeks. He sang with the right mixture of lyrical sensitivity and heroic dash, with stylistic mastery of the Italian cantilena – in short, he was the embodiment of perfection.' As a postscript to this extraordinary achievement I hope it is not too mundane to mention that it also brought with it certain practical advantages. In order to pursue the many golden opportunities which were opening up for him elsewhere Tauber had left the Dresden ensemble while his contract still had some time to run, and the Dresden Opera quite justifiably insisted on a heavy financial penalty. Included in what one might call 'the TURANDOT rescue package' was an agreement that as well as paying him a hefty fee the Opera should write off his substantial outstanding debt, making his Calaf performances possibly the best paid of his entire career.

Another CD which concentrates on Tauber's early recordings is Pearl's GEMM 9327, entitled 'The Vocal Prime of Richard Tauber'. Several operatic titles from the Nimbus selection reappear but there are numerous other delights as well, such as the Prize Song from DIE MEISTERSINGER, which lies rather less comfortably for him than 'Am stillen Herd', but is sung with enough freshness and verve to make it credible that we are listening to a Walther who really did write the song himself. There is a dramatic monologue from TIEFLAND, in which Pedro, the role Tauber so yearned to sing when he was a boy, describes how he once throttled a wolf with his bare hands, and in the duet 'Solenne in quest' ora' from LA FORZA DEL DESTINO we have one of the finest of all his offerings from the Italian repertoire. He spins out the arching phrases of the Verdian line with immaculate smoothness and poise, and once again achieves the miracle of combining a genuinely Italianate legato with flawless articulation of the German text.

With some of the Italian tracks on this particular disc we are into territory where other singers are more at home than Tauber – 'Di quella pira' for instance, from IL TROVATORE – and in numbers like the Duke's two light-hearted caperings from

RIGOLETTO, or the 'All'idea' duet from IL BARBIERE not even Tauber can disguise the basic incompatibility of the German language with such airy music. One cannot help admiring his skill even when he may not seem to be quite at the right address, but one listens to him with a certain detachment; whereas with the three last tracks on the disc he is standing with both feet firmly planted in his own domain, and this transforms him into a veritable weaver of spells. Grieg's 'Letzter Frühling', Tosti's 'Chanson de l'Adieu' and Liszt's 'Es muss ein Wunderbares sein' are three songs with much in common – romantic melodies, romantic texts and romantic orchestrations. It is scarcely possible to analyse what qualities of style or technique go to the making of a romantic singer, it lies so much in the personality behind the voice; but even if, like Tamino, one 'cannot put a name to this indefinable something' it is safe to say that it was Tauber's magic ingredient. The Grieg song was one of his favourites – he included it in a special recital which he gave for President Roosevelt in the White House in 1937 – and the mood of nostalgic enchantment which the composer achieves with the very first chord of the brief orchestral introduction is exactly mirrored by the warmth and tenderness of Tauber's opening phrase 'Ja, noch einmal ist das Wunder gescheh'n' ('Yes, once again the miracle has happened'). In his operatic repertoire Tauber was not one of those singers of whom it could be said that they were incapable of making an ugly sound, as his tone occasionally tightened under pressure. In his vast repertoire of songs, however, he could pick and choose what suited him, and he could sing them in the key of his choice. There is nothing harsh, nothing that is not entirely beautiful in these three songs, and all of them glow with Tauber's own delight in the act of singing them.

Tauber's fame as an opera singer and subsequently as an operetta star have tended to overshadow his reputation as an interpreter of songs, yet I would have no hesitation in placing him amongst the great Lieder singers of the gramophone era. It so happens that he made his very first public appearance with a programme of songs by Schubert and Schumann, in Freiburg's Festhalle on 17 May 1912, when the critics responded warmly to the new tenor's individual timbre and natural musicianship, and both of these composers feature prominently on a Pearl CD, GEMM *9370*, entitled 'Tauber Sings Lieder'. The Schubert section consists of the WINTERREISE songs to which I referred in my opening paragraph, and they are sung in a delightfully straightforward manner. I sometimes feel that during my lifetime Lieder singing has become too solemn an affair, as if it were something to be approached above all with the intellect. I have occasionally felt almost sheepish about the degree to which I enjoy Tauber in this repertoire, and I was quite relieved when I read some time ago in an article by Dietrich Fischer-Dieskau that in his authoritative opinion 'the ease of Tauber's delivery and his musicianship make his early Lieder recordings quite exceptional even today'.

The feeling imparted by Tauber's treatment of these songs is that of an Austrian singer faced with his natural birthright, namely a group of songs by an Austrian composer, and the treatment they receive is something utterly free of artifice. In 'Die Post' (another of his special favourites) he does not hesitate to put a dash of emotion into his apostrophising of his own over-eager heart – his head knows that the sound of the posthorn will not herald the arrival of a letter for him, but his heart cannot help hoping – and when his voice fades away to nothing on the final phrase of 'Der Lindenbaum' it is in no way with a sense of 'Ladies and gentlemen, kindly observe the exquisite quality of my soft singing', but merely the natural resignation of one whose hope has expired. The same unselfconscious alliance of personality, voice and technique places the four Schumann songs on this disc firmly amongst my favourite Tauber recordings; they were also recorded eight or nine years later with greatly improved sound quality, and they benefit too from the piano playing of Tauber's faithful accompanist Percy Kahn, who was invariably addressed by Tauber with the affectionate nickname 'Percy-Boy'. The gentle humour of 'Der Nussbaum', the fervour of 'Widmung', and the understated devotion of 'Aus den östlichen Rosen' find ideal expression in Tauber's endless gradations of colour and effortless breadth of phrasing, while the diminuendo on 'flog durch die stillen Lande', the penultimate phrase of 'Mondnacht', is one of those things which send shivers down the spine. The disc is completed by the twelve recordings which Tauber made of German folksongs under the title 'Das deutsche Volkslied', and the very simplicity of the material underlines what a mastersinger is at work. The songs are all strophic – several verses set to the same tune – but never, in Tauber's hands, do they become repetitive or dull, and never does he slip into the trap of archness, which floors certain 'great artists' when they set about proving that they too are human. He emerges furthermore as an unaffected master of dialect, putting the final touch to a set which I personally would rank as a minor classic.

Happily there are two more Pearl CDs of Tauber the Lieder singer. One, GEMM *9901*, concentrates on his early acoustic recordings, and as many of these are by now considerable rarities it is no wonder that some of the 78s from which the tracks are taken show signs of wear. Those who are prepared to overlook such imperfections will find much to enjoy in this selection, especially several of Schumann's DICHTERLIEBE songs, all imbued with the poetic delicacy which these exquisite miniatures require, and an irresistible version of Loewe's ballad 'Tom der Reimer'. Once again there are cuts to fit the time limit imposed by the 78 format, but no one can tell a musical story such as this more engagingly than Tauber. Another track of particular interest is Wagner's 'Träume', recorded in Tauber's very first session on 26 June 1919, with his teacher Carl Beines at the piano; the twenty-eight-year-old singer is revealed as an interpreter of remarkable maturity, and the débutant recording artist already sounds totally at home with this unfamiliar medium. The other Pearl disc, GEMM *9381*, consists of Lieder with orchestral accompaniment, mostly recorded a decade or so later than the acoustics and with considerably more amplitude of tone. Schubert once again predominates, with contributions by Schumann, Mendelssohn, Wolf, Grieg and others, and though some of the orchestral arrangements will not suit sticklers for musical *Echtheit* I am perfectly happy to capitulate to Tauber and his winning ways. To some people, I know, his musical persona was irritating rather than infectious but I am not of that group, and it is clearly no coincidence that I have known several instances of children being won over to 'serious' music by the voice of Richard Tauber and the sense of friendliness which it imparts. That eminent *aficionado* of great singing Lord Harewood wrote in his memoirs: 'I think it was listening to Tauber sing Schubert in a romantic film about the composer's life* that first turned me firmly towards music, or at least towards singing. I came back from the cinema in a daze of pleasure at what I had heard, and Tauber's records, particularly of Schubert, were very often to be heard at Harewood when I was about ten or eleven years old.'

Lord Harewood goes on to say (and I agree with him whole-heartedly), 'Tauber's constant characteristic was the ability to catch the lilt of a tune, the balance of a phrase, so that it haunts the listener's memory as if it had never been properly sung before,' and it was of course this potent appeal of the Tauber voice and style which made him the operetta tenor *sans pareil*. In the German-speaking countries certain roles in the 'classical' operettas always fall to the operatic tenor – Tauber had made frequent appearances in Dresden and elsewhere in Strauss's DIE FLEDERMAUS and DER ZIGEUNERBARON – and in 1921 he trod the stage for the first time in a piece by Franz Lehár, singing the role of Joszi in ZIGEUNERLIEBE in the Stadttheater, Salzburg.† The following year, shortly after he had started his first season with the Vienna

---

*   *Blossom Time* with Jane Baxter and Athene Seyler.

---

† Tauber made a point of visiting Salzburg whenever possible because his mother had spent the last years of her stage career in the Stadttheater playing the type of operetta role charmingly categorised in German as '*Die komische Alte*' ('the funny old woman'). She subsequently retired there, and died in 1938 at the age of ninety-one.

State Opera, he went to a performance of Lehár's new piece FRASQUITA in the Theater an der Wien, with Hubert Marischka in the role of Armand. Marischka was at the top of the tree in the operetta business, being Vienna's resident matinée idol and also the director of the theatre, but Tauber came away convinced that Lehár's music was being short-changed by Marischka's limitations as a singer. He asked if he could try his hand at the role during the State Opera's summer break, and the results were remarkable. Although bookings for the piece had been flagging during the heat of July they suddenly picked up, and the manner in which the new tenor 'Tauberised' the hit song 'Hab' ein blaues Himmelbett' set a pattern which was to be repeated in every new Lehár operetta from then onwards. Unfortunately Tauber's only German recording of this number is technically an exceptionally poor one, but through all the hiss and crackle one can tell without much difficulty what it was that so enchanted the Vienna public. The text of the song is highly suggestive, all about Armand's nice blue double bed, in which it is so pleasant to dream as long as one is not on one's own, and Tauber makes it quite simply as seductive as he knows how. It is personally addressed to each and every one of his female listeners, the long melodic phrases floating tantalisingly on the surface of that rhythmical buoyancy of which he was such a master; and the final utterance, complete with an elegantly turned little piece of fioriture, culminates in a high A which is the merest whisper, but which still contains all the core of the often imitated but in fact inimitable Tauber sound.

The first of the operettas which Lehár wrote specially for Tauber, and with Tauber's active collaboration – Lehár would often ask Tauber at rehearsals 'was that bit by you or by me?' – was PAGANINI, but Tauber's contract with the Berlin State Opera prevented him from singing the world première in Vienna and the piece flopped. When it opened in Berlin, however, with Tauber heading the cast, it was rapturously received and the tradition was established of the big song in Act II, the so-called

'Tauberlied', being encored as often as Tauber was prepared to sing it. Every reprise was delivered with different inflections, sometimes Tauber appeared in the stage box or down in the auditorium, and occasionally, when Lehár himself was conducting, he would indulge in flights of musical improvisation while the composer beamed up at him from the pit, secure in the knowledge that if he just kept going Tauber would rejoin him when he felt inclined.

Needless to say there were plenty of people who regarded Tauber's defection to the operetta stage as a prostitution of his art, and after his appearances in FRASQUITA Franz Schalk, the director of the Vienna State Opera, made noises about his contract not being renewed. This, however, was not how things turned out. Until the coming of the Nazis Tauber retained his contracts with the two State Operas, Vienna and Berlin, leaving him three months free each year to appear in operetta. On the subject of the vocal strain of singing in a long run Tauber held some interesting views. 'The many reprises of a song or a duet on operetta evenings', he was to write, 'were a technical exercise for me. I was always extremely careful not to demand more of my voice than my technique permitted, but I am always in top form when I sing a hundred performances on the trot!' On days when he had an opera or a concert to sing he would habitually rest his voice, but if he was singing operetta in the evening he would happily work in the film or gramophone studios during the day.

Those who could not imagine why an artist of Tauber's stature should have wanted to mess around with light music simply did not understand what made the man tick. The qualities of a great Mozart singer and a natural showman are not of necessity mutually exclusive, and it was mostly operetta that Tauber had been soaking up in his days as a backstage urchin. He loved the razzmatazz of the operetta world, and it was operetta which lifted him to the status of a superstar, recognised wherever he went. It would indeed be difficult to exaggerate the extent of Tauber's popularity in the Berlin of those days. This is the Tauber we encounter in the old photographs, leaning nonchalantly against the radiator of his 140 horse-power Mercedes, hat at a snappy angle, monocle firmly in the right eye, his face suffused with a happy grin. He revelled in the adulation of his operetta audiences, and he adored performing for them – your contact with the public is much more direct in operetta than in opera – and in any case he could frankly use the money. He lived in a luxurious villa in Berlin (and owned several others) but he found it more practical during the run of an operetta to base himself in a suite in the exclusive Hotel Adlon. He maintained a travelling retinue of manager, secretary, valet and chauffeur, and another expensive luxury was his brief marriage to a soprano named Carlotta Vanconti, who starred with him in Lehár's DER ZAREWITSCH. Had this hectic programme and glamorous life-style had a damaging effect on his 'serious' singing such expressions as 'the prostitution of his art' might have a ring of truth, but one only has to listen to certain recordings made right at the end of his career – the FREISCHÜTZ aria, for instance, or the Richard Strauss songs 'Allerseelen' and 'Ich trage meine Minne' – to realise that Tauber the 'serious' artist never went out of business.

There are numerous CDs of Tauber's operetta recordings. Nimbus *NI 7833* is shared between Tauber and that delightful soprano Lotte Schöne, with the tenor tracks including the first of the 'Tauberlieder', 'Gern hab' ich die Frau'n geküsst', from PAGANINI. If one wants a demonstration of how to sing operetta there is no need to look further than this performance, in which the skills of the Mozartian, the smooth legato, the elegance of phrasing and the subtleties of nuance, are perfectly allied with the *élan*, the humour, the extrovert charm which you need for the selling of the lighter muse. Another track which serves as an object lesson is a pot-pourri of waltz tunes from DIE LUSTIGE WITWE. There are few things in singing more elusive than the knack of keeping a Viennese waltz airborne rather than letting it clump around the floor, but this is second nature to Tauber –

his voice has wings on its heels. On EMI *CDC 7 54838 2* there is a fascinating selection of Lehár numbers conducted by the composer with four outstanding sopranos involved – Esther Réthy, Maria Reining, Vera Schwarz and Jarmila Novotná – and this time Tauber's contribution consists of the original cast recordings from DAS LAND DES LÄCHELNS (1929) and Lehár's final operetta GIUDITTA, which achieved its world première in the Vienna State Opera in 1934. The former, of course, includes the song which became, more than any other, Tauber's signature tune – 'Dein ist mein ganzes Herz', or 'You are my heart's delight'; and the contemplative introduction to the GIUDITTA 'Tauberlied', 'Du bist meine Sonne', offers a perfect demonstration of Tauber's ability to create a musical mood in only a couple of bars. Another selection of Lehár conducting his own works, this time featuring Tauber almost throughout, is to be found on Pearl, GEMM *9310*, and one particularly attractive item here is the duet 'Wenn zwei sich lieben' from Lehár's early operetta DER RASTELBINDER, in which Tauber is partnered, and very nicely too, by his first wife, Carlotta Vanconti.

A soprano of exceptional physical beauty who also featured prominently in Tauber's private life was the Russian-born Mary (or Mara) Losseff. She was his partner in his own operetta DER SINGENDE TRAUM which was produced with great success in Vienna in 1934, and four numbers from the score are included in another selection of Tauber's operetta recordings, Pearl GEMM *9444*. This disc includes the FRASQUITA Serenade which I have discussed above, and also a number from a piece called LIEBESKOMMANDO by Robert Stolz. I myself sang frequently under Stolz's baton during the last decade of his very long life, and I remember him telling me that he regarded Tauber as the greatest artist with whom he had ever worked. 'We never needed to rehearse,' he said. 'He looked into my eyes and knew what I wanted; I looked into his eyes and knew what he wanted' – a very time-saving method. Another beautifully Tauberised rendering on this disc is the number 'Was weiss ein nie geküsster Rosenmund?'

from Kálmán's DAS VEILCHEN VON MONTMARTRE. Here we have Tauber the arch-communicator, not in seductive mood, as in the FRASQUITA song, but teasing this time, as he enquires of the eponymous heroine of the piece how two rosy lips which have never been kissed can possibly know about love. It is sung with an exquisite line, but how the man *speaks* to the listener!

Another track in this selection ranks amongst Tauber's most persuasive operetta recordings, but it is redolent of the intrusion of catastrophe into his life. In the middle of January 1933 he opened in a new operetta called FRÜHLINGSSTÜRME by Jaromir Weinberger (of SCHWANDA fame) in the Theater am Admiralspalast in Berlin. It had a splendid score and Tauber achieved his customary triumph with the big number 'Du wär'st für mich die Frau gewesen', but by the end of that month Hitler had assumed power and not even Tauber's unique standing in the theatrical life of Berlin could save him from the fact that on his father's side he had Jewish blood in his veins. The performance on 9 March had to be stopped because of organised rioting in the auditorium. When Tauber complained to the Minister of Labour, a man by the name of Seldte, he was assured that the demonstration was aimed at the Jewish composer, not at Tauber himself, and Seldte accepted an invitation to dine with the star in one of Berlin's most luxurious restaurants in order to talk the situation over. As Tauber left the restaurant, however, he was set on by a gang of Nazi thugs, from whom he was rescued by his two half-brothers and by Bischof, his chauffeur; Arbeitsminister Seldte had vanished as if by magic.

Tauber, like so many musicians a total political innocent, was completely bewildered by his sudden transformation from idol of the Berlin public to enemy of the people, and he took the obvious step, a speedy departure for Vienna. All his money and property in Berlin were confiscated by the Nazis, and he had to make a fresh start, only to find himself in exactly the same position once again when, in 1938, Hitler annexed Austria. At the time of the Anschluss Tauber was on an operetta tour of

Italy. When the news arrived he shut himself in his hotel room for three days, where he sat playing the piano and refusing to speak to anyone. He had arranged that Bischof, who had been with Tauber for years and was almost regarded as a member of the family, should join him with Tauber's pride and joy, the 140 horse-power Mercedes. When he failed to arrive, preferring to stay in Vienna and act as chauffeur to Nazi bigwigs in Tauber's beloved car, it was one of the unkindest cuts of all.

Tauber's next move was to London, where he was to sing his long awaited opening season at Covent Garden. He was already well known to the British public through his appearances in the London productions of PAGANINI and THE LAND OF SMILES, as well as several concert tours, and the appearance as Tamino of someone almost exclusively regarded as a popular entertainer naturally aroused widespread interest. Ernest Newman of *The Sunday Times*, a critic who enjoyed putting star singers in their place, reported: 'Richard Tauber began rather badly, but steadily improved as he seemed to forget, and allowed us in the audience to forget, that he was Richard Tauber and became more and more Mozart's Tamino.' Another of the most respected British critics, Richard Capell of *The Daily Telegraph*, wrote:

> Better late than never, Tauber is welcome at Covent Garden . . . and his Tamino earned him new respect. A trace of a mannerism in his singing – his way sometimes of spreading his vowels a little in the upper part of his range – detracted somewhat from the effect of youthful energy proper to the adventurous Prince. But the hero of the Flute is too often hard and wooden, and it was no unpleasant change to hear one who is inclined to be luscious and what the Germans call '*weich*' ('soft').*

---

* This distortion of vowel sounds in the upper register was one of the Tauber mannerisms which was frequently picked on by British critics, and it was usually attributed (as by Desmond Shawe-Taylor in *Grove's Dictionary*) to the strain of his endless operetta appearances. In fact, though, it had been a habit of Tauber's from the beginning of his career. On the 1919 recording from DER EVANGELIMANN, for instance, referred to earlier on, the diphthong

Tauber's second Covent Garden role, Belmonte in DIE ENT-
FÜHRUNG, was not an entirely happy experience as he had
to cancel the first night owing to a tiresome throat condition,
which had begun to plague him with increasing frequency. When
he did sing, however, Francis Toye of *The Daily Telegraph*, after
complimenting Sir Thomas Beecham on 'dancing his way through
the score with incomparable elegance', found that Tauber 'provided a flavour of genuine if refreshingly refined light opera'; and
while noticing that Tauber clearly felt nervous about his voice he
described his phrasing and diction as 'a delight'.

Tauber's return to Covent Garden in May the following year
gave rise to one of the few recorded instances of Sir Thomas
being worsted in a verbal exchange. The opera was Smetana's
THE BARTERED BRIDE and the cast was an international one of
considerable distinction. The atmosphere at rehearsals, however,
was unrelaxed, as it frequently was in those days if singers who
were refugees from Germany were cast alongside others who
were known to be supporters of the Nazi party. To make matters
worse, Sir Thomas had not yet entirely familiarised himself with
the score and, as conductors sometimes will, he was taking out
his own insecurity on the singers, finding fault with every little
thing they did. Tears were flowing and it seemed unlikely that
the rehearsal would be able to continue, until Tauber, with his
usual beaming smile, strolled down to the footlights and said, 'I'm
sorry, Sir Thomas, but we've been singing it wrong for so many
years in Prague and Vienna that you can't expect us to get it right
in only one rehearsal!' In fact when the first night came conditions
were more comfortable on stage than they were in the auditorium.
It had been raining ceaselessly in London for the last three days
and half the audience arrived soaked to the skin. As the reporter
of the *Scotsman* put it: 'Box and stall holders too came in for a

---

'ei' in 'Himmelreich', which when sung should start on an 'ah' sound, distinctly
does not do so even on a humble F sharp, and this is something which I attribute much more to the inflections of his native Austrian dialect than to any
technical expedient.

wetting, for many of them, determined not to incur the wrath of Sir Thomas Beecham by arriving late, deserted cars and taxicabs some distance from the Opera House and dashed the rest of the way on foot, the puddles splashing the women's silk stockings and long dresses.'

Tauber's second role in the 1939 Covent Garden season was Don Ottavio, and this time it was Newman who smiled, while Capell frowned. 'Mr Tauber's Ottavio was the best thing I have seen him do on the stage in recent years,' Newman wrote, 'and he was always dignified and sympathetic, while his handling of the two tenor arias showed that he still retains much of the skill that made him so exceptional a Mozart singer in the earlier part of his career.' Capell, however, felt that tenors 'should go into training for "Il mio tesoro", otherwise they will, as Tauber did, cut out beats and scramble the semi-quavers'. Tauber did in fact record both Ottavio arias in London at this time, and 'Il mio tesoro' can be heard as part of an operatic selection on EMI *CDH 7 64029 2*. While the semiquavers to which Capell refers are not taken with the sovereign ease displayed on the celebrated McCormack recording, or indeed in several more modern versions, Tauber, to my mind, makes excellent sense of why Mozart put them there. Don Ottavio, as the orchestra plainly tells us, is at this point an angry man. He is hell-bent on catching the villain who tried (perhaps successfully?) to rape his fiancée, and when he hurls out phrases such as 'Tell her I am off to avenge the wrongs that have been done her', surely a sweet and honeyed tone is not what is required. I suspect that the correspondent of the *Glasgow Herald* would have been on my side. He found a nice phrase to describe Tauber's contribution at Covent Garden – 'For once we begin with Don Ottavio, not because Tauber's name was writ large on the bill, but because Tauber's personality was writ large on the performance . . . he made Ottavio the chairman of whatever meeting he happened to attend.'

Sadly the EMI issue mentioned above, though it offers an interesting selection of arias and duets, is not an impressive dubbing. Another EMI disc, *CDM 7 69476 2*, is more successful in this respect, and as it includes opera, operetta, Lieder and lighter songs it comes near to justifying its title of 'Richard Tauber, ein Porträt', though the disappointing feature this time is the rather unimaginative choice of the operatic items. In general, considering how many Tauber CDs there are in existence it is frustrating how few can be unreservedly recommended. It is annoying, too, how many obvious gaps there are. He made four outstanding Mozart recordings in 1938–9, of which only the 'Il mio tesoro', mentioned above, has been reissued,* and all the post-war operatic and Lieder titles are certainly worthy of transfer to CD. Where too are his exquisite renderings of so many Richard Strauss songs, including the most persuasive version I know of that old favourite 'Ständchen'? Where are his genial Heurigenlieder? We must keep hoping!

Tauber's output as a recording artist was truly remarkable. Back in the days of 78s very few singers recorded more than a couple of hundred titles, whereas Tauber notched up some 735. In every aspect of his career, though, he was a man of astonishing energy. It might be supposed that after the sudden loss of his Vienna contract he would have been at least temporarily stranded, but nothing could be further from the truth. His concert schedule for the eleven months between his two Covent Garden seasons of 1938 and 1939 makes extraordinary reading, comprising as it did (in chronological order) Bournemouth, Colombo, thirty-seven concerts all over Australia, including seven in a fortnight in Melbourne alone, with an eighth tacked on for those who had not secured tickets, eleven in South Africa, an extensive tour of Great Britain, including five concerts in one week, guest performances in the opera houses of Basle, Berne and Zurich, and a tour of the North American continent which took him straight across Canada and to half the major cities in the United States. This was his third tour of the States and the public's appetite for Tauber's style of

---

* One company has issued all four, but unfortunately dubbed at the wrong speed.

concert seemed to be insatiable. One contemporary description of these occasions caught the mood very well – 'He comes bounding onto the stage, beaming at his audience, as if to say "We're all here to have a marvellous time!" which is precisely what occurs.' Despite this alarming workload Tauber was always ready in each new venue to give spirited interviews to the press and to pose for pictures with whatever piece of local colour the photographers dreamt up – riding an elephant in Ceylon, hugging a koala bear in Melbourne, or kissing his old friend Marlene Dietrich in Hollywood.

When the Second World War broke out Tauber was in South Africa with THE LAND OF SMILES, but after various vicissitudes he found his way back to England and in 1940 he was granted British nationality. A glance at Tauber's wartime activities gives further evidence of his unflagging stamina. Apart from innumerable broadcasts, recordings and concerts he starred in several new operetta productions, including OLD CHELSEA, a piece which he composed himself and appeared in no less than 700 times. There can be no greater proof, I think, of the mesmeric effect of the Tauber voice than the fact that he could still get away with playing the romantic lead. He was well into middle age, he had always been stout and was now stouter, he had never been what anyone would normally call handsome, and a crippling bout of rheumatoid arthritis, which had nearly put paid to his career as early as 1929, had left him with a severe limp. From time to time during these wartime years he would give his voice a rest by returning to his old activity as a conductor, usually with the London Philharmonic Orchestra. Orchestral musicians, like all his colleagues in the theatre, adored working with him – his two outstanding characteristics as a human being were generosity and jocularity – and Felix Aprahamian, for many years music critic on *The Sunday Times* and previously assistant secretary to the London Philharmonic Orchestra, once described him to me as 'not just a gifted conductor, but a conductor of genius'.

The sheer multiplicity of Tauber's activities was understandably confusing to the public – could a man who had appeared in a run-down touring production of an operetta one week really make a good job of conducting Wagner in the Albert Hall the next? Then there was the bewildering question of his recordings – would this month's release be Mozart, or Irving Berlin's 'White Christmas'?* Tauber, however, had always enjoyed recording unashamedly popular numbers, and a selection of ditties from his Berlin days has been reissued on Pearl GEMM *9416*. They have titles such as 'Darf ich um den nächsten Tango bitten?' and several of them were penned by Tauber himself. It is not perhaps the selection which I personally would have made from Tauber's bottom drawer, but it does include one track which I find totally irresistible. It is a song called 'Das alte Lied', all about a girl who has gone away, a heart that will never mend and so on, and it is sung throughout in the merest whisper, to Tauber's own piano accompaniment. One has the feeling of eavesdropping on a private moment – this is how Tauber must have sounded during the countless hours that he spent playing and singing for his own amusement, in hotel rooms (where he always insisted on a piano being installed), backstage during breaks in rehearsals, or wherever he happened to be.

The salient point about the pot-boilers which Tauber recorded in London is that he had never so urgently needed to boil the pot – he was permanently frantic for ready cash. The Anschluss meant that he had once again lost everything, or at least everything except his expensive habits. His idea of home was a suite in London's Grosvenor House Hotel and he was an inveterate user of the telephone, endlessly ringing Britain from America or vice versa, an even more expensive habit then than it is today. Despite his apparently invincible good humour an element of desperation was entering his life. He was being troubled more and more by a persistent cough and the wartime tours, involving

---

* Many of these 'lowbrow' recordings are wonderfully well sung. Jerome Kern's 'All the things you are' and 'Long ago and far away', most certainly haunt the memory.

endless uncomfortable and even dangerous rail travel, were not all roses. In September 1940 he wrote to his second wife, the film actress Diana Napier, from a hotel in Manchester: 'Very quickly to let you have press cuttings and a little money. It is horrible here. I had just put the telephone down after speaking to you this morning when the sirens went. They go two or three times a night.' His wife, who was away with the armed forces, took a tolerant attitude when Tauber fell deeply in love with another woman; indeed the two ladies formed a kind of alliance in the business of looking after him and both were to remain his devoted friends until the last moment of his life. As if this situation were not in itself a trifle bizarre Tauber had also assumed financial responsibility for his old flame Mary Losseff, although their love affair had ended long before; and up till the time of his father's death in a Lugano sanatorium in 1942 he was doing his best to support him as well.

When the war ended Tauber's mind turned again to foreign travel. He paid a visit to his old friend Franz Lehár, now living in Zurich, and when Lehár conducted a concert of his own works for Radio Beromünster Tauber agreed to join in and sing four arias. It was to be the last time that they made music together, and a recording of the concert discovered a few years ago in the radio station's vaults and now available on a CD with the label KOCH *310982* makes it evident that this had been one of Tauber's most moving performances. A production of the inevitable LAND OF SMILES in New York, in a heavily and hammily rewritten version, was a flop, but once again Tauber was able to rescue the situation by setting out on yet another concert tour. When he came back to England, though, he was troubled more than ever by his recurrent cough and to save his voice he concentrated on conducting – massive income tax arrears precluded the possibility of his taking a real rest. Tauber believed his trouble to be bronchitis but unknown to him his doctor had already diagnosed lung cancer, and it became essential that he go into hospital for an operation. Before doing so, however, there was one more artistic appointment which Tauber was determined to keep, and the story of this, his last stage appearance, has become part of operatic legend.

In September 1947 the company of the Vienna State Opera was coming for a brief season to Covent Garden. It was Tauber's dearest wish to appear again with his old company and he wrote to David Webster, the general administrator of Covent Garden, asking if he could sing just one performance. Webster replied that the decision did not lie with him but with the director of the Vienna Opera, Josef Krips. Krips agreed, the tenor Anton Dermota, the company's Don Ottavio, was prepared to stand down from the last performance of DON GIOVANNI, and Tauber was engaged. Both Krips and he were taking an appalling risk. He had not appeared on the operatic stage for over eight years, Ottavio's two solos are amongst the most demanding in the lyric tenor repertoire, and now, a sick man, he was proposing to step in without rehearsal alongside a new generation of brilliant young stars. Yet he managed to conjure up a performance of which one of the most brilliant of these, Elisabeth Schwarzkopf, was later to say: 'I had never heard any tenor sing with this beauty of tone before, plus the breathing control, the expression and the clean intonation. I don't think any of us in the company had ever come across – much less been on stage with – a singer of the calibre of Richard Tauber.'

After the performance Tauber was exhausted, but the next day he went to the BBC for two of his 'Tauber Half-Hour' programmes, one pre-recorded and the other transmitted live. Then he was ready to go into hospital and the operation revealed the full extent of his achievement – he had been performing with one lung totally destroyed by cancer. Three months later it became evident that the other lung was also affected and on 18 January 1948 he died at the age of fifty-six.

Tauber's affairs were found to be in chaos. There was not enough money to pay the hospital bill and he owed the Inland Revenue £22,000, equivalent at the time of writing to roughly

£400,000.* More significantly, perhaps, he died mourned by countless people, and when a memorial concert was put on in the Albert Hall a month after his death, with the participants including Elisabeth Schwarzkopf, Sir Adrian Boult, the ever-faithful Percy-Boy and many others, the rush for tickets was such that it could have been sold twice over.

There had undeniably been occasions in Tauber's career when, either through necessity or of his own free will, he had stooped to conquer, but time has served to erase the trivia and it seems to me that today his artistic reputation stands as high as it ever did. Amongst the singers of the past there are some who come across to us now as nothing much more than outstanding voices on old recordings but there are others who, through some extra dimension to their singing, emerge from those recordings as vital and familiar personalities – almost like old friends. For me the first name on any list of tenors such as this would have to be Enrico Caruso. The second would be Richard Tauber.

---

* It was to be fourteen years before his tax arrears were cleared by the royalties on his recordings.

RECOMMENDED CDs: INDIVIDUAL SINGERS

A special compilation has been issued by Nimbus to accompany this book. The number is *NI 7864* and each singer is represented by one, or in some instances two, of their finest recordings.

For readers who would like to sample any of my chosen singers via a single complete disc the following suggestions might be helpful:

Maria Callas – *EMI CDC 5 55016 2* (Sixteen arias by ten different composers)

Feodor Chaliapin – *EMI CDH 7 61009 2* (Thirteen scenes from Russian opera)

Kathleen Ferrier – *Decca 414 194–2* (Mahler – DAS LIED VON DER ERDE)

Beniamino Gigli – *Nimbus NI 7807* (Sixteen arias and six songs, 1918–24)

Maria Jeritza – *Lebendige Vergangenheit 89079* (Twenty arias by ten different composers)

John McCormack – *Pearl GEMM 9338* (Twenty-two Irish songs)

Lauritz Melchior – *EMI CDH 7 69789 2* (Fifteen Wagner tracks)

Claudia Muzio – *Nimbus NI 7814* (Fourteen arias and six songs)

Titta Ruffo – *Nimbus NI 7810* (Twenty arias and one song)

Elisabeth Schumann – *Lebendige Vergangenheit 89031* (Mozart arias, oratorio and Lieder)

Conchita Supervia – *EMI CDH 7 63499 2* (CARMEN extracts, Rossini arias)

Richard Tauber – *Nimbus NI 7830* (Twenty arias by twelve different composers)

(The various compilations in which these singers feature are now too numerous to be listed, usually under such titles as 'Divas', 'Great Singers', 'Covent Garden on Record', 'Immortal Voices of the Vienna Opera' etc.)

SELECT BIBLIOGRAPHY

Ardoin, John, *The Callas Legacy*. (Charles Scribner's Sons, New York, 1982)

Bing, Sir Rudolf, *5000 Nights at the Opera*. (Hamish Hamilton, London, 1974)

Borovsky, Victor, *Chaliapin*. (Hamish Hamilton, London, 1988)

Campion, Paul, *Ferrier, a Career Recorded*. (Julia MacRae, London, 1929)

Cardus, Sir Neville (ed.), *Kathleen Ferrier, a Memoir*. (Hamish Hamilton, London, 1954)

Castle, Charles and Diana Napier Tauber, *This was Richard Tauber*. (W. H. Allen, London and New York, 1971)

Celletti, Rodolfo, *Le grandi voci*. (Rome, 1964)

Chaliapin, Feodor, *Pages From My Life*. (London, 1927)

Chaliapin, Feodor, *Mask and Soul*. (London, 1932)

Culshaw, John, *Putting the Record Straight*. (Secker and Warburg, London, 1981)

Emmons, Shirlee, *Tristanissimo*. (Schirmer Books, New York, 1990)

Farkas, Andrew (ed.), *Titta Ruffo, an Anthology*. (Greenwood Press, Connecticut, 1984)

Farrar, Geraldine, *Such Sweet Compulsion*. (The Greystone Press, New York, 1938)

Ferrier, Winifred, *The Life of Kathleen Ferrier*. (Hamish Hamilton, London, 1955)

Gatti-Casazza, Giulio, *Memoirs of the Opera*. (John Calder, London, 1977)

Glass, Beaumont, *Lotte Lehmann*. (Capra Press, Santa Barbara, 1988)

Gigli, Beniamino, *The Memoirs of Beniamino Gigli*. (Cassell and Company, London, 1957)

Gobbi, Tito, *My Life*. (Macdonald and Jane's, London, 1979)

Gorky, Maxim, *Chaliapin: an Autobiography as told to Maxim Gorky*. (London, 1968)

Hamilton, David (ed.), *The Metropolitan Opera Encyclopedia*. (Thames and Hudson, London, 1987)

Heyworth, Peter, *Otto Klemperer*. (Cambridge University Press, Cambridge, 1983)

Horgan, Paul, *A Book of Partial Portraits*. (Farrar, Strauss, Giroux, New York, 1993)

Kesting, Jürgen, *Maria Callas*. (Claassen Verlag GmbH, Düsseldorf, 1990)

Kolodin, Irving, *The Opera Omnibus*. (E. P. Dutton and Co., Inc., New York, 1976)

Ledbetter, Gordon T., *The Great Irish Tenor*. (Charles Scribner's Sons, New York, 1977)

Leonard, Maurice, *Kathleen – the Life of Kathleen Ferrier*. (Hutchinson, London, 1988)

Marek, George R., *The Eagles Die*. (Hart-Davis, MacGibbon, London, 1974)

McCormack, Lily, *I Hear You Calling Me*. (Milwaukee, 1949)

Moore, Gerald, *Am I Too Loud?* (Hamish Hamilton, London, 1962)

Newton, Ivor, *At the Piano*. (Hamish Hamilton, London, 1966)

Osborne, Charles (ed.), *Opera 66*. (Alan Ross Ltd, London, 1967)

Pleasants, Henry, *The Great Singers*. (Simon and Schuster, New York, 1961)

Puritz, Gerd, *Elisabeth Schumann*. (André Deutsch, London, 1993)

Rosenthal, Harold, *Two Centuries of Opera at Covent Garden*. (Putnam, London, 1958)

Ruffo, Titta, *La mia parabola*. (Staderini, Rome, 1977)

Schönherr, Max (ed. Andrew Lamb), *Unterhaltungsmusik aus Oesterreich*. (Peter Lang Publishing, Bern, 1993)

Schwarzkopf, Elisabeth, *On and Off the Record*. (Faber and Faber Ltd, London, 1982)

Scott, Michael, *Maria Meneghini Callas*. (Simon and Schuster, London, 1991)

Steane, J. B., *The Grand Tradition*. (Duckworth, London, 1994)

Steane, J. B., *Voices, Singing and Critics*. (Duckworth, London, 1992)

Strong, L. A. G., *John McCormack*. (Peter Nevill Ltd, London, 1949)

Tuggle, Robert, *The Golden Age of Opera*. (Holt, Rinehart and Winston, New York, 1983)

Valenti Ferro, Enzo, *Las Voces: Teatro Colón, 1908–1982*. (Gaglianone, Buenos Aires, 1983)

INDEX

INDEX OF INDIVIDUAL NUMBERS

ABOUT THE AUTHOR

After being President of the University Opera Club at Oxford, Nigel Douglas studied in the Opera School of the Vienna Music Academy and made his professional début with the Vienna Kammeroper in 1959 as Rodolfo in LA BOHEME. Since then he has appeared in over eighty roles in leading houses throughout the world in a repertoire extending from Danilo in DIE LUSTIGE WITWE at the Vienna Volksoper to Aschenbach in DEATH IN VENICE at the Royal Opera House, Covent Garden. He has directed productions for Sadler's Wells and the Australian Opera, and written and presented over two hundred programmes on opera and operetta for the BBC, including the Radio 4 series 'Singer's Choice'. During the year in which this book was written, he appeared in the Teatro Massimo, Catania, the Teatro Colón, Buenos Aires, with the company of the Opéra La Bastille in Seoul, with Scottish Opera and with the Welsh National Opera. He lives in Kent with his wife, two daughters and a son.